"AI is the most transformative technology of our era. Agrawal, Gans, and Goldfarb not only understand its essence but also deliver deep insights into its economic implications and intrinsic trade-offs. If you want to clear the fog of AI hype and see clearly the core of AI's challenges and opportunities for society, your first step should be to read this book."

—ERIK BRYNJOLFSSON, MIT professor; author, *The Second Machine Age* and *Machine, Platform, Crowd*

"*Prediction Machines* is a must-read for business leaders, policy makers, economists, strategists, and anyone who wants to understand the implications of AI for designing business strategies, decisions, and how AI will have an impact on our society."

—RUSLAN SALAKHUTDINOV, Carnegie Mellon professor; Director of AI Research, Apple

"I encounter so many people who feel excited but overwhelmed by AI. This book will ground those feeling lost by giving them a practical framework."

—SHIVON ZILIS, OpenAI Director and Partner, Bloomberg Beta

"The current AI revolution will likely result in abundance, but the process of getting there requires deliberation on tough topics that include increasing unemployment and income disparity. This book presents frameworks that allow decision makers to deeply understand the forces at play."

—VINOD KHOSLA, Khosla Ventures; founding CEO, Sun Microsystems

"What does AI mean for your business? Read this book to find out."

—HAL VARIAN, Chief Economist, Google

"AI may transform your life. And *Prediction Machines* will transform your understanding of AI. This is the best book yet on what may be the best technology that has come along."

—LAWRENCE H. SUMMERS, Charles W. Eliot Professor, former president, Harvard University; former secretary, US Treasury; and former chief economist, World Bank

"*Prediction Machines* is a path-breaking book that focuses on what strategists and managers really need to know about the AI revolution. Taking a grounded, realistic perspective on the technology, the book uses principles of economics and strategy to understand how firms, industries, and management will be transformed by AI."

—SUSAN ATHEY, Economics of Technology Professor, Stanford University; former consulting researcher, Microsoft Research New England

"*Prediction Machines* achieves a feat as welcome as it is unique: a crisp, readable survey of where artificial intelligence is taking us separates hype from reality, while delivering a steady stream of fresh insights. It speaks in a language that top executives and policy makers will understand. Every leader needs to read this book."

—DOMINIC BARTON, Global Managing Partner, McKinsey & Company

"This book makes artificial intelligence easier to understand by recasting it as a new, cheap commodity—predictions. It's a brilliant move. I found the book incredibly useful."

—KEVIN KELLY, founding executive editor, *Wired*; author, *What Technology Wants* and *The Inevitable*

Prediction Machines

Prediction Machines

The Simple Economics of Artificial Intelligence

| AJAY AGRAWAL | JOSHUA GANS | AVI GOLDFARB |

Harvard Business Review Press

Boston, Massachusetts

Library of Congress Cataloging-in-Publication Data

Names: Agrawal, Ajay, author. | Gans, Joshua, 1968- author. | Goldfarb, Avi, author.
    Title: Prediction machines : the simple economics of artificial intelligence
      / by Ajay Agrawal, Joshua Gans, and Avi Goldfarb.
    Description: Boston, Massachusetts : Harvard Business Review Press, [2018]
    Identifiers: LCCN 2017049211 | ISBN 9781633695672 (hardcover : alk. paper)
    Subjects: LCSH: Artificial intelligence—Economic aspects. | Decision making—Statistical
      methods. | Forecasting—Statistical methods.
    Classification: LCC TA347.A78 A385 2018 | DDC 658/.0563—dc23 LC record available at
      https://lccn.loc.gov/2017049211

*To our families, colleagues, students,
and startups who inspired us to think clearly
and deeply about artificial intelligence.*

Contents

Part Three: Tools

Part Four: Strategy

Part Five: Society

Acknowledgments

We express our thanks to the people who contributed to this book with their time, ideas, and patience. In particular, we thank Abe Heifets of Atomwise, Liran Belanzon of BenchSci, Alex Shevchenko of Grammarly, Marc Ossip, and Ben Edelman for the time they spent with us in interviews, as well as Kevin Bryan for his comments on the overall manuscript. Also, we thank our colleagues for discussions and feedback, including Nick Adams, Umair Akeel, Susan Athey, Naresh Bangia, Nick Beim, Dennis Bennie, James Bergstra, Dror Berman, Vincent Bérubé, Jim Bessen, Scott Bonham, Erik Brynjolfsson, Andy Burgess, Elizabeth Caley, Peter Carrescia, Iain Cockburn, Christian Catalini, James Cham, Nicolas Chapados, Tyson Clark, Paul Cubbon, Zavain Dar, Sally Daub, Dan Debow, Ron Dembo, Helene Desmarais, JP Dube, Candice Faktor, Haig Farris, Chen Fong, Ash Fontana, John Francis, April Franco, Suzanne Gildert, Anindya Ghose, Ron Glozman, Ben Goertzel, Shane Greenstein, Kanu Gulati, John Harris, Deepak Hegde, Rebecca Henderson, Geoff Hinton, Tim Hodgson, Michael Hyatt, Richard Hyatt, Ben Jones, Chad Jones, Steve Jurvetson, Satish Kanwar, Danny Kahneman, John Kelleher, Moe Kermani, Vinod Khosla, Karin Klein, Darrell Kopke, Johann Koss, Katya Kudashkina, Michael Kuhlmann, Tony Lacavera, Allen Lau, Eva Lau, Yann LeCun, Mara Lederman, Lisha Li, Ted Livingston, Jevon MacDonald, Rupam Mahmood, Chris Matys, Kristina McElheran, John McHale, Sanjog Misra, Matt Mitchell, Sanjay Mittal, Ash Munshi, Michael Murchison, Ken Nickerson, Olivia Norton, Alex Oettl, David Ossip, Barney Pell, Andrea Prat, Tomi Poutanen, Marzio

Pozzuoli, Lally Rementilla, Geordie Rose, Maryanna Saenko, Russ Salakhutdinov, Reza Satchu, Michael Serbinis, Ashmeet Sidana, Micah Siegel, Dilip Soman, John Stackhouse, Scott Stern, Ted Sum, Rich Sutton, Steve Tadelis, Shahram Tafazoli, Graham Taylor, Florenta Teodoridis, Richard Titus, Dan Trefler, Catherine Tucker, William Tunstall-Pedoe, Stephan Uhrenbacher, Cliff van der Linden, Miguel Villas-Boas, Neil Wainwright, Boris Wertz, Dan Wilson, Peter Wittek, Alexander Wong, Shelley Zhuang, and Shivon Zilis. We also thank Carl Shapiro and Hal Varian for their book *Information Rules*, which served as a source of inspiration for our project. The Creative Destruction Lab and Rotman School staffs have been fantastic, particularly Steve Arenburg, Dawn Bloomfield, Rachel Harris, Jennifer Hildebrandt, Anne Hilton, Justyna Jonca, Aidan Kehoe, Khalid Kurji, Mary Lyne, Ken McGuffin, Shray Mehra, Daniel Mulet, Jennifer O'Hare, Gregory Ray, Amir Sariri, Sonia Sennik, Kristjan Sigurdson, Pearl Sullivan, Evelyn Thomasos, and the rest of the Lab team and Rotman staff. We thank our dean, Tiff Macklem, for his enthusiastic support of our work on AI at the Creative Destruction Lab and throughout the Rotman School. Thanks also to the leadership and staff at The Next 36 and The Next AI. We also thank Walter Frick and Tim Sullivan for stellar editing, as well as our agent, Jim Levine. Many of the ideas in the book build on research supported by the Social Sciences and Humanities Research Council of Canada, the Vector Institute, the Canadian Institute for Advanced Research under the leadership of Alan Bernstein and Rebecca Finlay, and the Sloan Foundation with Danny Goroff's support under the Economics of Digitization grant, managed by Shane Greenstein, Scott Stern, and Josh Lerner. We are grateful for their support. We also thank Jim Poterba for his support of our conference on the economics of AI through the National Bureau of Economic Research. Finally, we thank our families for their patience and contributions during this process: Gina, Amelia, Andreas, Rachel, Anna, Sam, Ben, Natalie, Belanna, Ariel, Annika.

1

Introduction

Machine Intelligence

If the following scenario doesn't already sound familiar, then it will soon. A kid is doing homework alone in another room. You hear a question, "What's the capital of Delaware?" The parent starts thinking: *Baltimore . . . too obvious . . . Wilmington . . . not a capital.* But before the thought is complete, a machine called Alexa says the correct answer: "The capital of Delaware is Dover." Alexa is Amazon's artificial intelligence, or AI, that interprets natural language and provides answers to questions at lightning speed. Alexa has replaced the parent as the all-knowing source of information in the eyes of a child.

AI is everywhere. It's in our phones, cars, shopping experiences, romantic matchmaking, hospitals, banks, and all over the media. No wonder corporate directors, CEOs, vice presidents, managers, team leaders, entrepreneurs, investors, coaches, and policy makers are anxiously racing to learn about AI: they all realize it is about to fundamentally change their businesses.

The three of us have observed the advances in AI from a distinctive vantage point. We are economists who built our careers studying the last great technology revolution: the internet. During years of research, we learned how to cut through the hype to focus on what technology means for decision makers.

We also built the Creative Destruction Lab (CDL), a seed-stage program that increases the probability of success for science-based startups. Initially, the CDL was open to all kinds of startups, but by 2015, many of the most exciting ventures were AI-enabled companies. As of September 2017, the CDL had, for the third year in a row, the greatest concentration of AI startups of any program on earth.

As a result, many leaders in the field regularly traveled to Toronto to participate in the CDL. For example, one of the primary inventors of the AI engine that powers Amazon's Alexa, William Tunstall-Pedoe, flew to Toronto every eight weeks from Cambridge, England, to join us throughout the duration of the program. So did San Francisco–based Barney Pell, who previously led an eighty-five-person team at NASA that flew the first AI in deep space.

The CDL's dominance in this domain resulted partly from our location in Toronto, where many of the core inventions—in a field called "machine learning"—that drove the recent interest in AI were seeded and nurtured. Experts who were previously based in the computer science department at the University of Toronto today head several of the world's leading industrial AI teams, including those at Facebook, Apple, and Elon Musk's Open AI.

Being so close to so many *applications* of AI forced us to focus on how this technology affects business strategy. As we'll explain, AI is a prediction technology, predictions are inputs to decision making, and economics provides a perfect framework for understanding the trade-offs underlying any decision. So, by dint of luck and some design, we found ourselves at the right place at the right time to form a bridge between the technologist and the business practitioner. The result is this book.

Our first key insight is that the new wave of artificial intelligence does not actually bring us intelligence but instead a critical component of intelligence—*prediction*. What Alexa was doing when the child asked a question was taking the sounds it heard and predicting the words the child spoke and then predicting what information the words were looking for. Alexa doesn't "know" the capital of Delaware. But Alexa is able to predict that, when people ask such a question, they are looking for a specific response: "Dover."

Each startup in our lab is predicated on exploiting the benefits of better prediction. Deep Genomics improves the practice of medicine by predicting what will happen in a cell when DNA is altered. Chisel improves the practice of law by predicting which parts of a document to redact. Validere improves the efficiency of oil custody transfer by predicting the water content of incoming crude. These applications are a microcosm of what most businesses will be doing in the near future.

If you're lost in the fog trying to figure out what AI means for you, then we can help you understand the implications of AI and navigate through the advances in this technology, even if you've never programmed a convolutional neural network or studied Bayesian statistics.

If you are a business leader, we provide you with an understanding of AI's impact on management and decisions. If you are a student or recent graduate, we give you a framework for thinking about the evolution of jobs and the careers of the future. If you are a financial analyst or venture capitalist, we offer a structure around which you can develop your investment theses. If you are a policy maker, we give you guidelines for understanding how AI is likely to change society and how policy might shape those changes for the better.

Economics provides a well-established foundation for understanding uncertainty and what it means for decision making. As better prediction reduces uncertainty, we use economics to tell you what AI means for the decisions you make in the course of your business. This, in turn, provides insight into which AI tools are likely to deliver the highest return on investment for the work flows inside your business. This then leads to a framework for designing business strategies, such as how you might rethink the scale and scope of your business to exploit the new economic realities predicated on cheap prediction. Finally, we lay out the major trade-offs associated with AI on jobs, on the concentration of corporate power, on privacy, and on geopolitics.

What predictions are important for your business? How will further advances in AI change the predictions you rely on? How will your industry redesign jobs in response to advances in prediction technology just as industries reconfigured jobs with the rise of the personal computer and then of the internet? AI is new and still poorly understood, but the economics toolkit for evaluating the implications of a drop in the cost of prediction is rock solid; although the examples we use will surely become dated, the framework in this book will not. The insights will continue to apply as the technology improves and predictions become more accurate and complex.

Prediction Machines is not a recipe for success in the AI economy. Instead, we emphasize *trade-offs*. More data means less privacy. More speed means less accuracy. More autonomy means less control. We don't prescribe the best strategy for your business. That's your job. The best strategy for your company or career or country will depend on how you weigh each side of every trade-off. This book gives you a structure for identifying the key trade-offs and how to evaluate the pros and cons in order to reach the best decision for you. Of course, even with our framework in hand, you will find that things are changing rapidly. You will need to make decisions without full information, but doing so will often be better than inaction.

KEY POINTS

- The current wave of advances in artificial intelligence doesn't actually bring us intelligence but instead a critical component of intelligence: prediction.

- Prediction is a central input into decision-making. Economics has a well-developed framework for understanding decision-making. The new and poorly understood implications of advances in prediction technology can be combined with the old and well-understood logic of decision theory from economics to deliver a series of insights to help navigate your organization's approach to AI.

- There is often no single right answer to the question of which is the best AI strategy or the best set of AI tools, because AIs involve trade-offs: more speed, less accuracy; more autonomy, less control; more data, less privacy. We provide you with a method for identifying the trade-offs associated with each AI-related decision so that you can evaluate both sides of every trade in light of your organization's mission and objectives and then make the decision that is best for you.

2

Cheap Changes
Everything

Everyone has had or will soon have an *AI moment*. We are accustomed to a media saturated with stories of new technologies that will change our lives. While some of us are technophiles and celebrate the possibilities of the future, and others are technophobes who mourn the passing of the good ole days, almost all of us are so used to the constant drumbeat of technology news that we numbly recite that the only thing immune to change is change itself. Until we have our AI moment. Then we realize that this technology is different.

Some computer scientists experienced their AI moment in 2012 when a student team from the University of Toronto delivered such an impressive win in the visual object recognition competition Image-Net that the following year all top finalists used the then-novel "deep learning" approach to compete. Object recognition is more than just a game; it enables machines to "see."

Some technology CEOs experienced their AI moment when they read the headline in January 2014 that Google had just paid more than $600 million to acquire UK-based DeepMind, even though the startup had generated negligible revenue relative to the purchase price but had demonstrated that its AI had learned—on its own, without being programmed—to play certain Atari video games with super-human performance.

Some regular citizens experienced their AI moment later that year when renowned physicist Stephen Hawking emphatically explained, "[E]verything that civilisation has to offer is a product of human intelligence . . . [S]uccess in creating AI would be the biggest event in human history."[1]

Others experienced their AI moment the first time they took their hands off the wheel of a speeding Tesla, navigating traffic using Autopilot AI.

The Chinese government experienced its AI moment when it witnessed DeepMind's AI, AlphaGo, beating Lee Se-dol, a South Korean master of the board game Go, and then later that year beating the world's top-ranked player, Ke Jie of China. The *New York Times* described this game as China's "Sputnik moment."[2] Just as massive American investment in science followed the Soviet Union's launch of Sputnik, China responded to this event with a national strategy to dominate the AI world by 2030 and a financial commitment to make that claim plausible.

Our own AI moment came in 2012 when a trickle and then a surge in the number of early-stage AI companies employing state-of-the-art machine-learning techniques applied to the CDL. The applications spanned industries—drug discovery, customer service, manufacturing, quality assurance, retail, medical devices. The technology was both powerful and general purpose, creating significant value across a wide range of applications. We set to work understanding what it meant in economics terms. We knew that AI would be subject to the same economics as any other technology.

The technology itself is, simply put, amazing. Early on, famed venture capitalist Steve Jurvetson quipped: "Just about any product that you experience in the next five years that seems like magic will almost certainly be built by these algorithms."[3] Jurvetson's characterization of AI as "magical" resonated with the popular narrative of AI in films like *2001: A Space Odyssey*, *Star Wars*, *Blade Runner*, and more recently *Her*, *Transcendence*, and *Ex Machina*. We understand

and sympathize with Jurvetson's characterization of AI applications as magical. As economists, our job is to take seemingly magical ideas and make them simple, clear, and practical.

Cutting through the Hype

Economists view the world differently than most people. We see everything through a framework governed by forces such as supply and demand, production and consumption, prices and costs. Although economists often disagree with each other, we do so in the context of a common framework. We argue about assumptions and interpretations but not about fundamental concepts, like the roles of scarcity and competition in setting prices. This approach to viewing the world gives us a unique vantage point. On the negative side, our viewpoint is dry and doesn't make us popular at dinner parties. On the positive side, it provides a useful clarity for informing business decisions.

Let's start with the basics—prices. When the price of something falls, we use more of it. That's simple economics and is happening right now with AI. AI is everywhere—packed into your phone's apps, optimizing your electricity grids, and replacing your stock portfolio managers. Soon it may be driving you around or flying packages to your house.

If economists are good at one thing, it is cutting through hype. Where others see transformational new innovation, we see a simple fall in price. But it is more than that. To understand how AI will affect your organization, you need to know precisely what price has changed and how that price change will cascade throughout the broader economy. Only then can you build a plan of action. Economic history has taught us that the impact of major innovations is often felt in the most unexpected places.

Consider the story of the commercial internet in 1995. While most of us were watching *Seinfeld*, Microsoft released Windows 95, its first multitasking operating system. That same year, the US government removed the final restrictions to carrying commercial traffic on the internet, and Netscape—the browser's inventor—celebrated the first major initial public offering (IPO) of the commercial internet. This marked an inflection point when the internet transitioned from a technological curiosity to a commercial tidal wave that would wash over the economy.

Netscape's IPO valued the company at more than $3 billion, even though it had not generated any significant profit. Venture capital investors valued startups in the millions even if they were, and this was a new term, "pre-revenue." Freshly minted MBA graduates turned down lucrative traditional jobs to prospect on the web. As the effects of the internet began to spread across industries and up and down the value chain, technology advocates stopped referring to the internet as a new technology and began referring to it as the "New Economy." The term caught on. The internet transcended the technology and permeated human activity at a fundamental level. Politicians, corporate executives, investors, entrepreneurs, and major news organizations started using the term. Everyone began referring to the New Economy.

Everyone, that is, *except economists*. We did not see a new economy or a new economics. To economists, this looked like the regular old economy. To be sure, some important changes had occurred. Goods and services could be distributed digitally. Communication was easy. And you could find information with the click of a search button. But you could do all of these things before. What had changed was that you could now do them cheaply. The rise of the internet was a drop in the cost of distribution, communication, and search. Reframing a technological advance as a shift from expensive to cheap or from scarce to abundant is invaluable for thinking about how it will affect your business. For instance, if you recall the first time you used Google, you may remember being mesmerized by the seemingly magical ability to access information. From the economist perspective, Google made search cheap. When search became cheap, companies that made money selling search through other means (e.g., the Yellow Pages, travel agents, classifieds) found themselves in a competitive crisis. At the same time, companies that relied on people finding them (for example, self-publishing authors, sellers of obscure collectibles, homegrown moviemakers) prospered.

This change in the relative costs of certain activities radically influenced some companies' business models and even transformed some industries. However, economic laws did not change. We could still understand everything in terms of supply and demand and could set strategy, inform policy, and anticipate the future using off-the-shelf economic principles.

Cheap Means Everywhere

When the price of something fundamental drops drastically, the whole world can change. Consider light. Chances are you are reading this book under some kind of artificial light. Moreover, you probably never thought about whether using artificial light for reading was worth it. Light is so cheap that you use it with abandon. But, as the economist William Nordhaus meticulously explored, in the early 1800s it would have cost you four hundred times what you are paying now for the same amount of light.[4] At that price, you would notice the cost and would think twice before using artificial light to read this book. The subsequent drop in the price of light lit up the world. Not only did it turn night into day, but it allowed us to live and work in big buildings that natural light could not penetrate. Virtually nothing we have today would be possible had the cost of artificial light not collapsed to almost nothing.

Technological change makes things cheap that were once expensive. The cost of light fell so much that it changed our behavior from thinking about whether we should use it to not thinking for even a second before flipping on a light switch. Such significant price drops create opportunities to do things we've never done; it can make the impossible possible. So, economists are unsurprisingly obsessed with the implications of massive price drops in foundational inputs like light.

Some of the impacts from producing cheaper light were easy to imagine, and others less so. What might be affected when a new technology makes something cheap is not always precisely obvious, whether the technology is artificial light, steam power, the automobile, or computing.

Tim Bresnahan, a Stanford economist and one of our mentors, pointed out that computers do arithmetic and nothing more. The advent and commercialization of computers made arithmetic cheap.[5] When arithmetic became cheap, not only did we use more of it for traditional applications of arithmetic, but we also used the newly cheap arithmetic for applications that were not traditionally associated with arithmetic, like music.

Heralded as the first computer programmer, Ada Lovelace was the first to see this potential. Working under very expensive light in the early 1800s, she wrote the earliest recorded program to compute a series of numbers (called Bernoulli numbers) on a still-theoretical computer that Charles Babbage designed. Babbage was also an economist, and as we will see in this book, that was not the only time economics and computer science intersected. Lovelace understood that arithmetic could, to use modern startup lingo, "scale" and enable so much more. She realized that applications of computers were not limited to mathematical operations: "Supposing, for instance, that the fundamental relations of pitched sounds in the science of harmony and of musical composition were susceptible of such expression and adaptations, the engine might compose elaborate and scientific pieces of music of any degree of complexity."[6] No computer had been invented yet, but Lovelace saw that an arithmetic machine could store and replay music—a form that defined art and humanity.

That is precisely what happened. When, a century and a half later, the cost of arithmetic fell low enough, there were thousands of applications for arithmetic that most had never dreamed of. Arithmetic was such an important input into so many things that, when it became cheap, just as light had before, it changed the world. Reducing something to pure cost terms has a way of cutting through hype, although it does not help make the latest and greatest technology seem exciting. You'd never have seen Steve Jobs announce "a new adding machine," even though that is all he ever did. By reducing the cost of something important, Jobs's new adding machines were transformative.

That brings us to AI. AI will be economically significant precisely because it will make something important much cheaper. Right now, you may be thinking about intellect, reasoning, or thought itself.

You might be imagining robots all over or non-corporeal beings, such as the friendly computers in *Star Trek*, letting you avoid the need to think. Lovelace had the same thought, but quickly dismissed it. At least insofar as a computer was concerned, she wrote, it "had no pretensions to originate anything. It can do whatever we know how to order it to perform. It can follow analysis; but it has no power of anticipating any analytical relations or truths."[7]

Despite all the hype and the baggage that comes with the notion of AI, what Alan Turing later called "Lady Lovelace's Objection" still stands. Computers still cannot think, so thought isn't about to become cheap. However, what will be cheap is something so prevalent that, like arithmetic, you are probably not even aware of how ubiquitous it is and how much a drop in its price could affect our lives and economy.

What will new AI technologies make so cheap? *Prediction.* Therefore, as economics tells us, not only are we going to start using a lot more prediction, but we are going to see it emerge in surprising new places.

Cheap Creates Value

Prediction is the process of filling in missing information. Prediction takes information you have, often called "data," and uses it to generate information you don't have. Much discussion about AI emphasizes the variety of prediction techniques using increasingly obscure names and labels: classification, clustering, regression, decision trees, Bayesian estimation, neural networks, topological data analysis, deep learning, reinforcement learning, deep reinforcement learning, capsule networks, and so on. The techniques are important for technologists interested in implementing AI for a particular prediction problem.

In this book, we spare you the details of the mathematics behind the methods. We emphasize that each of these methods is about prediction: using information you have to generate information you don't have. We focus on helping you identify situations in which prediction will be valuable, and then on how to benefit as much as possible from that prediction.

Cheaper prediction will mean more predictions. This is simple economics: when the cost of something falls, we do more of it. For example, as the computer industry began to take off in the 1960s and the cost of arithmetic began to fall rapidly, we used more arithmetic in applications where it was already an input, such as at the US Census Bureau, the US Department of Defense, and NASA (recently depicted in the film *Hidden Figures*). We later began to use the newly cheap arithmetic on problems that *weren't* traditionally arithmetic problems, such as photography. Whereas we once solved photography with chemistry, when arithmetic became cheap enough, we transitioned to an arithmetic-based solution: digital cameras. A digital image is just a string of zeros and ones that can be reassembled into a viewable image using arithmetic.

The same goes for prediction. Prediction is being used for traditional tasks, like inventory management and demand forecasting. More significantly, because it is becoming cheaper it is being used for problems that were not traditionally prediction problems. Kathryn Hume, of Integrate.ai, calls the ability to see a problem and reframe it as a prediction problem "AI Insight," and, today, engineers all over the world are acquiring it. For example, we are transforming transportation into a prediction problem. Autonomous vehicles have existed in controlled environments for over two decades. They were limited, however, to places with detailed floor plans such as factories and warehouses. The floor plans meant engineers could design their robots to maneuver with basic "if-then" logical intelligence: if a person walks in front of the vehicle, then stop. If the shelf is empty, then move to the next one. However, no one could use those vehicles on a regular city street. Too many things could happen—too many "ifs" to possibly code.

Autonomous vehicles could not function outside a highly predictable, controlled environment—until engineers reframed navigation as a prediction problem. Instead of telling the machine what to do in each circumstance, engineers recognized they could instead focus on a single prediction problem: *"What would a human do?"* Now, companies are investing billions of dollars in training machines to drive autonomously in uncontrolled environments, even on city streets and highways.

Imagine an AI sitting in the car with a human driver. The human drives for millions of miles, receiving data about the environment through their eyes and ears, processing that data with their human brain, and then acting in response to the incoming data: drive straight or turn, brake or accelerate. Engineers give the AI its own eyes and ears by outfitting the car with sensors (e.g., cameras, radar, lasers). So, the AI observes the incoming data as the human drives and simultaneously observes the human's actions. When particular environmental data comes in, does the human turn right, brake, or accelerate? The more the AI observes the human, the better it becomes at predicting the specific action the driver will take, given the incoming environmental data. The AI learns to drive by predicting what a human driver would do given specific road conditions.

Critically, when an input such as prediction becomes cheap, this can enhance the value of other things. Economists call these "complements." Just as a drop in the cost of coffee increases the value of sugar and cream, for autonomous vehicles, a drop in the cost of prediction increases the value of sensors to capture data on the vehicle's surroundings. For example, in 2017, Intel paid more than $15 billion for the Israeli startup Mobileye, primarily for its data-collection technology that allows vehicles to effectively see objects (stop signs, people, etc.) and markings (lanes, roads).

When prediction is cheap, there will be more prediction and more complements to prediction. These two simple economic forces drive the new opportunities that prediction machines create. At low levels, a prediction machine can relieve humans of predictive tasks and so save on costs. As the machine cranks up, prediction can change and improve decision-making quality. But at some point, a prediction machine may become so accurate and reliable that it changes how an organization does things. Some AIs will affect the economics of a business so dramatically that they will no longer be used to simply enhance productivity in executing against the strategy; they will change the strategy itself.

From Cheap to Strategy

The single most common question corporate executives ask us is: "How will AI affect our business strategy?" We use a thought experiment to answer that question. Most people are familiar with shopping at Amazon. As with most online retailers, you visit its website, shop for items, place them in your cart, pay for them, and then Amazon ships them to you. Right now, Amazon's business model is shopping-then-shipping.

During the shopping process, Amazon's AI offers suggestions of items that it predicts you will want to buy. The AI does a reasonable job. However, it is far from perfect. In our case, the AI accurately predicts what we want to buy about 5 percent of the time. We actually purchase about one of every twenty items it recommends. Considering the millions of items on offer, that's not bad!

Imagine that the Amazon AI collects more information about us and uses that data to improve its predictions, an improvement akin to turning up the volume knob on a speaker dial. But rather than volume, it's turning up the AI's prediction accuracy.

At some point, as it turns the knob, the AI's prediction accuracy crosses a threshold, changing Amazon's business model. The prediction becomes sufficiently accurate that it becomes more profitable for Amazon to ship you the goods that it predicts you will want rather than wait for you to order them.

With that, you won't need to go to other retailers, and the fact that the item is there may well nudge you to buy more. Amazon gains a higher share of wallet. Clearly, this is great for Amazon, but it is also great for you. Amazon ships before you shop, which, if all goes well, saves you the task of shopping entirely. Cranking up the prediction dial changes Amazon's business model from shopping-then-shipping to shipping-then-shopping.

Of course, shoppers would not want to deal with the hassle of returning all the items they don't want. So, Amazon would invest in infrastructure for the product returns, perhaps a fleet of delivery-style trucks that do pickups once a week, conveniently collecting items that customers don't want.[8]

If this is a better business model, then why hasn't Amazon done it already? Because if implemented today, the cost of collecting and handling returned items would outweigh the increase in revenue from a greater share of wallet. For example, today we would return 95 percent of the items it ships to us. That is annoying for us and costly for Amazon. The prediction isn't good enough for Amazon to adopt the new model.

We can imagine a scenario where Amazon adopts the new strategy even *before* the prediction accuracy is good enough to make it profitable because the company *anticipates* that at some point it will be profitable. By launching sooner, Amazon's AI will get more data sooner and improve faster. Amazon realizes that the sooner it starts, the harder it will be for competitors to catch up. Better predictions will attract more shoppers, more shoppers will generate more data to train the AI, more data will lead to better predictions, and so on, creating a virtuous cycle. Adopting too early could be costly, but adopting too late could be fatal.[9]

Our point is not that Amazon will or should do this, although skeptical readers may be surprised to learn that Amazon obtained a US patent for "anticipatory shipping" in 2013.[10] Instead, the salient insight is that turning the prediction dial has a significant impact on strategy. In this example, it shifts Amazon's business model from shopping-then-shipping to shipping-then-shopping, generates the incentive to vertically integrate into operating a service for product returns (including a fleet of trucks), and accelerates the timing of investment. All this is due simply to turning up the dial on the prediction machine.

What does this mean for strategy? First, you must invest in gathering intelligence on how fast and how far the dial on the prediction machines will turn for your sector and applications. Second, you must invest in developing a thesis about the strategic options created from turning the dial.

To get started on this "science fictioning" exercise, close your eyes, imagine putting your fingers on the dial of your prediction machine, and, in the immortal words of Spinal Tap, turn it to eleven.

The Plan for the Book

You need to build foundations before the strategic implications of prediction machines for your organization become apparent. That is precisely how we structured this book, building a pyramid from the ground up.

We lay the foundation in part one and explain how machine learning makes *prediction* better. We move to why these new advances are different from the statistics you learned in school or that your analysts might already conduct. We then consider a key complement to prediction, data, especially the types of data required to make good predictions, and how to know whether you have it. Finally, we delve into when prediction machines perform better than humans and when people and machines might work together for even better predictive accuracy.

In part two, we describe the role of prediction as an input into *decision making* and explain the importance of another component that the AI community has so far neglected: judgment. Prediction facilitates decisions by reducing uncertainty, while judgment assigns value. In economists' parlance, judgment is the skill used to determine a payoff, utility, reward, or profit. The most significant implication of prediction machines is that they increase the value of judgment.

Practical matters are the focus of part three. AI *tools* make prediction machines useful and are implementations of prediction machines designed to perform a specific task. We outline three steps that will help you figure out when building (or buying) an AI tool will generate the highest return on investment. Sometimes such tools slot neatly into an existing work flow; at other times, they motivate redesigning the work flow. Along the way, we introduce an important aid for specifying the key features of an AI tool: the AI canvas.

We turn to *strategy* in part four. As we describe in our Amazon thought experiment, some AIs will have such a profound effect on the economics of a task that they will transform a business or industry. That's when AI becomes the cornerstone of an organization's strategy. AIs that have an impact on strategy shift the attention on

AI from product managers and operations engineers to the C-suite. Sometimes, it's hard to tell in advance when a tool will have such a powerful effect. For example, few people predicted, when they tried it for the first time, that the Google search tool would transform the media industry and become the basis of one of the most valuable companies on earth.

In addition to upside opportunities, AI poses systemic risks that may hit your business unless you take preemptory actions. Popular discussion seems to focus on the risks AI poses to humanity, but people pay much less attention to the dangers AI poses to organizations. For instance, some prediction machines trained on human-generated data have already "learned" treacherous biases and stereotypes.

We end the book in part five by applying our economists' tool kit to questions that affect *society* more broadly, examining five of the most common AI debates:

1. Will there still be jobs? *Yes.*

2. Will this generate more inequality? *Perhaps.*

3. Will a few large companies control everything? *It depends.*

4. Will countries engage in race-to-the-bottom policy making and forfeit our privacy and security to give their domestic companies a competitive advantage? *Some will.*

5. Will the world end? *You still have plenty of time to derive value from this book.*

KEY POINTS

- Economics offers clear insights regarding the business implications of cheaper prediction. Prediction machines will be used for traditional prediction tasks (inventory and demand forecasting) and new problems (like navigation and translation). The drop in the cost of prediction will impact the value of other things, increasing the value of complements (data, judgment, and action) and diminishing the value of substitutes (human prediction).

- Organizations can exploit prediction machines by adopting AI tools to assist with executing their current strategy. When those tools become powerful, they may motivate changing the strategy itself. For instance, if Amazon can predict what shoppers want, then they may move from a shop-then-ship model to a ship-then-shop model—bringing goods to homes before they are ordered. Such a shift will transform the organization.

- As a result of the new strategies that organizations pursue to take advantage of AI, we will be faced with a new set of trade-offs related to how AI will impact society. Our choices will depend on our needs and preferences, and will almost surely be different across different countries and cultures. We structured this book in five sections to reflect each layer of impact from AI, building from the foundations of prediction all the way up to the trade-offs for society: (1) Prediction, (2) Decision making, (3) Tools, (4) Strategy, and (5) Society.

PART ONE

Prediction

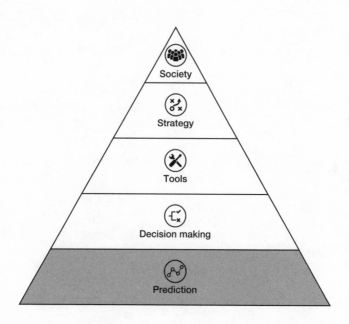

- Society
- Strategy
- Tools
- Decision making
- Prediction

3

Prediction Machine Magic

What do Harry Potter, Snow White, and Macbeth have in common? These characters are all motivated by a prophecy, a prediction. Even in *The Matrix*, a film seemingly about intelligent machines, the human characters' belief in predictions drives the plot. From religion to fairy tales, knowledge of the future is consequential. Predictions affect behavior. They influence decisions.

The ancient Greeks revered their many oracles for an apparent ability to predict, sometimes in riddles that fooled the questioners. For example, King Croesus of Lydia was considering a risky assault on the Persian Empire. The king did not trust any particular oracle, so he decided to test each before asking for advice about attacking Persia. He sent messengers to each oracle. On the hundredth day, the messengers were to ask the various oracles what Croesus was doing *at that moment*. The oracle at Delphi predicted most accurately, so the king asked for and trusted its prophecy.[1]

As in Croesus's case, predictions can be about the *present*. We predict whether a current credit card transaction is legitimate or fraudulent, whether a tumor in a medical image is malignant or benign, whether the person looking into the iPhone camera is the owner or not. Despite its Latin root verb (*praedicere*, meaning to make known beforehand), our cultural understanding of prediction emphasizes the ability to see otherwise hidden information, whether in the past, present, or future. The crystal ball is perhaps the most familiar symbol of magical prediction. While we may associate crystal balls with fortune-tellers predicting someone's future wealth or love life, in *The Wizard of Oz*, the crystal ball allowed Dorothy to see Auntie Em in the present. This brings us to our definition of prediction:

> PREDICTION is the process of filling in missing information.
> Prediction takes information you have, often called "data,"
> and uses it to generate information you don't have.

The Magic of Prediction

Several years ago, Avi (one of the authors) noticed a large, unusual transaction in a Las Vegas casino on his credit card. He hadn't been in Las Vegas. He had only been there once a long time before; the losing bet of gambling doesn't appeal to his economist way of seeing the world. After an extensive conversation, his card provider reversed the transaction and replaced the card.

Recently, a similar problem occurred. Someone had used Avi's credit card for a purchase. This time Avi didn't see it on his statement and didn't have to deal with the painstaking process of explaining it to a polite but firm customer service representative. Instead, he received a proactive call that his card had been compromised and that a new card was already in the mail.

The credit card provider had accurately inferred, based on Avi's spending habits and a myriad of other available data, that the transaction was fraudulent. The credit card company was so confident that they did not even block his card for a few days while they carried out an investigation. Instead, like magic, the company sent a replacement without his having to do anything. Of course, the credit card provider did not have a crystal ball. It had data and a good predictive model: a prediction machine. Better prediction allowed it to reduce fraud while, as Ajay Bhalla, Mastercard's president of enterprise risk and security, put it, "solving a major consumer pain point of being falsely declined."[2]

Business applications are well aligned with our definition of prediction as the process of filling in missing information. Credit card networks find it is useful to know whether a recent credit card transaction is fraudulent. The card network uses information about past fraudulent (and nonfraudulent) transactions to predict whether a particular recent transaction is fraudulent. If so, then the credit card provider can prevent future transactions on that card and, if the prediction is made quickly enough, then, perhaps even the current one.

This notion—taking information of one kind and turning it into information of another kind—is at the heart of one of AI's recent main achievements: language translation, a goal that has been around for all of human civilization, even enshrined in the millennia-old story of the Tower of Babel. Historically, the approach to automatic language translation was to hire a linguist—an expert on the rules of language—to exposit rules and translate them into a way they could be programmed.[3] This is how, for instance, you might take a Spanish phrase and, beyond simply substituting word for word, understand that you need to swap the order of nouns and adjectives to make it a readable English sentence.

The recent advances in AI, however, have enabled us to recast translation as a prediction problem. We can see the seemingly magical nature of the use of prediction for translation in the sudden change in the quality of Google's translation service. Ernest Hemingway's *The Snows of Kilimanjaro* begins beautifully:

> Kilimanjaro is a snow-covered mountain 19,710 feet high, and is said to be the highest mountain in Africa.

One day in November 2016, in translating a Japanese version of Hemingway's classic short story into English via Google, Professor Jun Rekimoto, a computer scientist at the University of Tokyo, read:

> Kilimanjaro is 19,710 feet of the mountain covered with snow, and it is said that the highest mountain in Africa.

The next day, the Google translation read:

> Kilimanjaro is a mountain of 19,710 feet covered with snow and is said to be the highest mountain in Africa.

The difference was stark. Overnight, the translation had gone from clearly automated and clunky to a coherent sentence, from someone struggling with a dictionary to seemingly fluent in both languages.

Admittedly, it wasn't quite at the Hemingway level, but the improvement was extraordinary. Babel appeared to have returned. And this change was no accident or quirk. Google had revamped the engine underlying its translation product to take advantage of the recent advances in AI that are our focus here. Specifically, Google's translation service now relied on deep learning to supercharge prediction.

Language translation from English to Japanese is about predicting the Japanese words and phrases that match the English. The missing information to be predicted is the set of Japanese words and the order in which they belong. Take data from a foreign language and predict the correct set of words in the right order in a language you know, and then you can understand another language. Do it really well, and you might not realize translation is taking place at all.

Companies have wasted no time in putting this magical technology to commercial use. For example, over 500 million people in China already use a deep learning–powered service developed by iFlytek to translate, transcribe, and communicate using natural language. Landlords use it to communicate with tenants in other languages, hospital patients use it to communicate with robots for directions, doctors use it to dictate a patient's medical details, and drivers use it to communicate with their vehicles.[4] The more the AI is used, the more data it collects, the more it learns, and the better it becomes. With so many users, the AI is improving rapidly.

How Much Better Is Prediction Than It Used to Be?

The changes in Google Translate illustrate how machine learning (of which deep learning is a subfield) has dramatically reduced the costs of quality-adjusted prediction. For the same cost in terms of computational capacity, Google can now provide higher-quality translations. The cost of producing the same quality of prediction has dropped significantly.

Innovations in prediction technology are having an impact on areas traditionally associated with forecasting, such as fraud detection. Credit card fraud detection has improved so much that credit card companies detect and address fraud before we notice anything amiss. Still, this improvement seems incremental. In the late 1990s, the leading methods caught about 80 percent of fraudulent transactions.[5] These rates improved to 90–95 percent in 2000 and to 98–99.9 percent today.[6] That last jump is a result of machine learning; the change from 98 percent to 99.9 percent has been transformational.

The change from 98 percent to 99.9 percent might *seem* incremental, but small changes are meaningful if mistakes are costly. An improvement from 85 percent to 90 percent accuracy means that mistakes fall by one-third. An improvement from 98 percent to 99.9 percent means mistakes fall by a factor of twenty. An improvement of twenty no longer seems incremental.

The drop in the cost of prediction is transforming many human activities. Just as the first applications of computing applied to familiar arithmetic problems like census tabulations and ballistics tables, many of the first applications of inexpensive prediction from machine learning applied to classic prediction problems. In addition to fraud detection, these included creditworthiness, health insurance, and inventory management. Creditworthiness involved predicting the likelihood that someone would pay back a loan. Health insurance involved predicting how much an individual would spend on medical care. Inventory management involved predicting how many items would be in a warehouse on a given day.

More recently, entirely new classes of prediction problems emerged. Many were nearly impossible before the recent advances in machine intelligence technology, including object identification, language translation, and drug discovery. For example, the ImageNet Challenge is a high-profile annual contest to predict the name of an object in an image. Predicting the object in an image can be a difficult task, even for humans. The ImageNet data contains a thousand categories of objects, including many breeds of dog and other similar images. It can be difficult to tell the difference between a Tibetan mastiff and a Bernese mountain dog, or between a safe and a combination lock. Humans make mistakes around 5 percent of the time.[7]

Between the first year of the competition in 2010 to the final contest in 2017, prediction got much better. Figure 3-1 shows the accuracy of the contest winners by year. The vertical axis measures the error rate, so lower is better. In 2010, the best machine predictions made mistakes in 28 percent of images. In 2012, the contestants used deep learning for the first time and the error rate plunged to 16 percent. As Princeton professor and computer scientist Olga Russakovsky notes,

FIGURE 3-1

Image classification error over time

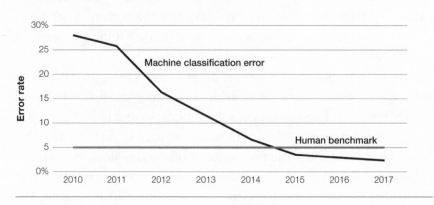

"2012 was really the year when there was a massive breakthrough in accuracy, but it was also a proof of concept for deep learning models, which had been around for decades."[8] Rapid improvements in the algorithms continued, and a team beat the human benchmark in the competition for the first time in 2015. By 2017, the vast majority of the thirty-eight teams did better than the human benchmark, and the best team had fewer than half as many mistakes. Machines could identify these types of images better than people.[9]

The Consequences of Cheap Prediction

The current generation of AI is a long way from the intelligent machines of science fiction. Prediction does not get us HAL from *2001: A Space Odyssey*, Skynet from *The Terminator*, or C3PO from *Star Wars*. If modern AI is just prediction, then why is there so much fuss? The reason is because prediction is such a foundational input. You might not realize it, but predictions are everywhere. Our businesses and our personal lives are riddled with predictions. Often our predictions are hidden as inputs into decision making. Better prediction means better information, which means better decision making.

Prediction is "intelligence" in the espionage sense of "obtaining of useful information."[10] Machine prediction is artificially generated useful information. Intelligence matters. Better predictions lead to better outcomes, as we illustrated with the fraud-detection example. As the cost of prediction continues to fall, we are discovering its usefulness for a remarkably broad range of *additional* activities and, in the process, enabling all sorts of things, like machine language translation, that were previously unimaginable.

KEY POINTS

- Prediction is the process of filling in missing information. Prediction takes information you have, often called "data," and uses it to generate information you don't have. In addition to generating information about the future, prediction can generate information about the present and the past. This happens when prediction classifies credit card transactions as fraudulent, a tumor in an image as malignant, or whether a person holding an iPhone is the owner.

- The impact of small improvements in prediction accuracy can be deceptive. For example, an improvement from 85 percent to 90 percent accuracy seems more than twice as large as from 98 percent to 99.9 percent (an increase of 5 percentage points compared to 2). However, the former improvement means that mistakes fall by one-third, whereas the latter means mistakes fall by a factor of twenty. In some settings, mistakes falling by a factor of twenty is transformational.

- The seemingly mundane process of filling in missing information can make prediction machines seem magical. This has already happened as machines see (object recognition), navigate (driverless cars), and translate.

4

Why It's Called Intelligence

In 1956, a group of scholars met at Dartmouth College in New Hampshire to map out a research path to artificial intelligence. They wanted to see if computers could be programmed to engage in cognitive thought, things like playing games, proving mathematical theorems, and the like. They also thought carefully about what language and knowledge are so that computers could describe things. Their efforts involved attempts to give computers choices and have them choose the best one. The researchers were optimistic about the possibilities of AI. When asking for funds from the Rockefeller Foundation, they wrote:

> An attempt will be made to find how to make machines use language, form abstractions and concepts, solve kinds of problems now reserved for humans, and improve themselves. We think that a significant advance can be made in one or more of these problems if a carefully selected group of scientists work on it together for a summer.[1]

This agenda turned out to be more visionary than practical. Among other challenges, the computers of the 1950s were not fast enough to do what the scholars envisioned.

After that original research statement, AI showed some early progress in translation, but it proved slow. Work on AI in very specific environments (for instance, one that bred an artificial therapist) failed to generalize. The early 1980s brought hope that engineers could carefully program expert systems to replicate skilled domains like medical diagnosis, but these were costly to develop, cumbersome, and could not address the myriad of exceptions and possibilities, leading to what became known as an "AI winter."

Winter, however, appears to be over. More data, better models, and enhanced computers have enabled recent developments in machine learning to improve prediction. Improvements in the collection and storage of big data have provided feedstock for new machine learning algorithms. Compared to their older statistical counterparts, and facilitated by the invention of more suitable processors, the new machine learning models are significantly more flexible and generate better predictions—so much better that some people have returned to describing this branch of computer science as "artificial intelligence."

Predicting Churn

Better data, models, and computers are at the core of progress in prediction. To understand their value, let's consider a long-standing problem of prediction: forecasting what marketers call "customer churn." For many businesses, customers are expensive to acquire and, therefore, losing customers through churn, is costly. Once acquired, businesses can capitalize on those acquisition costs by reducing churn. In service industries like insurance, financial services, and telecommunications, managing churn is perhaps the most important marketing activity. The first step in reducing churn is to identify at-risk customers. Companies can use prediction technologies to do that.

Historically, the core method for predicting churn was a statistical technique called "regression." Research focused on improving regression techniques. Researchers proposed and tested hundreds of different regression methods in academic journals and in practice.

What does regression do? It finds a prediction based on the average of what has occurred in the past. For instance, if all you have to go on to determine whether it is going to rain tomorrow is what happened each day last week, your best guess might be an average. If it rained on two of the last seven days, you might predict that the probability of rain tomorrow is around two in seven, or 29 percent. Much of what we know about prediction has been making our calculations of the average better by building models that can take in more data about the context.

We have done this by using something called "the conditional average." For instance, if you live in northern California, you may have past knowledge that the likelihood of rain depends on the season—low in the summer and high in the winter. If you observe that during the winter, the probability of rain on any given day is 25 percent, while during the summer, it is 5 percent, you would not assess that the probability of rain tomorrow is the average—15 percent. Why? Because you know whether tomorrow is winter or summer, so you would condition your assessment accordingly.

Adjusting for seasons is just one way we condition averages (although a popular one in the retail trade). We can condition averages on time of day, pollution, cloud cover, ocean temperature, or any other available information.

It is even possible to condition on multiple things at once: Will it rain tomorrow if it rained today, it is winter, it is raining two hundred miles to the west, it is sunny a hundred miles to the south, the ground is wet, the Arctic Ocean temperature is low, and the wind is blowing from the southwest at fifteen miles per hour? However, this quickly gets rather unwieldy. Calculating the average for these seven types of information alone creates 128 different combinations. Adding more types of information creates exponentially more combinations.

Before machine learning, multivariate regression provided an efficient way to condition on multiple things, without the need to calculate dozens, hundreds, or thousands of conditional averages.

Regression takes the data and tries to find the result that minimizes prediction mistakes, maximizing what is called "goodness of fit."

Thankfully, this term is more precise mathematically than verbally. Regression minimizes prediction mistakes on average and punishes large errors more than small ones. It is a powerful method, especially with relatively small data sets and a good sense of what will be useful in prediction. For churn in cable television, it might be how frequently people watch TV; if they aren't using their cable subscription, then they are likely to stop subscribing.

In addition, regression models aspire to generate unbiased results, so with enough predictions, those predictions will be exactly correct on average. Although we prefer unbiased over biased predictions (that systematically overestimate or underestimate a value, for example), predictions that are unbiased are still not perfect. We can illustrate this point with an old statistics joke:

> A physicist, an engineer, and a statistician are on a hunting trip. They are walking through the woods when they spot a deer in the clearing.
>
> The physicist calculates the distance to the target, the velocity and drop of the bullet, adjusts, and fires, missing the deer by five feet to the left.
>
> The engineer looks frustrated. "You forgot to account for the wind. Give it here." After licking a finger to determine the wind speed and direction, the engineer snatches the rifle and fires, missing the deer by five feet to the right.
>
> Suddenly, without firing a shot, the statistician cheers, "Woo hoo! We got it!"

Being precisely perfect on average can mean being actually wrong each time. Regression can keep missing several feet to the left or several feet to the right. Even if it averages out to the correct answer, regression can mean never actually hitting the target.

Unlike regression, machine learning predictions might be wrong on average, but when the predictions miss, they often don't miss by much. Statisticians describe this as allowing some bias in exchange for reducing variance.

An important difference between machine learning and regression analysis is the way in which new techniques are developed. Inventing a new machine learning method involves proving that it works better in practice. In contrast, inventing a new regression method requires first proving it works in theory. The focus on working in practice gave machine learning innovators more room to experiment, even if their methods generated estimates that were incorrect on average, or biased. This freedom to experiment drove rapid improvements that take advantage of the rich data and fast computers that appeared over the last decade.

Throughout the late 1990s and early 2000s, experiments with machine learning to predict customer churn had limited success. Machine learning methods were improving, but regression still generally performed better. The data wasn't rich enough, and the computers weren't good enough to take advantage of what machine learning could do.

For example, Duke University's Teradata Center held a data science tournament in 2004 to predict churn. Such tournaments were unusual then. Anyone could submit, and winning submissions received cash prizes. The winning submissions used regression models. Some machine learning methods performed adequately, but the neural net methods that would later drive the AI revolution did not perform well. By 2016, that had all changed. The best churn models used machine learning, and (neural net) deep learning models generally outperformed all others.

What changed? First, the data and computers were finally good enough to enable machine learning to dominate. In the 1990s, it was difficult to build large enough data sets. For example, a classic study of churn prediction used 650 customers and fewer than 30 variables.

By 2004, computer processing and storage had improved. In the Duke tournament, the training data set contained information on hundreds of variables for tens of thousands of customers. With these additional variables and customers, machine learning methods started to perform as well, if not better, than regression.

Now researchers base churn prediction on thousands of variables and millions of customers. Improvements in computing power mean it is possible to include enormous amounts of data, including text and images as well as numbers. For example, in a mobile phone churn model, researchers utilized data on hour-by-hour call records in addition to standard variables such as bill size and payment punctuality.

The machine learning methods also got better at leveraging the data available. In the Duke competition, a key component of success was choosing which of the hundreds of available variables to include and choosing which statistical model to use. The best methods at the time, whether machine learning or classic regression, used a combination of intuition and statistical tests to select the variables and model. Now, machine learning methods, and especially deep learning methods, allow flexibility in the model and this means variables can combine with each other in unexpected ways. People with large phone bills who rack up minutes early in the billing month might be less likely to churn than people with large bills who rack up their minutes later in the month. Or people with large weekend long-distance bills who also pay late and tend to text a lot may be particularly likely to churn. Such combinations are difficult to anticipate, but they can help prediction a great deal. Because they are hard to foresee, modelers do not include them when predicting with standard regression techniques. Machine learning gives the choices of which combinations and interactions might matter to the machine and not the programmer.

Improvements in machine learning methods, generally, and deep learning, in particular, mean that it is possible to efficiently turn available data into accurate predictions of churn. And machine learning methods now clearly dominate regression and various other techniques.

Beyond Churn

Machine learning is improving prediction in a variety of other settings beyond churn, from financial markets to the weather.

The financial crisis of 2008 was a spectacular failure of regression-based prediction methods. Partly driving the financial crisis were predictions of the likely default of collateralized debt obligations, or CDOs. In 2007, ratings agencies like Standard & Poor's forecasted that AAA-rated CDOs had a less than one in eight hundred chance of failing to deliver a return in five years. Five years later, more than one in four CDOs failed to deliver a return. The initial prediction was staggeringly wrong despite very rich data on past defaults.

The failure was not due to insufficient data, but instead how analysts used that data to form a prediction. Ratings agencies based their prediction on multiple regression–like models that assumed house prices in different markets were not correlated with one another. That turned out to be false, not just in 2007 but also previously. Include the possibility that a shock might hit many housing markets simultaneously, and the probability goes way up that you lose out on CDOs, even if they are distributed across many US cities.

Analysts built their regression models on hypotheses of what they believed mattered and how—beliefs unnecessary for machine learning. Machine learning models are particularly good at determining which of many possible variables will work best and recognizing that some things don't matter and others, perhaps surprisingly, do. Now, an analyst's intuition and hypotheses are less important. In this way, machine learning enables predictions based on unanticipated correlations, including that housing prices in Las Vegas, Phoenix, and Miami might move together.

If It's Just Prediction, Then Why Is It Called "Intelligence"?

Recent advances in machine learning have transformed how we use statistics to predict. It is tempting to consider the most recent developments in AI and machine learning as just "traditional statistics on steroids." In one sense that is true, since the ultimate goal is to generate a prediction to fill in missing information. Moreover, the process of machine learning involves searching for a solution that tends to minimize errors.

So what makes machine learning a transformative computing technology that might deserve the label "artificial intelligence"? In some cases, the predictions are so good that we can use prediction instead of rule-based logic.

Effective prediction changes the way computers are programmed. Neither traditional statistical methods nor algorithms of if-then statements operate well in complex environments. Want to identify a cat in a group of pictures? Specify that cats come in many colors and textures. They may be standing, sitting, lying, jumping, or looking grumpy. They may be inside or outside. It quickly becomes complicated. Thus, even doing a passable job requires much careful tending. And that is just for cats. What if we want a way to describe all the objects in a picture? We need a separate specification for each one.

A key technology underpinning recent advances, labeled "deep learning," relies on an approach called "back propagation." It avoids all this in a way similar to how natural brains do, by learning through example (whether artificial neurons mimic real ones is an interesting distraction from the usefulness of the technology). If you want a child to know the word for "cat," then every time you see a cat, say the word. It is basically the same for machine learning. You feed it a number of photos of cats with the label "cat" and a number of photos without cats that do not have the label "cat." The machine learns to recognize the patterns of pixels associated with the label "cat."

If you have a series of pictures with cats and dogs, the link between cats and four-legged objects will strengthen, but so will the same link with dogs. Without having to specify more, once you have fed several million pictures with different variations (including some without dogs) and labels into your machine, it develops many more associations and learns to distinguish between cats and dogs.

Many problems have transformed from algorithmic problems ("what are the features of a cat?") to prediction problems ("does this image with a missing label have the same features as the cats I have seen before?"). Machine learning uses probabilistic models to solve problems.

So why do many technologists refer to machine learning as "artificial intelligence"? Because the output of machine learning—prediction—is a key component of intelligence, the prediction accuracy improves by learning, and the high prediction accuracy often enables machines to perform tasks that, until now, were associated with human intelligence, such as object identification.

In his book *On Intelligence*, Jeff Hawkins was among the first to argue that prediction is the basis for human intelligence. The essence of his theory is that human intelligence, which is at the core of creativity and productivity gains, is due to the way our brains use memories to make predictions: "We are making continuous low-level predictions in parallel across all our senses. But that's not all. I am arguing a much stronger proposition. Prediction is not just one of the things your brain does. It is the primary function of the neocortex, and the foundation of intelligence. The cortex is an organ of prediction."[2]

Hawkins argues that our brains are constantly making predictions regarding what we are about to experience—what we will see, feel, and hear. As we develop and mature, our brains' predictions are increasingly accurate; the predictions often come true. However, when predictions do not accurately predict the future, we notice the anomaly, and this information is fed back into our brain, which updates its algorithm, thus learning and further enhancing the model.

Hawkins's work is controversial. His ideas are debated in the psychology literature, and many computer scientists flatly reject his emphasis on the cortex as a model for prediction machines. The notion that an AI that could pass the Turing test (a machine being able to deceive a human into believing that the machine is actually a human) in its strongest sense remains far from reality. Current AI algorithms cannot reason, and moreover it is difficult to interrogate them to understand the source of their predictions.

Irrespective of whether the underlying model is appropriate, his emphasis on prediction as the basis for intelligence is useful for understanding the impact of recent changes in AI. Here we emphasize the consequences of dramatic improvements in prediction technology. Many of the scholars' aspirations at the 1956 Dartmouth conference are now within reach. In various ways, prediction machines can "use language, form abstractions and concepts, solve the kinds of problems now [as of 1955] reserved for humans, and improve themselves."[3]

We do not speculate on whether this progress heralds the arrival of general artificial intelligence, "the Singularity," or Skynet. However, as you will see, this narrower focus on prediction still suggests extraordinary changes over the next few years. Just as cheap arithmetic enabled by computers proved powerful in ushering in dramatic changes to business and personal lives, similar transformations will occur due to cheap prediction.

Overall, whether or not it is intelligence, this progression from deterministic to probabilistic programming of computers is an important step-function transition, albeit consistent with progress in the social and physical sciences. Philosopher Ian Hacking, in his book *The Taming of Chance*, said that, before the nineteenth century, probability was the domain of gamblers.[4] By the nineteenth century, the rise of government census data applied the newly emerging mathematics of probability to the social sciences. The twentieth century saw a fundamental reordering of our understanding of the physical world, moving from a Newtonian deterministic perspective to the uncertainties of quantum mechanics. Perhaps the most important advance of twenty-first-century computer science matches these previous advances in social and physical sciences: the recognition that algorithms work best when structured probabilistically, based on data.

KEY POINTS

- Machine learning science had different goals from statistics. Whereas statistics emphasized being correct on average, machine learning did not require that. Instead, the goal was operational effectiveness. Predictions could have biases so long as they were better (something that was possible with powerful computers). This gave scientists a freedom to experiment and drove rapid improvements that take advantage of the rich data and fast computers that appeared over the last decade.

- Traditional statistical methods require the articulation of hypotheses or at least of human intuition for model specification. Machine learning has less need to specify in advance what goes into the model and can accommodate the equivalent of much more complex models with many more interactions between variables.

- Recent advances in machine learning are often referred to as advances in artificial intelligence because: (1) systems predicated on this technique *learn* and improve over time; (2) these systems produce significantly more-accurate predictions than other approaches under certain conditions, and some experts argue that prediction is central to intelligence; and (3) the enhanced prediction accuracy of these systems enable them to perform tasks, such as translation and navigation, that were previously considered the exclusive domain of human intelligence. We remain agnostic on the link between prediction and intelligence. None of our conclusions rely on taking a position on whether advances in prediction represent advances in intelligence. We focus on the consequences of a drop in the cost of prediction, not a drop in the cost of intelligence.

5

Data Is the New Oil

Hal Varian, the chief economist at Google, channeling Coca-Cola's Robert Goizueta, said in 2013, "[A] billion hours ago, modern homo sapiens emerged. A billion minutes ago, Christianity began. A billion seconds ago, the IBM PC was released. A billion Google searches ago . . . was this morning."[1] Google isn't the only company with extraordinary amounts of data. From large companies like Facebook and Microsoft to local governments and startups, data collection is cheaper and easier than ever before. This data has value. Billions of searches mean billions of lines of data with which Google can improve its services. Some have called data "the new oil."

Prediction machines rely on data. More and better data leads to better predictions. In economic terms, data is a key complement to prediction. It becomes more valuable as prediction becomes cheaper.

With AI, data plays three roles. First is *input data*, which is fed to the algorithm and used to produce a prediction. Second is *training data*, which is used to generate the algorithm in the first place. Training data is used to train the AI to become good enough to predict in the wild. Finally, there is *feedback data*, which is used to improve the algorithm's performance with experience. In some situations, considerable overlap exists, such that the same data plays all three roles.

But data can be costly to acquire. Thus, the investment involves a trade-off between the benefit of more data and the cost of acquiring it. To make the right data investment decisions, you must understand how prediction machines use data.

Prediction Requires Data

Before the recent enthusiasm over AI, there was excitement about big data. The variety, quantity, and quality of data have increased substantially over the last twenty years. Images and text are now in digital form, so machines can analyze them. Sensors are ubiquitous. The enthusiasm is predicated on the ability of this data to help people reduce uncertainty and know more about what is happening.

Consider the improved sensors that monitor peoples' heart rates. Various companies and nonprofits with medical-sounding names like AliveCor and Cardiio are building products that use heart rate data. For example, the startup Cardiogram provides an iPhone app that uses heart rate data from an Apple Watch to generate an extraordinary amount of information: a second-by-second measure of heart rates for everyone who uses the app. Users can see when and if their heart rates spike over the course of a day and whether their heart rates have sped up or slowed down over a year or even a decade.

But the potential power of such products comes from combining this rich data with a prediction machine. Both academic and industry researchers have shown that smartphones can predict irregular heart rhythms (medically, atrial fibrillation).[2] So, with their prediction machines, the products that Cardiogram, AliveCor, Cardiio, and others are building use heart rate data to help diagnose heart disease. The general approach is to use heart rate data to predict the unknown information of whether a particular user has an abnormal heart rhythm.

This input data is necessary to operate the prediction machine. Because prediction machines cannot run without input data, we often label it simply "data," in contrast to training and feedback data.

The uninitiated consumer cannot see the link between heart rate data and an abnormal heart rhythm from raw data. In contrast,

Cardiogram can detect an irregular heart rhythm with 97 percent accuracy using its deep neural network.[3] Such abnormalities cause about a quarter of strokes. With better prediction, doctors can deliver better treatment. Certain drugs can prevent strokes.

For this to work, individual consumers have to provide their heart rate data. Without personal data, a machine cannot predict the risk for that particular person. The combination of a prediction machine with an individual's personal data enables a prediction for that person's likelihood of an irregular heart rhythm.

How Machines Learn from Data

The current generation of AI technology is called "machine learning" for a reason. The machines learn from data. In the case of heart rate monitors, in order to predict an irregular heart rhythm (and an increased likelihood of a stroke) from heart rate data, the prediction machine has to learn how the data is associated with actual incidences of irregular heart rhythms. To do so, the prediction machine needs to combine the input data coming from the Apple Watch—which statisticians call "independent variables"—with information on irregular heart rhythms ("the dependent variable").

For the prediction machine to learn, the information on irregular heart rhythms has to come from the same people as the Apple Watch heart rate data. So, the prediction machine needs data from many people with an irregular heart rhythm, along with their heart rate data. Importantly, it also needs data from many people *who do not have* irregular heart rhythms, along with their heart rate data. The prediction machine then compares the heart rate patterns for those with and without irregular rhythms. This comparison enables the prediction. If a new patient's heart rate pattern is more similar to the "training" sample of people with an irregular rhythm than to the sample of those with a regular rhythm, then the machine will predict that this patient has an irregular heart rhythm.

Like many medical applications, Cardiogram collects its data by working with academic researchers who monitored six thousand users to assist in the study. Of the six thousand users, approximately two hundred had already been diagnosed with an irregular heart rhythm. So, all Cardiogram did was collect data on heart rate patterns from the Apple Watch and compare.

Such products continue to improve their prediction accuracy even after they launch. The prediction machine needs feedback data on whether its predictions are correct. So, it needs data on the incidence of irregular heart rhythms among the product's users. The machine combines this data with the input data on cardio-monitoring to generate feedback that continually improves prediction accuracy.

However, acquiring training data can be challenging. To predict the same group of items (in this case, heart patients), you need information on the outcome of interest (irregular heart rhythms) as well as information on something that will be useful for predicting that outcome in a new context (cardio-monitoring).

This is particularly challenging when the prediction is about some future event. The prediction machine can only be fed information that is known at the time you want to predict. For example, suppose you are thinking of buying season tickets for your favorite sports team next year. In Toronto, for most people that would be the Toronto Maple Leafs ice hockey team. You like going to the games when the team wins but dislike supporting a losing team. You decide it is only worth buying the tickets if the team will win at least half the games it plays next year. To make this decision, you need to predict the number of wins.

In ice hockey, the team that scores the most goals wins. So, you intuit that teams scoring lots of goals tend to win and teams scoring few goals tend to lose. You decide to feed your prediction machine with data from past seasons on goals scored by each team, goals scored against each team, and the number of wins for each team. You feed this data to the prediction machine and find that this is indeed an excellent predictor of the number of wins. Then you get ready to use this information to predict the number of wins next year.

You can't. You're stuck. You don't have information on the number of goals the team will score next year. So, you cannot use that data to predict the number of wins. You do have data on goals scored last year, but that won't work because you trained the prediction machine to learn from the current year's data.

To make this prediction, you need data that you will have on hand at the time you make the prediction. You could retrain your prediction machine using goals scored the previous year to predict the current year's wins. You could use other information like wins during the previous year or the age of the players on the team and their past performance on the ice.

Many commercial AI applications have this structure: use a combination of input data and outcome measures to create the prediction machine, and then use input data from a new situation to predict the outcome of that situation. If you can obtain data on outcomes, then your prediction machine can learn continually through feedback.

Decisions about Data

Data is often costly to acquire, but prediction machines cannot operate without it. They require data to create, operate, and improve.

You therefore must make decisions around the scale and scope of data acquisition. How many different types of data do you need? How many different objects are required for training? How frequently do you need to collect data? More types, more objects, and more frequency mean higher cost but also potentially higher benefit. In thinking through this decision, you must carefully determine what you want to predict. The particular prediction problem will tell you what you need.

Cardiogram wanted to predict strokes. It used irregular heart rhythms as a (medically validated) proxy.[4] Once it had set this prediction objective, it needed only heart rate data for each person who used its app. It might also use information on sleep, physical activity, family, medical history, and age. After asking some questions to collect age and other information, it needed just one device to measure one thing well: heart rate.

Cardiogram also needed data for training—the six thousand people in its training data, a fraction of whom have an irregular heart rhythm.

Despite the vast array of sensors and variety of details about users potentially available, Cardiogram only had to collect a small amount of information on most of its users. And it only required access to abnormal heart rhythm information for the people it was using to train its AI. In this way, the number of variables was relatively small.

In order to make a good prediction, the machine must have enough individuals (or units of analysis) in the training data. The number of individuals required depends on two factors: first, how reliable the "signal" is relative to the "noise," and second, how accurate the prediction must be to be useful. In other words, the number of required people depends on whether we expect heart rates to be a strong or a weak predictor of irregular heart rhythms and how costly a mistake will be. If heart rate is a strong predictor and mistakes are not a big deal, then we only need a few people. If heart rate is a weak predictor or if each mistake puts lives at risk, then we need thousands or even millions. Cardiogram, in its preliminary study, used six thousand people, including just two hundred with an irregular heart rhythm. Over time, one way to collect further data is through feedback on whether the app's users have or develop irregular heart rhythms.

Where did the six thousand come from? Data scientists have excellent tools for assessing the amount of data required given the expected reliability of the prediction and the need for accuracy. These tools are called "power calculations" and tell you how many units you need to analyze to generate a useful prediction.[5] The salient management point is that you must make a trade-off: more accurate predictions require more units to study, and acquiring these additional units can be costly.

Cardiogram requires a high frequency of data collection. Its technology uses the Apple Watch to collect data on a second-by-second basis. It needs this high frequency because heart rates vary during the day, and correct measurement requires repeated assessment of whether the measured rate is the true value for the person being studied. To work, Cardiogram's algorithm uses the steady stream of measurement that a wearable device provides, rather than a measurement taken only when the patient is in the doctor's office.

Collecting this data was a costly investment. Patients had to wear a device at all times, so it intruded on their regular routines (particularly for those without an Apple Watch). Because it involved health data, there were privacy concerns, so Cardiogram developed its system in a way that improved privacy but at the expense of increased development costs and reduced ability of the machine to improve predictions from feedback. It collected the data it used in the predictions through the app; the data remained on the watch.

Next, we discuss the difference between statistical and economic thinking in how much data to collect. (We consider issues associated with privacy when we discuss strategy in part four.)

Economies of Scale

More data improves prediction. But how much data do you need? The benefit of additional information (whether in terms of number of units, types of variables, or frequency) may increase or decrease with the existing amount of data. In economist speak, data may have increasing or decreasing returns to scale.

From a purely statistical point of view, data has decreasing returns to scale. You get more useful information from the third observation than the hundredth, and you learn much more from the hundredth observation than the millionth. As you add observations to your training data, it becomes less and less useful to improving your prediction.

Each observation is an additional piece of data that helps inform your prediction. In the case of Cardiogram, an observation is the time between each recorded heartbeat. When we say "data has decreasing returns," we mean that the first hundred heartbeats give you a good sense of whether the person has an irregular heart rhythm. Each additional heartbeat is less important than the ones before for improving the prediction.

Consider the time at which you need to leave when you are going to the airport. If you have never been to the airport, the first time you go provides a lot of useful information. The second and third times also give you a sense of how long it typically takes. However, by the hundredth time, you are unlikely to learn much about how long it takes to get there. In this way, data has decreasing returns to scale: as you get more data, each additional piece is less valuable.

This might not be true from an economic point of view, which is not about how data improves prediction. It is about how data improves the value you get from the prediction. Sometimes prediction and outcome go together, so the decreasing returns to observations in statistics imply decreasing returns in terms of the outcomes you care about. Sometimes, however, they are different.

For example, consumers can choose to use your product or your competitor's. They may only use your product if it is almost always as good as or better than your competitor's. In many cases, all competitors will be equally good for situations with readily available data. For example, most search engines provide similar results to common searches. Whether you use Google or Bing, the results from a search for "Justin Bieber" are similar. The value of a search engine is driven by its ability to give better results for unusual searches. Try typing "disruption" into Google and Bing. At the time of this writing, Google showed both the dictionary definition and results related to Clay Christensen's ideas on disruptive innovation. Bing's first nine results provided dictionary definitions. A key reason Google's results were better is that figuring out what the searcher needs in an unusual search requires data on such searches. Most people use Google for both rare and common searches. Being even a little better in search can lead to a big difference in market share and revenue.

So, while the data technically has decreasing returns to scale—the billionth search is less useful for improving the search engine than the first—from a business viewpoint, data might be most valuable if you have more and better data than your competitor. Some have argued that more data about unique factors brings disproportionate rewards in the market.[6] Increasing data brings disproportionate rewards in the market. Thus, from an economic point of view, in such cases data may have increasing returns to scale.

KEY POINTS

- Prediction machines utilize three types of data: (1) training data for training the AI, (2) input data for predicting, and (3) feedback data for improving the prediction accuracy.

- Data collection is costly; it's an investment. The cost of data collection depends on how much data you need and how intrusive the collection process is. It is critical to balance the cost of data acquisition with the benefit of enhanced prediction accuracy. Determining the best approach requires estimating the ROI of each type of data: how much will it cost to acquire, and how valuable will the associated increase in prediction accuracy be?

- Statistical and economic reasons shape whether having more data generates more value. From a statistical perspective, data has diminishing returns. Each additional unit of data improves your prediction less than the prior data; the tenth observation improves prediction by more than the one thousandth. In terms of economics, the relationship is ambiguous. Adding more data to a large existing stock of data may be greater than adding it to a small stock—for example, if the additional data allows the performance of the prediction machine to cross a threshold from unusable to usable, or from below a regulatory performance threshold to above, or from worse than a competitor to better. Thus, organizations need to understand the relationship between adding more data, enhancing prediction accuracy, and increasing value creation.

6

The New Division
of Labor

Every time you change an electronic document, those changes can be recorded. For most of us, this is little more than a useful way to track revisions, but for Ron Glozman, it was an opportunity to use AI on data to predict changes. In 2015, Glozman launched a startup called Chisel, whose first product took legal documents and predicted which information was confidential. This product is valuable to law firms because, when they are required to disclose documents, they have to black out, or redact, confidential information. Historically, redaction was done by hand, with humans reading documents and blacking out confidential information. Glozman's approach promised to save time and effort.

Machine redaction worked, but imperfectly. On occasion, the machine erroneously redacted information that should be disclosed. Or it failed to pick up something confidential. To achieve legal standards, humans had to help. In its testing phase, Chisel's machine suggested what to redact, and the human rejected or accepted the suggestion. In effect, working together meant saving a lot of time, while achieving an error rate lower than the humans had achieved on their own. This human-machine division of labor worked because it overcame human weaknesses in speed and attention, and machine weaknesses in interpreting text.

Humans and machines both have failings. Without knowing what they are, we cannot assess how machines and humans should work together to generate predictions. Why? Because of an idea that dates back to Adam Smith's eighteenth-century economic thinking on the division of labor that involves allocating roles based on relative strengths. Here, the division of labor is between humans and machines in generating predictions. Understanding the division of labor involves determining which aspects of prediction are best performed by humans or machines. This enables us to identify their distinctive roles.

Where Humans Are Poor at Prediction

An old psychology experiment gives subjects a random series of Xs and Os and asks them to predict what the next one will be. For instance, they may see:

OXXOXOXOXOXOXXOOXXOXOXOXXXOXX

For a sequence like this, most people realize that there are slightly more Xs than Os—if you count, you'll see it's 60 percent Xs, 40 percent Os—so they guess X most of the time, but throw in some Os to reflect that balance. However, if you want to maximize your chances of a correct prediction, you would always choose X. Then you would be right 60 percent of the time. If you randomize 60/40, as most participants do, your prediction ends up being correct 52 percent of the time, only slightly better than if you had not bothered to assess relative frequencies of Xs and Os and instead just guessed one or the other (50/50).[1]

What such experiments tell us is that humans are poor statisticians, even in situations when they are not too bad at assessing probabilities. No prediction machine would make an error like this. But perhaps humans don't take such tasks seriously, since they may feel as if they are playing a game. Would they make similar errors if the consequences are decidedly not game-like?

The answer—demonstrated over many experiments by psychologists Daniel Kahneman and Amos Tversky—is decidedly yes.[2] When they told people to consider two hospitals—one with forty-five births per day and another with fifteen births per day—and asked which hospital would have more days when 60 percent or more of the babies born are boys, very few gave the correct answer—the smaller hospital. The smaller hospital is correct because the larger the number of events (in this case, births), the likelier each daily outcome will be close to the average (in this case, 50 percent). To see how this works, imagine you are flipping coins. You are more likely to get heads every time if you flip five coins than if you flip fifty coins. Thus, the smaller hospital—precisely because it has fewer births—is more likely to have more extreme outcomes away from the average.

Several books have been written about such heuristics and biases.[3] Many people find it challenging to make predictions based on sound statistical principles, which is precisely why they bring in experts. Unfortunately, those experts can exhibit the same biases and difficulties with statistics when making decisions. These biases plague fields as diverse as medicine, law, sports, and business. Tversky, along with researchers at Harvard Medical School, presented physicians with two treatments for lung cancer: radiation or surgery. The five-year survival rate recommends surgery. Two groups of participants received different ways of presenting information about the short-term survival rate of surgery, which is riskier than radiation. When told that "the one-month survival rate is 90 percent," 84 percent of physicians chose surgery, but that rate fell to 50 percent when told that "there is a 10 percent mortality in the first month." Both these phrases said the same thing, but how the researchers framed the information resulted in major changes in the decision. A machine would not have this outcome.

Kahneman identifies many other situations where experts did not predict well when facing complex information. Experienced radiologists contradicted themselves one in five times when evaluating X-rays. Auditors, pathologists, psychologists, and managers exhibited similar inconsistencies. Kahneman concludes that if there is a way of predicting using a formula instead of a human, the formula should be considered seriously.

Poor expert prediction was the centerpiece of Michael Lewis's *Moneyball*.[4] The Oakland Athletics baseball team faced a problem when, after three of their best players left, the team did not have the financial resources to recruit replacements. The A's general manager, Billy Beane (played by Brad Pitt in the film), used a statistical system developed by Bill James to predict player performance. With this "sabermetrics" system, Beane and his analysts overruled the recommendations of the A's scouts and picked their own team. Despite a modest budget, the A's outperformed their rivals all the way to the playoffs in 2002. At the heart of the new approach was a move away from indicators they had previously thought important (such as stolen bases and batting average) to others (such as on-base performance and slugging percentage). It was also a move away from the scout's sometimes bizarre heuristics. As one scout in the movie remarks, "He's got an ugly girlfriend. Ugly girlfriend means no confidence." In light of decision-making algorithms like that, it's no surprise that data-driven predictions were often able to outcompete human ones in baseball.

The newly emphasized metrics accounted for a player's contribution to the performance of the team as a whole. The new prediction machine enabled the Oakland A's to identify players who were lesser known quantities compared to those evaluated traditionally and thus better value in terms of lower price relative to their impact on team performance. Absent prediction, these were prospects that other teams had undervalued. The A's capitalized on those biases.[5]

Perhaps the clearest indication of difficulties with human prediction, even by experienced and powerful experts, comes from a study of US judges' bail-granting decisions.[6] In the United States, there are 10 million such decisions each year, and whether someone receives bail or not is very consequential for family, job, and other personal issues, not to mention the cost of prison for the government. Judges must base their decisions on whether the defendant will flee or commit other crimes if released on bail, not whether an eventual conviction is likely. The decision criteria are clear and well defined.

The study used machine learning to develop an algorithm that predicted the probability that a given defendant would reoffend or flee while on bail. The training data was extensive: three-quarters of a million people who were granted bail in New York City between 2008 and 2013. The information included prior rap sheets, the crimes people were accused of, and demographic information.

The machine made better predictions than the human judges. For instance, for the 1 percent of defendants that the machine classified as riskiest, it predicted that 62 percent would commit crimes while out on bail. Nevertheless, the human judges (who did not have access to the machine predictions) opted to release almost half of them. The machine predictions were reasonably accurate, with 63 percent of the machine-identified high-risk offenders actually committing a crime while on bail and over half not appearing at the next court date. Five percent of those the machine identified as high risk committed rape or murder while on bail.

By following the recommendations of the machine, the judges could have released the same number of defendants and reduced the crime rate of those let out on bail by three-quarters. Or they could have kept the crime rate the same and jailed half as many additional defendants.[7]

What is going on here? Why do judges assess so differently than prediction machines? One possibility is that judges use information unavailable to the algorithm, such as the defendant's appearance and demeanor in court. That information might be useful—or it might be deceiving. Given the high crime rate of those released, it's not unreasonable to conclude that it is more likely the latter; the judges' predictions are fairly horrible. The study provides plenty of additional evidence to support this unfortunate conclusion.

Prediction proves so difficult for humans in this situation because of the complexity of the factors that might explain crime rates. Prediction machines are much better than humans at factoring in complex interactions among different indicators. So, while you might believe that a past criminal record may mean that a defendant is a bigger flight risk, the machine may have discovered that is only the case if the defendant has been unemployed for a certain period of time. In other words, the interaction effect may be the most important, and as the number of dimensions for such interactions grows, humans' ability to form accurate predictions diminishes.

These biases don't just show up in medicine, baseball, and law; they are a constant feature of professional work. Economists have found that managers and workers often engage in prediction—and prediction with confidence—unaware they are doing a poor job. In a study of hiring across fifteen low-skilled service firms, Mitchell Hoffman, Lisa Kahn, and Danielle Li found that when the firms used an objective and verifiable test along with normal interviews, there was a 15 percent bump in the job tenure of hires relative to when they made hiring decisions based on interviews alone.[8] For these jobs, managers were instructed to maximize tenure.

The test itself was extensive, including cognitive abilities and fit-for-job indicators. Also, when the discretion of hiring managers was restricted—preventing managers from overruling test scores when those scores were unfavorable—an even higher job tenure and a reduced quit rate occurred. So, even when instructed to maximize tenure, when experienced at hiring, and when given fairly accurate machine predictions, the managers still made poor predictions.

Where Machines Are Poor at Prediction

Former Secretary of Defense Donald Rumsfeld once said:

> There are known knowns; there are things we know we know. We also know there are known unknowns; that is to say we know there are some things we do not know. But there are also unknown unknowns—the ones we don't know we don't know. And if one looks throughout the history of our country and other free countries, it is the latter category that tend to be the difficult ones.[9]

This provides a useful structure for understanding the conditions under which prediction machines falter. First, *known knowns* are when we have rich data, so we know we can make good predictions. Second, *known unknowns* are when there is too little data, so we know that prediction will be difficult. Third, *unknown unknowns* are those events that are not captured by past experience or what is present in the data but are nonetheless possible, so prediction is difficult, although we may not realize it. Finally, a category Rumsfeld did not recognize, *unknown knowns*, is when an association that appears to be strong in the past is the result of some unknown or unobserved factor that changes over time and makes predictions we thought we could make unreliable. Prediction machines fail precisely where it is hard to predict based on the well-understood limits in statistics.

Known Knowns

With rich data, machine prediction can work well. The machine knows the situation, in the sense that it supplies a good prediction. And we know the prediction is good. This is the sweet spot for the current generation of machine intelligence. Fraud detection, medical diagnosis, baseball players, and bail decisions all fall under this category.

Known Unknowns

Even the best prediction models of today (and in the near future) require large amounts of data, meaning we know our predictions will be relatively poor in situations where we do not have much data. We know that we don't know: known unknowns.

We might not have much data because some events are rare, so predicting them is challenging. US presidential elections happen only every four years, and the candidates and political environment change. Predicting a presidential election outcome a few years out is nearly impossible. The 2016 election showed that even predicting the outcome a few days out, or on the day of the election, is difficult. Major earthquakes are sufficiently (and thankfully) rare that predicting when, where, and how large they will be has thus far proven elusive. (Yes, seismologists are working on this.[10])

In contrast to machines, humans are sometimes extremely good at prediction with little data. We can recognize a face after seeing it only once or twice, even if we see it from a different angle. We can identify a fourth-grade classmate forty years later, despite numerous changes in appearance. From a very young age, we can guess the trajectory of a ball (even if we aren't always coordinated enough to catch it). We are also good at analogy, taking new situations and identifying other circumstances that are similar enough to be useful in a new environment. For example, scientists imagined the atom as a miniature solar system for decades, and it is still taught that way in many schools.[11]

While computer scientists are working to reduce machines' data needs, developing techniques such as "one-shot learning" in which machines learn to predict an object well after seeing it just once, current prediction machines are not yet adequate.[12] Because these are *known* unknowns and because humans are still better at decisions in the face of known unknowns, the people managing the machine know that such situations may arise and thus they can program the machine to call a human for help.

Unknown Unknowns

In order to predict, someone needs to tell a machine what is worth predicting. If something has never happened before, a machine cannot predict it (at least without a human's careful judgment to provide a useful analogy that allows the machine to predict using information about something else).

Nassim Nicholas Taleb emphasizes unknown unknowns in his book *The Black Swan*.[13] He highlights that we cannot predict truly new events from past data. The book's title refers to the Europeans' discovery of a new type of swan in Australia. To eighteenth-century Europeans, swans were white. Upon arrival in Australia, they saw something totally new and unpredictable: black swans. They had never seen black swans and therefore had no information that could predict the existence of such a swan.[14] Taleb argues that the appearances of other unknown unknowns have important consequences—unlike the appearance of black swans, which had little meaningful impact on the direction of European or Australian society.

For example, the 1990s were a good time to be in the music industry.[15] CD sales were growing and revenue climbed steadily. The future looked bright. Then, in 1999, eighteen-year-old Shawn Fanning developed Napster, a program that allowed people to share music files for free over the internet. Soon, people had downloaded millions of such files, and music industry revenues began to fall. The industry still hasn't recovered.

Fanning was an unknown unknown. Machine prediction could not predict his arrival. Admittedly, as Taleb and others emphasized, humans are also relatively bad at predicting unknown unknowns. Faced with unknown unknowns, both humans and machines fail.

Unknown Knowns

Perhaps the biggest weakness of prediction machines is that they sometimes provide wrong answers that they are confident are right. As we describe above, in the case of known unknowns, humans understand the inaccuracy of the prediction. The prediction comes with a confidence range that reveals its imprecision. In the case of unknown unknowns, humans don't think they have any answers. In contrast, with unknown knowns, prediction machines appear to provide a very precise answer, but that answer can be very wrong.

How does that occur? Because, while data informs decisions, data can also come from decisions. If the machine does not understand the decision process that generated the data, its predictions can fail. For example, suppose you are interested in predicting whether you will use prediction machines in your organization. You are off to a good start. It turns out that reading this book is almost surely an excellent predictor of being a manager who will use prediction machines.

Why? For at least three possible reasons. First, and most directly, the insights in this book will prove useful, so the act of reading the book causes you to learn about prediction machines and therefore to bring these tools into your business effectively.

Second is a reason called "reverse causality." You are reading this book because you already use prediction machines or have definite plans to do so in the near future. The book didn't cause the technology adoption; instead, the (perhaps pending) technology adoption caused you to read this book.

Third is a reason called "omitted variables." You are the kind of person who is interested in technological trends and management. Therefore, you decided to read this book. You also use new technologies such as prediction machines in your work. In this case, your underlying preferences for technology and management caused both the book reading and the use of prediction machines.

Sometimes this distinction does not matter. If all you care about is knowing whether a person reading this book will adopt prediction machines, then it doesn't matter what causes what. If you see someone reading this book, then you can make an informed prediction that such a person will use prediction machines in their work.

Sometimes this distinction does matter. If you are thinking of recommending this book to your friends, you will do so if it caused you to be a better manager with respect to prediction machines. What would you like to know? You'd start with the fact that you read the book. Then you'd like to peer into the future and observe how well you do in managing AI. Suppose you see the future perfectly. You have been fabulously successful at managing prediction machines, it becomes core to your organization, and you and your organization succeed beyond your wildest dreams. Can you then say that reading this book caused that success?

No.

To figure out if reading this book had an impact, you also need to know what would have happened if you *hadn't* read this book. You don't have that data. You need to observe what economists and statisticians call the "counterfactual": what would have happened if you took a different action. Determining whether an action causes an outcome requires two predictions: first, what outcome will happen after the action is taken, and second, what outcome would have happened had a different action been taken. But that's impossible. You will never have data on the action *not* taken.[16]

This is a recurrent problem for machine prediction. In his book, *Deep Thinking*, chess grandmaster Garry Kasporov discusses a related issue with an early machine-learning algorithm for chess:

> When Michie and a few colleagues wrote an experimental data-based machine-learning chess program in the early 1980s, it had an amusing result. They fed hundreds of thousands of positions from Grandmaster games into the machine, hoping it would be able to figure out what worked and what did not. At first it seemed to work. Its evaluation of positions was more accurate than conventional programs. The problem came when they let it actually play a game of chess. The program developed its pieces, launched an attack, and immediately sacrificed its queen! It lost in just a few moves, having given up the queen for next to nothing. Why did it do it? Well, when a Grandmaster sacrifices his queen it's nearly always a brilliant and decisive blow. To the machine, educated on a diet of GM games, giving up its queen was clearly the key to success![17]

The machine reversed the causal sequence. Without understanding that grandmasters sacrifice the queen only when doing so creates a short and clear path to victory, the machine learned that winning occurs shortly after sacrificing the queen. So sacrificing the queen wrongly appears to be the way to win. While this particular issue in machine prediction has been solved, reverse causality remains a challenge for prediction machines.

This issue appears frequently in business, too. In many industries, low prices are associated with low sales. For example, in the hotel industry, prices are low outside the tourist season, and prices are high when demand is highest and hotels are full. Given that data, a naive prediction might suggest that increasing the price would lead to more rooms sold. A human—at least one with some training in economics—would understand that the price changes are likely caused by the high level of demand, not vice versa. So increasing price is unlikely to increase sales. This human can then work with the machine to identify the right data (such as individual-level choices of hotel rooms based on price) and appropriate models (that take into account seasonality and other demand and supply factors) to better predict sales at different prices. Thus, to the machine, this is an unknown known, but a human, with an understanding of how prices are determined, will see this as a known unknown or perhaps even a known known if the human can properly model the pricing decision.

The issue of unknown knowns and causal inference is even more important in the presence of others' strategic behavior. Google's search results come from a secret algorithm. That algorithm is largely determined by prediction machines that predict which links someone is likely to click. For a website manager, a higher ranking means more visitors to the website and more sales. Most website managers recognize this and perform search engine optimization: they adapt their websites to try to improve their ranking in Google's search results. These adaptations are often ways to game idiosyncratic aspects of the algorithm, so as time passes, the search engine becomes filled with spam, links that are not what the person searching really wanted but instead the results of website managers gaming the quirks in the algorithm.

Prediction machines do a great job in the short run in terms of predicting what people will click. But after weeks or months, enough website managers find ways to game the system that Google needs to substantially change the prediction model. This back-and-forth between the search engine and the search engine spammers occurs because the prediction machine can be gamed. While Google has tried to create a system that makes such gaming unprofitable, it also recognizes the weaknesses of relying fully on prediction machines and uses human judgment to re-optimize the machine in the face of such spam.[18] Instagram is also in a constant battle with spammers, updating the algorithms it uses to regularly catch spam and offensive material.[19] More generally, once humans have identified such problems, they are no longer unknown knowns. Either they find solutions to generate good predictions, so the problems become known knowns that may require humans and machines to work together, or they cannot find solutions, so they become known unknowns.

Machine prediction is extremely powerful but has limitations. It does not perform well with limited data. Some well-trained humans can recognize these limitations, whether because of rare events or causal inference problems, and improve the machine predictions. To do so, those humans need to understand the machine.

Predicting Better Together

Sometimes, the combination of humans and machines generates the best predictions, each complementing the other's weaknesses. In 2016, a Harvard/MIT team of AI researchers won the Camelyon Grand Challenge, a contest that produces computer-based detection of metastatic breast cancer from slides of biopsies. The team's winning deep-learning algorithm made the correct prediction 92.5 percent of the time compared with a human pathologist whose performance was at 96.6 percent. While this seemed like a victory for humanity, the researchers went further and combined the predictions of their algorithm and a pathologist's. The result was an accuracy of 99.5 percent.[20] That is, the human error rate of 3.4 percent fell to just 0.5 percent. Errors fell by 85 percent.

This is a classic division of labor, but not physically as Adam Smith described. Rather, it is a cognitive division of labor that economist and computer pioneer Charles Babbage initially described in the nineteenth century: "the effect of the division of labour, both in mechanical and mental processes, is, that it enables us to purchase and apply precisely the quantity of skill and knowledge which is required for it."[21]

The human and the machine are good at different aspects of prediction. The human pathologist was usually right when saying there was cancer. It was unusual to have a situation in which the human said there was cancer but was mistaken. In contrast, the AI was much more accurate when saying the cancer wasn't there. The human and the machine made different types of mistakes. By recognizing these different abilities, combining human and machine prediction overcame these weaknesses, so their combination dramatically reduced the error rate.

How does such collaboration translate into a business environment? Machine prediction can enhance the productivity of human prediction via two broad pathways. The first is by providing an initial prediction that humans can use to combine with their own assessments. The second is to provide a second opinion after the fact, or a path for monitoring. In this way, the boss can ensure the human is working hard and putting effort into the prediction. In the absence of such monitoring, the human may not work hard enough. The theory is that humans who must answer for why their prediction differed from an objective algorithm might only overrule machines if they put in extra effort to ensure they are sufficiently confident.

One excellent place to examine such interactions is the prediction regarding the creditworthiness of loan applicants. Daniel Paravisini and Antoinette Schoar examined a Colombian bank's evaluation of small enterprise loan applicants after the introduction of a new credit scoring system.[22] The computerized scoring system took a variety of information about the applicants and aggregated it into a single measure that predicted risk. Then a loan committee of bank employees used the score and their own processes to approve, reject, or refer the loan to a regional manager to decide.

A randomized controlled trial, not management decree, determined whether the score was introduced before or after the decision. Thus, the score provided a good place to scientifically evaluate its impact on decision making. One group of employees was provided the score just before they met to deliberate. This is analogous to the first way to collaborate with a machine, in which the machine prediction informs the human decision. Another group of employees was not given the score until after they had made an initial evaluation. This is analogous to the second way to collaborate with a machine, in which the machine prediction helps monitor the quality of the human decision. The difference between the first and second treatments was whether the score was providing information or not to the human decision makers.

In both cases, the score helped, though the improvement was largest when the score was provided in advance. In that case, the committee made better decisions and asked the manager for help less often. The predictions empowered the lower level managers by providing information. In the other case, when the committee had the score after, decision making improved because the predictions helped the higher level managers monitor the committees. It increased the incentives of the committee to ensure the quality of their decisions.

For a human–prediction machine pair to generate a better prediction requires an understanding of the limits of the human and the machine. In the case of the loan application committees, humans might make biased predictions, or they might shirk on effort. Machines might lack important information. While we often place an emphasis on teamwork and collegiality when humans collaborate, we might not think of human-machine pairs as teams. For humans to make machine prediction better, and vice versa, it is important to understand the weaknesses of both humans and machines and combine them in a way that overcomes these flaws.

Prediction by Exception

One major benefit of prediction machines is that they can scale in a way that humans cannot. One downside is that they struggle to make predictions in unusual cases for which there isn't much historical data. Combined, this means that many human-machine collaborations will take the form of "prediction by exception."

As we've discussed, prediction machines learn when data is plentiful, which happens when they are dealing with more routine or frequent scenarios. In these situations, the prediction machine operates without the human partner expending attention. By contrast, when an exception arises—a scenario that is non-routine—it is communicated to the human, and then the human puts in more effort to improve and verify the prediction. This "prediction by exception" is precisely what happened with the Colombian bank loan committee.

The idea of prediction by exception has its antecedents in the managerial technique of "management by exception." In coming up with predictions, the human is, in many respects, the prediction machine's supervisor. A human manager has many difficult tasks; to economize on the human's time, the working relationship is to engage the human's attention only when really needed. That it is needed only infrequently means that one human can easily leverage a prediction machine's advantages in routine predictions.

Prediction by exception is integral to how Chisel's initial product worked. Chisel's first product, which we discussed at the beginning of the chapter, took various documents and identified and redacted confidential information. This otherwise laborious procedure arises in many legal situations where documents may be disclosed to other parties or publicly, but only if certain information is hidden.

The Chisel redactor relied on prediction by exception taking a first-pass at that task.[23] In particular, a user could effectively set the redactor to be aggressive or light. An aggressive redactor's threshold for what might be blocked out would be higher than a lighter-touch version. For instance, if you are worried about leaving confidential information un-redacted, you choose an aggressive setting. But if you are worried about disclosing too little, you choose a lighter setting. Chisel provided an easy-to-use interface for a person to review redactions and accept or reject them. In other words, each redaction was a recommendation rather than a final decision. The ultimate authority still rested with a human.

Chisel's product combines humans and machines to overcome the weaknesses of both. The machine works faster than a human and provides a consistent measure across documents. The human can intervene when the machine does not have enough data to make a good prediction.

KEY POINTS

- Humans, including professional experts, make poor predictions under certain conditions. Humans often overweight salient information and do not account for statistical properties. Many scientific studies document these shortcomings across a wide variety of professions. The phenomenon was illustrated in the feature film *Moneyball*.

- Machines and humans have distinct strengths and weaknesses in the context of prediction. As prediction machines improve, businesses must adjust their division of labor between humans and machines in response. Prediction machines are better than humans at factoring in complex interactions among different indicators, especially in settings with rich data. As the number of dimensions for such interactions grows, the ability of humans to form accurate predictions diminishes, especially relative to machines. However, humans are often better than machines when understanding the data generation process confers a prediction advantage, especially in settings with thin data. We describe a taxonomy of prediction settings (i.e., known knowns, known unknowns, unknown knowns, and unknown unknowns) that is useful for anticipating the appropriate division of labor.

- Prediction machines scale. The unit cost per prediction falls as the frequency increases. Human prediction does not scale the same way. However, humans have cognitive models of how the world works and thus can make predictions based on small amounts of data. Thus, we anticipate a rise in *human prediction by exception* whereby machines generate most predictions because they are predicated on routine, regular data, but when rare events occur the machine recognizes that it is not able to produce a prediction with confidence, and so calls for human assistance. The human provides prediction by exception.

PART TWO

Decision Making

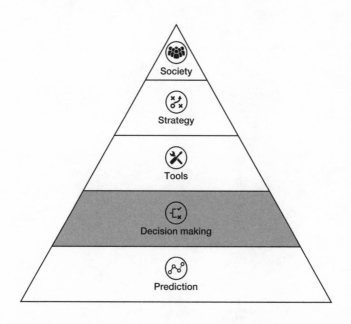

- Society
- Strategy
- Tools
- Decision making
- Prediction

7

Unpacking Decisions

We typically associate decision making with big decisions: Should I buy this house? Should I attend this school? Should I marry this person? No doubt, these life-changing decisions, while rare, are important.

But we also make small decisions all the time: Should I keep sitting in this chair? Should I keep walking down this street? Should I keep paying this monthly bill? And, as the great Canadian rock band Rush quips in its anthem to free will: "If you choose not to decide, you still have made a choice." We handle many of our smaller decisions on autopilot, perhaps by accepting the default, choosing to focus all our attention on bigger decisions. However, deciding not to decide is still a decision.

Decision making is at the core of most occupations. Schoolteachers decide how to educate their students, who have different personalities and learning styles. Managers decide who to recruit for their team and who to promote. Janitors decide how to deal with unexpected events such as spills and safety hazards. Truck drivers decide how to respond to route closures and traffic accidents. Police officers decide how to handle suspicious individuals and potentially dangerous situations. Doctors decide what medicine to prescribe and when to administer costly tests. Parents decide how much screen time is suitable for their children.

Decisions like these usually occur under conditions of uncertainty. The teacher doesn't know for sure whether a particular child will learn better from one teaching approach or another. The manager doesn't know for sure whether a job applicant will perform well or not. The doctor doesn't know for sure whether it is necessary to administer a costly exam. Each of them must predict.

But a prediction is not a decision. Making a decision requires applying judgment to a prediction and then acting. Before recent advances in machine intelligence, this distinction was only of academic interest because humans always performed prediction and judgment together. Now, advances in machine prediction mean that we have to examine the anatomy of a decision.

The Anatomy of a Decision

Prediction machines will have their most immediate impact at the decision level. But decisions have six other key elements (see figure 7-1). When someone (or something) makes a decision, they take *input data* from the world that enables a *prediction*. That prediction is possible because *training* occurred about relationships between different types of data and which data is most closely associated with a situation. Combining the prediction with *judgment* on what matters, the decision maker can then choose an *action*. The action leads to an *outcome* (which has an associated reward or payoff). The outcome is a consequence of the decision. It is needed to provide a complete picture. The outcome may also provide *feedback* to help improve the next prediction.

Imagine you have a pain in your leg and go to the doctor. The doctor sees you, takes an X-ray and a blood test and asks you a few questions, resulting in input data. Using that input, and based on years in medical school and many other patients who are more or less like you (that's training and feedback), the doctor makes a prediction: "You most

FIGURE 7-1

Anatomy of a task

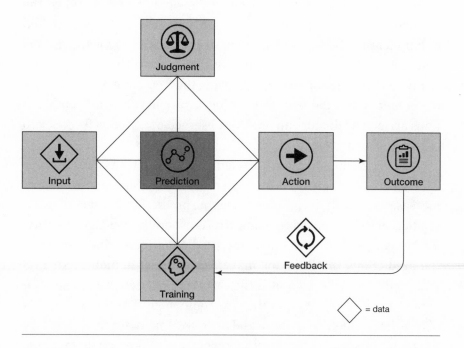

likely have muscle cramps, although there is a small chance you have a blood clot."

Alongside this assessment is judgment. The doctor's judgment takes into account other data (including intuition and experience). Suppose that, if it is a muscle cramp, then the treatment is rest. If a blood clot, then the treatment is a drug with no long-term side effects, but it causes mild discomfort for many people. If the doctor mistakenly treats your muscle cramp with the blood clot treatment, then you are uncomfortable for a short time. If the doctor mistakenly treats the blood clot with rest, then there is a chance of serious complications or even death. Judgment involves determining the relative payoff associated with each possible outcome, including those associated with "correct" decisions as well as those associated with mistakes (in this case, the payoffs associated with healing, mild discomfort, and serious complications). Determining the payoffs for all possible outcomes is a necessary step for deciding when to choose the drug treatment, opting for the mild discomfort and reducing the risk of a serious complication, versus when to choose rest. So, applying judgment to the prediction, the doctor makes a decision, perhaps, given your age and risk preferences, that you should have the treatment for the muscle cramp, even though there is some tiny likelihood you have a blood clot.

Finally is the action in administering the treatment and observing the outcome: Did the pain in your leg go away? Did other complications arise? The doctor can use this observed outcome as feedback to inform the next prediction.

By breaking up a decision into elements, we can think clearly about which parts of human activities will diminish in value and which will increase as a result of enhanced machine prediction. Most clearly, for prediction itself, a prediction machine is generally a better substitute for human prediction. As machine prediction increasingly replaces the predictions that humans make, the value of human prediction will decline. But a key point is that, while prediction is a key component of any decision, it is not the only component. The other elements of a decision—judgment, data, and action—remain, for now, firmly in the realm of humans. They are complements to prediction, meaning they increase in value as prediction becomes cheap. For example, we may be more willing to exert effort by applying judgment to decisions where we previously had decided not to decide (e.g., accepted the default) because prediction machines now offer better, faster, and cheaper predictions. In that case, the demand for human judgment will increase.

Losing the Knowledge

"The Knowledge" is the subject matter of a test that London cabbies take to drive the city's celebrated black taxis. The test involves knowing the location of thousands of points and streets around the city and—this is the harder part—predicting the shortest or fastest route between any two points at any time of day. The amount of information for even an ordinary city is staggering, but London is not ordinary. It is a mass of formerly independent villages and towns that have grown together over the past two thousand years into a global metropolis. To pass the test, potential cabbies need a near-perfect score. Not surprisingly, passing the test takes, on average, *three years*, including not only time spent poring over maps but also riding around the city on mopeds memorizing and visualizing. But once they have achieved this, honored green badge recipients are a font of knowledge.[1]

You know where this story is going. A decade ago, London cab drivers' knowledge was their competitive advantage. No one could provide the same degree of service. People who would otherwise have walked would hop in a cab just because the cab drivers knew the way. But just five years later, a simple mobile GPS or satellite navigation system gave drivers access to data and predictions that had once been the cabbies' superpower. Today, the same superpowers are available for free on most mobile phones. People do not get lost. People know the fastest route. And now the phone is one step better because it is updated in real time with traffic information.

Cabbies who invested three years of studying to learn "The Knowledge" did not know they would someday be competing with prediction machines. Over the years, they uploaded maps into their memory, tested routes, and filled in the blanks with their common sense. Now, navigation apps have access to the same map data and are able, through a combination of algorithms and predictive training, to find the best route whenever requested, using real-time data about traffic that the taxi driver cannot hope to know.

But the fate of London cabbies rested not just on the ability for navigation apps to predict "The Knowledge" but also on other crucial elements to take the best path from point A to point B. First, the cabbies could control a motor vehicle. Second, they had sensors affixed to them—their eyes and ears most importantly—that fed contextual data to their brains to ensure that they put their knowledge to good use. But so did other people. No London cabbie became worse at their job because of navigation apps. Instead, millions of other non-cabbies became a lot better. The cabbies' knowledge was no longer a scarce commodity, opening up cabbies to competition from ride-sharing platforms like Uber.

That other drivers could show up with "The Knowledge" on their phones and predictions of the fastest routes meant they could provide equivalent service. When high-quality machine prediction became cheap, human prediction declined in value, so the cabbies were worse off. The number of rides in London's black cabs fell. Instead, other people provided the same service. These others also had driving skills and human sensors, complementary assets that went up in value as prediction became cheap.

Of course, self-driving cars might themselves end up substituting for those skills and senses, but we will return to that story later. Our point here is that understanding the impact of machine prediction requires an understanding of the various aspects of decisions, as described by the anatomy of a decision.

Should You Take an Umbrella?

Until now, we've been a little imprecise about what judgment actually is. To explain it, we introduce a decision-making tool: the decision tree.[2] It is especially useful for decisions under uncertainty, when you are not sure what will happen if you make a particular choice.

Let's consider a familiar choice you might face. Should you carry an umbrella on a walk? You might think that an umbrella is a thing you hold over your head to stay dry, and you'd be right. But an umbrella is also a kind of insurance, in this case, against the possibility of rain. So, the following framework applies to any insurance-like decision to reduce risk.

Clearly, if you knew it was not going to rain, you would leave the umbrella at home. On the other hand, if you knew it would rain, then you would certainly take it with you. In figure 7-2, we represent this using a tree-like diagram. At the root of the tree are two branches representing the choices you could make: "leave umbrella" or "take umbrella." Extending from these are two branches that represent what you are uncertain about: "rain" versus "shine." Absent a good weather forecast, you do not know. You might know that, at this time of the year, sun is three times more likely than rain. This would give

FIGURE 7-2

Should you take an umbrella?

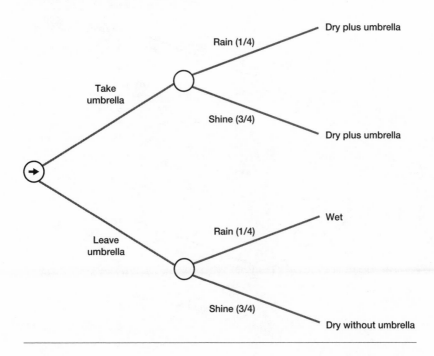

you a three-quarters chance of sun and a one-quarter chance of rain. This is your prediction. Finally, at the tips of the branches are the consequences. If you don't take an umbrella and it rains, you get wet, and so on.

What decision should you make? This is where judgment comes in. Judgment is the process of determining the reward to a particular action in a particular environment. It is about working out the objective you're actually pursuing. Judgment involves determining what we call the "reward function," the relative rewards and penalties associated with taking particular actions that produce particular outcomes. Wet or dry? Burdened by carrying an umbrella or unburdened?

Let's assume that you prefer being dry without an umbrella (you rate it a 10 out of 10) more than being dry, but carrying an umbrella (8 out of 10) more than being wet (a big, fat 0). (See figure 7-3.) This gives you enough to act. With the prediction of rain one-quarter of the time

FIGURE 7-3

Average payoff from taking or leaving an umbrella

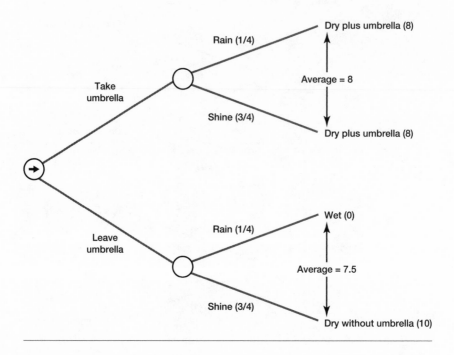

and the judgment of the payoffs to being wet or carrying an umbrella, you can work out your average payoff from taking versus leaving the umbrella. Based on this, you are better off taking the umbrella (an average payoff of 8) than leaving it (an average payoff of 7.5).[3]

If you really hate toting an umbrella (a 6 out of 10), your judgment about preferences can also be accommodated. In this case, the average payoff from leaving an umbrella at home is unchanged (at 7.5), while the payoff from taking one is now 6. So, such umbrella haters will leave the umbrella at home.

This example is trivial: of course, people who hate umbrellas more than getting wet will leave them home. But the decision tree is a useful tool for figuring out payoffs for nontrivial decisions, too, and that is at the heart of judgment. Here, the action is taking the umbrella, the prediction is rain or shine, the outcome is whether you get wet, and judgment is anticipating happiness you will feel ("payoff") from being wet or dry, with or without an umbrella. As prediction becomes better, faster, and cheaper, we'll use more of it to make more decisions, so we'll also need more human judgment and thus the value of human judgment will go up.

KEY POINTS

- Prediction machines are so valuable because (1) they can often produce better, faster, and cheaper predictions than humans can; (2) prediction is a key ingredient in decision making under uncertainty; and (3) decision making is ubiquitous throughout our economic and social lives. However, a prediction is not a decision—it is only a component of a decision. The other components are judgment, action, outcome, and three types of data (input, training, and feedback).

- By breaking down a decision into its components we can understand the impact of prediction machines on the value of humans and other assets. The value of substitutes to prediction machines, namely human prediction, will decline. However, the value of complements, such as the human skills associated with data collection, judgment, and actions, will become more valuable. In the case of the London cabbies who each invested three years to learn "The Knowledge"—how to predict the fastest route from one location to another at a particular time of day—none became worse at their job because of prediction machines. Rather, many other drivers became a lot better at choosing the best route by using prediction machines. The cabbies' prediction skills were no longer a scarce commodity. Drivers who weren't cabbies had driving skills and human sensors (eyes and ears) that were effectively enhanced by prediction machines, enabling them to compete.

- Judgment involves determining the relative payoff associated with each possible outcome of a decision, including those associated with "correct" decisions as well as those associated with mistakes. Judgment requires specifying the objective you're actually pursuing and is a necessary step in decision making. As prediction machines make predictions increasingly better, faster, and cheaper, the value of human judgment will increase because we'll need more of it. We may be more willing to exert effort and apply judgment to decisions where we previously had chosen not to decide (by accepting the default).

8

The Value of Judgment

Having better prediction raises the value of judgment. After all, it doesn't help to know the likelihood of rain if you don't know how much you like staying dry or how much you hate carrying an umbrella.

Prediction machines don't provide judgment. Only humans do, because only humans can express the relative rewards from taking different actions. As AI takes over prediction, humans will do less of the combined prediction-judgment routine of decision making and focus more on the judgment role alone. This will enable an interactive interface between machine prediction and human judgment, much the same way that you run alternative queries when interacting with a spreadsheet or database.

With better prediction come more opportunities to consider the rewards of various actions—in other words, more opportunities for judgment. And that means that better, faster, and cheaper prediction will give us more decisions to make.

Judging Fraud

Credit card networks such as Mastercard, Visa, and American Express predict and judge all the time. They have to predict whether card applicants meet their standards for credit worthiness. If the individual doesn't, then the company will deny them credit. You might think that's pure prediction, but a significant element of judgment is involved as well. Being credit worthy is a sliding scale, and the credit card company has to decide how much risk it's willing to take on at different interest and default rates. Those decisions lead to significantly different business models—the difference between American Express's high-end platinum card and an entry-level card aimed at college students.

The company also needs to predict whether any given transaction is legitimate. As with your decision to carry an umbrella or not, the company must weigh four distinct outcomes (see figure 8-1). The

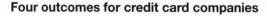

FIGURE 8-1

Four outcomes for credit card companies

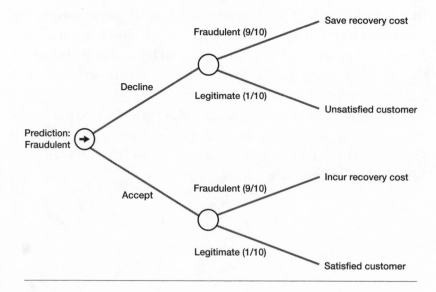

company has to predict if the charge is fraudulent or legitimate, decide whether to authorize or decline the transaction, and then to evaluate each outcome (denying a fraudulent charge is good, angering a customer with the denial of a legitimate transaction is bad). If the credit card companies were perfect at predicting fraud, all would be well. But they're not.

For instance, Joshua (one of the authors) has had his credit card company routinely deny transactions when he is shopping for running shoes, something he does about once a year, usually at an outlet mall when he is on vacation. For many years, he had to call the credit card company to lift a restriction.

Credit card theft often happens at malls, and the first few fraudulent purchases might be things like shoes and clothing (easy to convert into cash as returns at a different branch of the same chain). And since Joshua is not in the habit of routinely buying clothes and shoes and rarely goes to a mall, the credit card company predicts that the card has likely been stolen. It's a fair guess.

Some factors that influence the prediction about whether a card has been stolen are generic (the type of transaction, such as purchasing running shoes), while others are specific to individuals (in this case, age and frequency). That combination of factors means that the eventual algorithm that flags transactions will be complex.

The promise of AI is that it can make prediction much more precise, especially in situations with a mix of generic and personalized information. For instance, given data on Joshua's years of transactions, a prediction machine could learn the pattern of those transactions, including the fact that he buys shoes around the same time each year. Rather than classifying such a purchase as an unusual event, it could classify it as a usual event for this particular person. A prediction machine may notice other correlations, such as how long it takes someone to shop, working out whether transactions in two different shops are too close together. As the prediction machine becomes more precise in flagging transactions, the card network can become more confident in imposing a restriction and even whether to contact a consumer. This is already happening. Joshua's last outlet mall purchase of running shoes went smoothly.

But until prediction machines become perfect at predicting fraud, credit card companies will have to figure out the costs of errors, which requires judgment. Suppose that prediction is imperfect and has a 10 percent chance of being incorrect. Then, if the companies decline the transaction, they will do the right thing with a 90 percent chance and save the network the costs of recovering the payment associated with the unauthorized transaction. But they also will decline a legitimate transaction with a 10 percent chance, leaving the network with a dissatisfied customer. To work out the right course of action, they need to be able to balance the costs associated with fraud discovery with the costs associated with customer dissatisfaction. Credit card companies don't automatically know the right answer to this trade-off. They need to figure it out. Judgment is the process of doing that.

It's the umbrella case all over again, but instead of burdened/ unburdened and wet/dry, there are fraud charges and customer satisfaction. In this case, because this transaction is nine times likelier to be fraudulent than legitimate, the company will deny the charge unless customer satisfaction is nine times more important than the possible loss.

For credit card fraud, many of these payoffs may be easy to judge. It is highly likely that the cost of recovery has a distinct monetary value that a network can identify. Suppose that for a $100 transaction, the recovery cost is $20. If the customer dissatisfaction cost is less than $180, it makes sense to decline the transaction (10 percent of $180 is $18, the same as 90 percent of $20). For many customers, being declined for a single transaction does not lead to the equivalent of $180 in dissatisfaction.

A credit card network also must assess whether that is likely to be the case for a particular customer. For example, a high-net-worth platinum cardholder may have other credit card options and might stop using that particular card if declined. And that person may be on an expensive vacation, so the card network could lose all of the expenditures associated with that trip.

Credit card fraud is a well-defined decision process, which is one reason we keep coming back to it, yet it's still complicated. By contrast, for many other decisions, not only are the potential actions more complex (not just a simple accept or decline), but the potential situations (or states) also vary. Judgment requires an understanding of the reward for each pair of actions and situations. Our credit card example had just four outcomes (or eight if you distinguish between high-net-worth customers and everyone else). But if you had, say, ten actions and twenty possible situations, then you're judging two hundred outcomes. As things get even more complicated, the number of rewards can become overwhelming.

The Cognitive Costs of Judgment

People who have studied decisions in the past have generally taken rewards as givens—they simply exist. You may like chocolate ice cream, while your friend may like mango gelato. How you two came to your different views is of little consequence. Similarly, we assume most businesses are maximizing profit or shareholder value. Economists looking at why firms choose certain prices for their products have found it useful to take those objectives on faith.

Payoffs are rarely obvious, and the process of understanding those payoffs can be time consuming and costly. However, the rise of prediction machines increases the returns to understanding the logic and motivation for payoff values.

In economic terms, the cost of figuring out the payoffs will mostly be time. Consider one particular pathway by which you might determine payoffs: deliberation and thought. Thinking through what you really want to achieve or what the costs of customer dissatisfaction might be takes time spent thinking, reflecting, and perhaps asking others for advice. Or it may be the time spent researching to better understand payoffs.

For credit card fraud detection, thinking through the payoffs of satisfied and unsatisfied customers and the cost of allowing a fraudulent transaction to proceed are necessary first steps. Providing different payoffs for high-net-worth customers requires more thought. Assessing whether those payoffs change when those customers are on vacation requires even more consideration. And what about regular customers when they are on vacation? Are the payoffs in that situation different? And is it worth separating work travel from vacation? Or trips to Rome from trips to the Grand Canyon?

In each case, judging the payoffs requires time and effort: more outcomes mean more judgment means more time and effort. Humans experience the cognitive costs of judgment as a slower decision-making process. We all have to decide how much we want to pin down the payoffs against the costs of delaying a decision. Some will choose not to investigate payoffs for scenarios that seem remote or unlikely. The credit card network might find it worthwhile to separate work trips from vacations but not vacations to Rome from the Grand Canyon.

In such unlikely situations, the card network may guess at the right decision, group things together, or just choose a safer default. But for more frequent decisions (such as travel in general) or ones that appear more important (such as high-net-worth customers), many will take the time to deliberate and identify the payoffs more carefully. But the longer it takes to experiment, the longer it will take before your decision making is performing as well as it could.

Figuring out payoffs might also be more like tasting new foods: try something and see what happens. Or, rather, in the vernacular of modern business: experiment. Individuals might take different actions in the same circumstances and learn what the reward actually is. They learn the payoffs instead of cogitating on them beforehand. Of course, because experimentation necessarily means making what you will later regard as mistakes, experiments also have costs. You will try foods you don't like. If you keep trying new foods in the hope of finding some ideal, you are missing out on a lot of good meals. Judgment, whether by deliberation or experimentation, is costly.

Knowing Why You Are Doing Something

Prediction is at the heart of a move toward self-driving cars and the rise of platforms such as Uber and Lyft: choosing a route between origin and destination. Car navigation devices have been around for a few decades, built into cars themselves or as stand-alone devices. But the proliferation of internet-connected mobile devices has changed the data that providers of navigation software receive. For instance, before Google acquired it, the Israeli startup Waze generated accurate traffic maps by tracking the routes drivers chose. It then used that information to provide efficient optimization of the quickest path between two points, taking into account the information it had from drivers as well as continual monitoring of traffic. It could also forecast how traffic conditions might evolve if you were traveling farther and could offer new, more efficient paths on route if conditions changed.

Users of apps like Waze don't always follow the directions. They don't disagree with the prediction per se, but their ultimate objective might include more elements than just speed. For instance, the app doesn't know if someone is running out of fuel and needs a gas station. But human drivers, knowing that they need gas, can overrule the app's suggestion and take another route.

Of course, apps like Waze can and will get better. For instance, in Tesla cars, which run on electricity, navigation takes into account the need to recharge and the location of charging stations. An app could simply ask you whether you are likely to need fuel or, in the future, even get that data directly from your car. This seems like a solvable problem, just as you can tweak the settings on navigation apps to avoid toll roads.

Other aspects of your preferences are harder to program. For instance, on a long drive, you might want to make sure you pass certain good areas to stop and eat. Or the fastest route might tax the driver by suggesting back roads that only save a minute or two but require a lot of effort. Or you may not enjoy taking winding roads. Again, apps might learn those behaviors, but at any given time, some factors are necessarily not part of a codified prediction to automate an action. A machine has fundamental limitations about how much it can learn to predict your preferences.

The broader point for decisions is that objectives rarely have only a single dimension. Humans have, explicitly and implicitly, their own knowledge of why they are doing something, which gives them weights that are both idiosyncratic and subjective.

While a machine predicts what is likely to happen, humans will still decide what action to take based on their understanding of the objective. In many situations, as with Waze, the machine will give the human a prediction that implies a certain outcome for one dimension (like speed); the human will then decide whether to overrule the suggested action. Depending on the sophistication of the prediction machine, the human may ask it for another prediction based on a new constraint ("Waze, take me past a gas station").

Hard-Coding Judgment

Ada Support, a startup, is using AI prediction to siphon off the easy from the difficult technical support questions. The AI answers the easy questions and sends the difficult ones to a human. For a typical mobile phone service provider, when consumers call for support, the vast majority of the questions they ask have also been asked by other people. The action of typing the answer is easy. The challenges are in predicting what the consumer wants and judging which answer to provide.

Rather than directing people to a "frequently asked questions" area of a web page, Ada identifies and answers these frequent questions right away. It can match a consumer's individual characteristics (such as past knowledge of technical competence, the type of phone they are calling from, or past calls) to improve its assessment of the question. In the process, it can diminish frustration, but more importantly, it can handle more interactions quickly without the need to spend money on costlier human call-center operators. The humans specialize in the unusual and more difficult questions, while the machine handles the easy ones.

As machine prediction improves, it will be increasingly worthwhile to prespecify judgment in many situations. Just as we explain our thinking to other people, we can explain our thinking to machines—in the form of software code. When we anticipate receiving a precise prediction, we can hard-code the judgment before the machine predicts. Ada does this for easy questions. Otherwise, it is too time consuming, with too many possible situations to specify what to do in each situation in advance. So, for the hard questions, Ada calls in the humans for their judgment.

Experience can sometimes make judgment codifiable. Much experience is intangible and so cannot be written down or expressed easily. As Andrew McAfee and Erik Brynjolfsson wrote: "[S]ubstitution (of computers for people) is bounded because there are many tasks that people understand tacitly and accomplish effortlessly but for which neither computer programmers nor anyone else can enunciate the explicit 'rules' or procedures."[1] That, however, is not true of all tasks. For some decisions, you can articulate the requisite judgment and express it as code. After all, we often explain our thinking to other people. In effect, codifiable judgment allows you to fill in the part after "then" in "if-then" statements. When this happens, then judgment can be enshrined and programmed.

The challenge is that, even when you can program judgment to take over from a human, the prediction the machine receives must be fairly precise. When there are too many possible situations, it is too time consuming to specify what to do in each situation in advance. You can easily program a machine to take a certain action when it is clear what is likely to be true; however, when there is still uncertainty, telling the machine what to do requires a more careful weighing of the costs of mistakes. Uncertainty means you need judgment when the prediction turns out to be wrong, not just when the prediction is right. In other words, uncertainty increases the cost of judging the payoffs for a given decision.

Credit card networks have embraced new machine-learning techniques for fraud detection. Prediction machines enable them to be more confident in codifying the decision about whether to block a card transaction. As the predictions on fraud become more precise, the likelihood of mislabeling legitimate transactions as fraudulent is reduced. If the credit card companies are not afraid of making a mistake on the prediction, then they can codify the machine's decision, with no need to judge how costly it might be to offend particular customers by declining their transaction. Making the decision is easier: if fraud, then reject; otherwise, accept the transaction.

Reward Function Engineering

As prediction machines provide better and cheaper predictions, we need to work out how to best use those predictions. Whether or not we can specify judgment in advance, someone needs to determine the judgment. Enter reward function engineering, the job of determining the rewards to various actions, given the predictions that the AI makes. Doing this job well requires an understanding of the organization's needs and the machine's capabilities.

Sometimes reward function engineering involves hard-coding judgment—programming the rewards in advance of the predictions in order to automate actions. Self-driving vehicles are an example of such hard-coded rewards. Once the prediction is made, the action is instant. But getting the reward right isn't trivial. Reward function engineering has to consider the possibility that the AI will over-optimize on one metric of success and, in doing so, act inconsistently with the organization's broader goals. Entire committees are working on this for self-driving cars; however, such analysis will be required for a variety of new decisions.

In other cases, the number of possible predictions may make it too costly for anyone to judge all the possible payoffs in advance. Instead, a human needs to wait for the prediction to arrive and then assess the payoff, which is close to how most decision making currently works, whether or not it includes machine-generated predictions. As we will see in the following chapter, machines are encroaching on this as well. A prediction machine can, in some circumstances, learn to predict human judgment by observing past decisions.

Putting It All Together

Most of us already do some reward function engineering, but for humans, not machines. Parents teach their children values. Mentors teach new workers how the system operates. Managers give objectives to their staff and then tweak them to get better performance. Every day, we make decisions and judge the rewards. But when we do this for humans, we group prediction and judgment together, and the role of reward function engineering is not distinct. As machines get better at prediction, the role of reward function engineering will become increasingly important.

To illustrate reward function engineering in practice, consider pricing decisions at ZipRecruiter, an online job board. Companies pay ZipRecruiter to find qualified candidates for job openings they wish to fill. The core product of ZipRecruiter is a matching algorithm that does this efficiently and at scale, a version of the traditional headhunter that matches job seekers to companies.[2]

ZipRecruiter wasn't clear what it should charge companies for its service. Charge too little, and it leaves money on the table. Charge too much, and customers switch to the company's competitors. To figure out its pricing, ZipRecruiter brought in two experts, J. P. Dubé and Sanjog Misra, economists from the University of Chicago's Booth School of Business, who designed experiments to determine the best prices. They randomly assigned different prices to different customer leads and determined the likelihood each group would purchase. This allowed them to determine how different customers responded to different price points.

The challenge was to figure out what "best" meant. Should the company just maximize short-term revenue? To do so, it might choose a high price. But a high price means fewer customers (even though each customer is more profitable). That would also mean less word of mouth. In addition, if it has fewer job postings, the number of people who use ZipRecruiter to find jobs might fall. Finally, the customers facing high prices might start looking for alternatives. While they might pay the high price in the short run, they might switch to a competitor in the long run. How should ZipRecruiter weigh these various considerations? What payoff should it maximize?

It was relatively easy to measure the short-run consequences of a price increase. The experts found that increasing prices for some types of new customers would increase profits on a day-to-day basis by over 50 percent. However, ZipRecruiter didn't act right away. It recognized the longer-term risk and waited to see if the higher-paying customers would leave. After four months, it found that the price increase was still highly profitable. It didn't want to forgo the higher

profits any longer and judged four months to be long enough to implement the price changes.

Figuring out the rewards from these various actions—the key
piece of judgment—is reward function engineering, a fundamental
part of what humans do in the decision-making process. Prediction
machines are a tool for humans. So long as humans are needed to
weigh outcomes and impose judgment, they have a key role to play as
prediction machines improve.

KEY POINTS

- Prediction machines increase the returns to judgment because,
  by lowering the cost of prediction, they increase the value of
  understanding the rewards associated with actions. However,
  judgment is costly. Figuring out the relative payoffs for different actions in different situations takes time, effort, and
  experimentation.

- Many decisions occur under conditions of uncertainty. We
  decide to bring an umbrella because we think it might rain,
  but we could be wrong. We decide to authorize a transaction
  because we think it is legitimate, but we could be wrong. Under
  conditions of uncertainty, we need to determine the payoff for
  acting on wrong decisions, not just right ones. So, uncertainty
  increases the cost of judging the payoffs for a given decision.

- If there are a manageable number of action-situation combinations associated with a decision, then we can transfer the
  judgment from ourselves to the prediction machine (this is
  "reward function engineering") so that the machine can make
  the decision itself once it generates the prediction. This enables
  automating the decision. Often, however, there are too many
  action-situation combinations, such that it is too costly to code
  up in advance all the payoffs associated with each combination,
  especially the very rare ones. In these cases, it is more efficient for
  a human to apply judgment after the prediction machine predicts.

9

Predicting Judgment

Companies like Google subsidiary Waymo have been successfully testing automated ways of transporting people between two points. But that is only part of creating autonomous vehicles. Driving also has an impact on the passengers in the car, which is much harder to observe. Human drivers, however, do take into account the other people in the car. One of the first things a new driver learns is to brake in a manner that is comfortable for others in the car. Waymo's cars had to be taught to avoid sudden stops and instead smoothly halt.

There are thousands of related decisions that are involved in driving.[1] It is impractical for humans to code their judgment about how to handle every possible situation. Instead, we train autonomous driving systems by showing them many examples so that they learn to predict human judgment: "What would a human do in this situation?" Driving is not unique. In any environment where humans make decisions over and over again and we are able to collect data about the data they receive and the decisions they make in response, we will likely be able to automate those decisions by rewarding the prediction machine for predicting: *What would a human do?*

A fundamental question, at least for humans, is whether AI can turn its predictive powers on human judgment and, in the process, circumvent the need for humans altogether.

Hacking the Humans

Many decisions are complex and predicated on judgment that is not easily codified. However, this does not guarantee that humans will remain a core part of these decisions. Instead, as with self-driving cars, the machine may learn to predict human judgment by observing many examples. The prediction problem becomes: "given the input data, what would a human do?"

The company Grammarly offers an example. Founded in 2009 by Alex Shevchenko and Max Lytvyn, Grammarly pioneered the use of machine learning to improve the composition of formal written materials. It's main focus is on improving grammer and spelling in sentences. For instance, put the previous sentence into Grammarly, and it will tell you that "It's" should be "Its" and "grammer" is misspelled (it should be "grammar"). It will also tell you that the word "main" is often overused.

Grammarly achieved these corrections both by examining a corpus of documents that skilled editors had corrected and by learning from the feedback of users who accepted or rejected the suggestions. In both cases, Grammarly predicted what a human editor would do. It goes beyond the mechanical application of grammar rules to also assess whether deviations from perfect grammar are preferred by human readers.

The idea that humans can train AI extends to a wide variety of situations. The AI at the heart of Lola, a startup automating the process of booking travel, began by finding good hotel options. But, as the *New York Times* reported:

> [I]t couldn't match the expertise of, for example, a human agent with years of experience booking family vacations to Disney World. The human can be more nimble—knowing, for instance, to advise a family that hopes to score an unobstructed photo with the children in front of the Cinderella Castle that they should book a breakfast reservation inside the park, before the gates open.[2]

This example shows that a machine finds it easy to apply judgment where it is describable (e.g., availability and price), but not to understand subtler human preferences. However, Lola can learn to predict what humans with a high level of experience and thought would do. The question for Lola is: How many observations of people booking Orlando vacations does the prediction machine need to get enough feedback to learn other relevant criteria? As Lola discovered, while its AI was challenged by some criteria, it was able to uncover decisions human agents had made that those agents were unable to describe in advance, such as preferences for modern hotels or hotels on a street corner.

Human trainers help AIs become good enough so that humans gradually become unnecessary for many aspects of a task. This is particularly important when the AI is automating a process with very little tolerance for error. A human may supervise the AI and correct mistakes. Over time, the AI learns from its mistakes until human correction is unnecessary.

X.ai, a startup focused on providing an assistant that can arrange meetings and put them into your calendar, is another example.[3] It interacts with the user and people the user wants to meet with through email to a digital personal assistant ("Amy" or "Andrew," depending upon your preference). For instance, you could send an email to Andrew to arrange a meeting between you and Mr. H next Thursday. X.ai then accesses your calendar and sends emails to Mr. H to schedule the meeting. Mr. H may well be none the wiser that Andrew is not human. The point is that you are freed from the task of communicating with Mr. H or his assistant (who ideally would be another Amy or Andrew).

Obviously, disaster might strike if scheduling mistakes occur or if the automated assistant offends a potential invitee. For a number of years, X.ai employed human trainers. They reviewed the AI's responses for accuracy and validated them. Every time a trainer made a change, the AI learned a better response.[4] The role of human trainers was more than just ensuring politeness. They also dealt with bad behavior from humans trying to trip up the assistant.[5] As of this writing, the question is still open as to how much automation this approach of predicting judgment can achieve.

Will Humans Be Pushed Out?

If the machines can learn to predict human behavior, will they push humans out completely? Given the current trajectory of prediction machines, we don't think so. Humans are a resource, so simple economics suggest they will still do something. The question is more whether the "something" for humans is high or low value, appealing or unappealing. What should the humans in your organization do? What should you look for in new hires?

Prediction relies on data. That means humans have two advantages over machines. We know some things that the machines don't (yet), and, more importantly, we are better at deciding what to do when there isn't much data.

Humans have three types of data that machines don't. First, human senses are powerful. In many ways, human eyes, ears, nose, and skin still surpass machine capabilities. Second, humans are the ultimate arbiters of our own preferences. Consumer data is extremely valuable because it gives prediction machines data about these preferences. Grocery stores provide discounts to consumers who use loyalty cards in order to obtain data on their behavior. Stores pay consumers to reveal their preferences. Google, Facebook, and others provide free services in exchange for data that they can use in other contexts to target advertising. Third, privacy concerns restrict the data available to machines. As long as enough people keep their sexual activity, financial situation, mental health status, and repugnant thoughts to themselves, the prediction machines will have insufficient data to predict many types of behavior. In the absence of good data, our understanding of other humans will provide a role for our judgment skills that machines cannot learn to predict.

Prediction with Little Data

Prediction machines may also lack data because some events are rare. If a machine cannot observe enough human decisions, it cannot predict the judgment underlying those decisions.

In chapter 6, we discussed "known unknowns," rare events that are difficult to predict due to lack of data, including presidential elections and earthquakes. In some cases, humans are good at prediction with little data; we can recognize faces, for instance, even as people age. We also discussed how "unknown unknowns" are, by definition, difficult to predict or respond to. AI cannot predict what a human would do if that human has never faced a similar situation. In this way, AI cannot predict the strategic direction of a company facing a new technology, such as the internet, bioengineering, or even AI itself. Humans are able to make analogies or recognize useful similarities in different contexts.

Eventually, prediction machines may get better at analogies. Still, our point that prediction machines will be bad at predicting rare events holds. For the foreseeable future, humans will have a role in prediction and judgment when unusual situations arise.

In chapter 6, we also highlighted "unknown knowns." For example, we discussed the challenges of deciding whether to recommend this book to your friend, even if you become fabulously successful at managing AI in the future. The challenge is that you do not have the data on what would have happened had you not read the book. If you want to understand what causes what, you need to observe what would have happened in the counterfactual situation.

Humans can provide two main solutions to this problem: experiments and modeling. If the situation arises often enough, you can run a randomized control trial. Assign some people to the treatment (force them to read the book, or at least give them the book and maybe hold some consequential exam on it) and others to the control (force them not to read the book, or at least don't advertise it to them). Wait and collect some measure of how they apply AI in their work. Compare the two groups. The difference between the treatment and control groups is the effect of reading the book.

Such experiments are very powerful. Without them, new medical treatments are not approved. They fuel many of the decisions at data-driven companies from Google to Capital One. Machines can also conduct experiments. As long as the situation arises enough, the ability to experiment is not unique to humans. The machine can experiment and learn to predict what causes what, just as humans do. This has been a key aspect of how machines can now outperform humans in a variety of video games.

Modeling, an alternative to experiments, involves having a deep understanding of the situation and the process that generated the data observed. It is particularly useful when experiments are impossible because the situation doesn't arise often enough or the cost of an experiment is too high.

Online job board ZipRecruiter's decision to find the best price, which we described in the previous chapter, involved two parts. First, it needed to figure out what "best" meant: short-term revenue or something longer term? More job seekers and more advertisers, or higher prices? Second, it needed to choose a specific price. To solve the second problem, it experimented. Expert humans designed the experiment, but in principle, as AI improves, with enough advertisers and enough time, such experiments could be automated.

Determining "best," however, is more difficult to automate. Since the number of job seekers depends on the number of job advertisements and vice versa, the overall market has just one observation. Get it wrong, and ZipRecruiter could go out of business and not get a second chance. So, it modeled its business. It explored the consequences of maximizing its short-term profit and compared it to alternative models in which its goal was to maximize profit over a longer time. Without data, modeling outcomes and engineering the reward function remain human abilities, albeit highly skilled ones.

Modeling also helped Allied bombing raids during World War II. Engineers recognized that they could better armor their bombers. In particular, they could add some weight to the planes without compromising performance. The question was where exactly to protect the planes. Experimentation was possible, but costly. Pilots would lose their lives.

For every bomber that returned from bombing raids over Germany, the engineers could see where they had been hit by antiaircraft fire. The bullet holes in the planes were their data. But were these the obvious places to better protect the plane?

They asked statistician Abraham Wald to assess the problem. After some thought and some rather thorough mathematics, he told them to protect the places *without* bullet holes. Was he confused? That seemed counterintuitive. Didn't he mean to protect the areas of the plane that did have bullet holes? No. He had a model of the process that generated the data. He recognized that some bombers did not come back from the raids and conjectured that these bombers got hit in places that were fatal. In contrast, the bombers that made it home were hit in places that were not fatal. With this insight, the air force engineers increased the armor in the places without bullet holes, and the planes were better protected.[6]

Wald's insight about the missing data required an understanding of where the data came from; given that the problem had not arisen before, the engineers did not have prior examples to draw from. For the foreseeable future, such calculations are beyond the abilities of prediction machines.

This problem was hard to solve. The solution came from a human, not a prediction machine. However, the human was one of the best statisticians in history. He had a deep understanding of the mathematics of statistics and a flexible enough mind to understand the process that generated the data.

Humans can learn such modeling skills with training. It is a core aspect of most economics PhD programs and part of the MBA curriculum in many schools (including courses we developed at the University of Toronto). Such skills matter when working with prediction machines. Otherwise, it is easy to fall into the trap of unknown knowns. You will think your predictions tell you what to do, but they may lead you astray, mixing cause and effect.

Just as Wald had a good model of the process generating the data about bullet holes, a good model of human behavior can help make better predictions when human decisions generate the data. For the foreseeable future, humans need to help develop such models and identify the relevant predictors of behavior. A prediction machine will struggle to extrapolate in a situation in which it has no data because behavior is likely to change. It needs to understand humans.[7]

Similar issues arise in many decisions that involve the question, "What will happen if I do this?" when you have never done it before. Should you add a new product to a product line? Should you merge with a competitor? Should you acquire an innovative startup or a channel partner?[8] If people will behave differently after the change, then past behavior is not a useful guide for future behavior. The prediction machine will not have relevant data. For rare events, prediction machines have limited use. Rare events therefore provide an important limit to the ability of machines to predict human judgment.

KEY POINTS

- Machines may learn to predict human judgment. An example is driving. It is impractical for humans to code their judgment about how to handle every possible situation. However, we train autonomous driving systems by showing them many examples and rewarding them for predicting human judgment: *What would a human do in this situation?*

- There are limits to the ability of machines to predict human judgment. The limits relate to lack of data. There is some data that humans have that machines do not, such as individual preferences. Such data has value, and companies currently pay to access it through discounts on using loyalty cards and free online services like Google and Facebook.

- Machines are bad at prediction for rare events. Managers make decisions on mergers, innovation, and partnerships without data on similar past events for their firms. Humans use analogies and models to make decisions in such unusual situations. Machines cannot predict judgment when a situation has not occurred many times in the past.

10

Taming Complexity

The TV show *The Americans*, a cold-war drama set in Washington, DC, in the 1980s, features a robot that delivers mail and classified documents around the FBI office. That an autonomous vehicle existed in the 1980s might seem surprising. Marketed as the Mailmobile, it had first appeared a decade earlier.[1]

To guide the Mailmobile, a technician would lay out a chemical trail that gave off ultraviolet light from the mail room along the carpeted floors to various offices. The robot used a sensor to slowly follow the trail (at less than one mile per hour) until the chemical markings signaled it to stop. The Mailmobile cost between $10,000 and $12,000 (about $50,000 in today's dollars), and for an extra fee, the company could attach a sensor to detect obstacles in its path. Otherwise, it just beeped a lot to warn people it was coming. In an office where a human took two hours to deliver the mail, the Mailmobile completed the job in twenty minutes, not stopping for office banter.

The mail robot required careful planning. Even some simple but perhaps costly office reallocations might have been necessary to accommodate the robot's operation. It could deal with only small variations in its environment.

Even today, many automated rail systems worldwide have extensive installation requirements. For example, the Copenhagen metro uses no drivers, but it works because trains operate in a carefully pre-planned setting; only a limited number of sensors inform the robot about its environment.

These limitations are a common feature of most machines and equipment. They are designed to operate in rigid environments. Compared with most equipment on factory floors, the mail robot was notable because many offices could install it relatively easily. But, for the most part, robots need a tightly controlled and standardized environment in which to operate because the equipment does not tolerate uncertainty.

More "Ifs"

All machines—both hard and soft—are essentially programmed using the classic if-then logic. The "if" part specifies a scenario, environmental condition, or piece of information. The "then" part tells the machine what to do for each of the "ifs" (and "if nots" and "elses"): "If the chemical trail is no longer detected, then stop." The mail robot had no ability to see its surroundings and could only operate in an environment that artificially reduced the "ifs" it could deal with.

If it could distinguish between more situations—more "ifs"—and even if it didn't change what it did, essentially stop or go at any point, it could have been used in many more places. A modern-day Roomba—the automated vacuum cleaning robot from iRobot—is able to do this and roam freely around rooms with sensors to prevent it from falling down stairs or getting stuck in corners, along with a memory to ensure it covers the floor in a timely fashion.

If a robot operates outside, it needs to move more slowly to avoid slipping when the ground is wet. Two possible situations (or states) arise—dry and wet. If the robot's motion is also influenced by whether it is light or dark, whether a human is moving in the vicinity or not, whether rush items are in that batch of mail, if it is okay to run over squirrels but not cats, and a variety of other factors, and if the rules are sensitive to interactions (it is okay to run over squirrels if it is dark, but not if it is light), then the number of situations—the number of "ifs"—grows radically.

Better prediction identifies more "ifs." With more "ifs," a mail robot can react to more situations. A prediction machine enables the robot to identify that wet dark environments with a human running twenty feet behind and a cat up ahead might require slowing down, but wet dark environments with a human standing twenty feet behind and a squirrel ahead might not. The prediction machine enables the robot to move around without a preplanned trail or track. Our new Mailmobile can operate in more environments without much additional cost.

Delivery robots abound. Warehouses have autonomous delivery systems that can predict their environment and adjust accordingly. Fleets of Kiva robots transport products inside Amazon's vast fulfillment centers. Startups are experimenting with delivery robots that take packages (or pizza) onto sidewalks and streets from businesses to homes and back again.

Robots can now do this because they can now use data from sophisticated sensors to predict their environment and then receive instructions for how to handle it. We don't often conceptualize this as prediction, but fundamentally it is. And as it keeps getting cheaper, the robots will get better and better.

More "Thens"

George Stigler, a Nobel Prize–winning economist, reportedly remarked: "People who have never missed a flight have spent too long in airports."[2] While a peculiar logic is in operation here, the counterargument is strong: you can get work done or relax just as easily at the airport as elsewhere, and it might give you some peace of mind to get there early to avoid the hassles of missing a flight. Thus, was born the airport lounge. Airlines invented it to provide passengers (or at least wealthy or frequent-flying ones) a convenient and quiet space to wait for their flights. The lounge exists because you are likely to arrive early for your flight. Someone who is perennially late would only use a lounge in transit or when a flight is delayed or to weep when they miss their flight to Bali. The lounge is there to provide some wiggle room, a bit of a buffer for when your arrival time is less than precise (which is likely to be quite often).

Suppose you have a flight at 10 a.m. Airline guidelines say you should arrive sixty minutes beforehand. You could arrive at 9 a.m. and make your flight. Given that, what time should you leave for the airport?

You usually can get to the airport in thirty minutes, which might allow you to leave at 8:30 a.m., but that does not account for traffic disruption. When flying back to Toronto from a New York meeting about this very book, we three experienced such bad traffic to LaGuardia Airport that we ended up walking the last mile along the freeway. That could easily add another thirty minutes (more, if you are risk averse). Now you are back to 8 a.m., which is when you leave *every time* you don't know what traffic is going to be like. As a result, you usually end up spending thirty minutes or more in the lounge.

Apps such as Waze provide very accurate travel times from your current location to the airport. Such apps monitor both real time and historic traffic patterns to both forecast and update the quickest routes. Pair that with Google Now, and you can account for any delays that might appear for your flights with other apps that monitor historical delays or the location of a connecting aircraft. Together, these apps mean that you can reliably trust the prediction, which opens up new options such as "unless there is a traffic problem, leave later and go directly to the gate" or "if there is flight delay, leave later."

Better prediction, by reducing or eliminating a key source of uncertainty, eliminates your need to have a place to wait at the airport. More critically, better prediction enables new actions. Rather than having a hard-wired rule to leave two hours before your flight, you can have a contingent rule that takes information and then tells you when to leave. Those contingent rules are if-then statements and enable more "thens" (leave early, on time, or later), depending on more reliable predictions. So, in addition to producing more "ifs," prediction expands opportunities by increasing the number of feasible "thens."

Mail robots and airport lounges have something in common: they are both imperfect solutions to uncertainty, and they both will be undermined by better prediction.

More "Ifs" and "Thens"

Better prediction allows you to predict more things more often, reducing uncertainty. Each new prediction also has an indirect effect: it makes choices feasible that you would not have considered before. And you don't have to explicitly code the "ifs" and "thens." You can train the prediction machine with examples. Voilà! Problems that were not previously understood as prediction problems may now be tackled as such. We were compromising without recognizing it.

Such compromises are a key aspect of how humans make decisions. Economics Nobel Prize–winner Herbert Simon called this "satisficing." While classical economics models superintelligent beings making perfectly rational decisions, Simon recognized and emphasized in his work that humans cannot cope with complexity. Instead, they satisfice, doing the best they can to meet their objectives. Thinking is difficult, so people take shortcuts.

Simon was a polymath. In addition to a Nobel, he also won the Turing Award, often called the Nobel of computing, for "contributions to artificial intelligence." His economics and computing contributions were related. Echoing his thoughts on humans, his 1976 Turing Award lecture emphasized that computers "have limited processing resources; in a finite number of steps over a finite interval of time, they can execute only a finite number of processes." He recognized that computers—like humans—satisfice.[3]

The mail robots and airport lounge are examples of satisficing in the absence of good prediction. Such examples are everywhere. It will take practice and time to imagine the possibilities enabled by better prediction. It is not intuitive for most people to think of airport lounges as a solution to poor prediction and that they will be less valuable in an era of powerful prediction machines. We are so used to satisficing that we don't even think of some decisions as involving a prediction.

In the translation example earlier in the book, specialists saw automatic language translation not as a prediction problem but as a linguistic one. The traditional linguistic approach used a dictionary to translate word by word, coupled with some grammatical rules. This was satisficing; it led to poor results because of too many ifs. Translation became a prediction problem when researchers recognized that translation could happen sentence by sentence or even paragraph by paragraph.

Translation with prediction machines involves predicting the likely equivalent sentence in the other language. Statistics enable the computer to choose the best translation by predicting the ifs—which sentence a professional translator is most likely to use based on translation matching in the data. It relies on, remarkably, no linguistic rules. A pioneer of this field, Frederick Jelinek remarked, "Every time I fire a linguist, the performance of the speech recognizer goes up."[4] Clearly, this is a scary development for linguists and translators. All sorts of other tasks—including image recognition, shopping, and conversation—are being identified as complex prediction problems that are amenable to the application of machine learning.

By enabling more complex decisions, better prediction can lower risk. For instance, one of the practical applications of recent AI is in radiology. Much of what radiologists currently do involves taking images and then identifying issues of concern. They predict abnormalities in images.

AIs are increasingly able to perform that prediction function at human levels of accuracy or better, which can assist radiologists and other medical specialists in making decisions that have an impact on patients. The critical performance metric is the accuracy of the diagnosis: whether the machine predicts a disease when the patient is ill and predicts no disease when the patient is healthy.

But we must consider what such decisions involve. Suppose doctors suspect a lump and must decide how to determine if it is cancerous. One option is medical imaging. Another option is something more invasive, like a biopsy. A biopsy has the advantage of being highly likely to provide an accurate diagnosis. The problem, of course, is that a biopsy is invasive; thus, both doctors and patients prefer to avoid it if the likelihood is low that the issue is serious. One job of a radiologist is to provide a reason not to conduct an invasive procedure. The ideal is to perform a procedure only to confirm a serious diagnosis. The biopsy offers insurance against the risk of not treating a deadly disease, but it comes at a cost. The decision to undertake the biopsy depends on how costly and invasive the biopsy itself is and how bad it would be to overlook the disease. Doctors use these factors to decide whether the biopsy is worth the physical and monetary costs of the invasive procedure.

With a reliable diagnosis from an image, patients can forgo the invasive biopsy. They can take an action that, absent the prediction, would be too risky. They no longer have to compromise. Advances in AI mean less need for satisficing and more "ifs" and more "thens." More complexity with less risk. This transforms decision making by expanding options.

KEY POINTS

- Enhanced prediction enables decision makers, whether human or machine, to handle more "ifs" and more "thens." That leads to better outcomes. For example, in the case of navigation, illustrated in this chapter with the mail robot, prediction machines liberate autonomous vehicles from their previous limitation of operating only in controlled environments. These settings are characterized by their limited number of "ifs" (or states). Prediction machines allow autonomous vehicles to operate in uncontrolled environments, like on a city street, because rather than having to code all the potential "ifs" in advance, the machine can instead learn to predict what a human controller would do in any particular situation. Similarly, the example of airport lounges illustrates how enhanced prediction facilitates more "thens" (e.g., "then leave at time X or Y or Z," depending on the prediction of how long it will take to get to the airport at a particular time on a particular day), rather than always leaving early "just in case" and then spending extra time waiting in the airport lounge.

- In the absence of good prediction, we do a lot of "satisficing," making decisions that are "good enough" given the information available. Always leaving early for the airport and often waiting once you arrive because you're early is an example of satisficing. That solution is not optimal, but it's good enough given the information available. The mail robot and the airport lounge are both inventions designed in response to satisficing. Prediction machines will reduce the need to satisfice and thus reduce the returns to investing in solutions like mail robot systems and airport lounges.

- We are so used to satisficing in our businesses and in our social lives that it will take practice to imagine the vast array of transformations possible as a result of prediction machines that can handle more "ifs" and "thens" and, thus, more complex decisions in more complex environments. It's not intuitive for most people to think of airport lounges as a solution to poor prediction and that they will be less valuable in an era of powerful prediction machines. Another example is the use of biopsies, which largely exist in response to weaknesses in prediction from medical images. As the confidence in prediction machines go up, the impact from medical imaging AIs may be much greater on the jobs associated with conducting biopsies because, like airport lounges, this costly and invasive procedure was invented in response to poor prediction. Airport lounges and biopsies are both risk management solutions. Prediction machines will provide new and better methods for managing risk.

11

Fully Automated Decision Making

On December 12, 2016, Tesla Motors Club member "jmdavis" posted to a forum on electric vehicles, reporting on an experience he had had in his Tesla. While driving to work on a Florida freeway at about sixty miles per hour, his Tesla dashboard indicated a car ahead that he could not see because the truck immediately in front of him blocked his view. Suddenly, his emergency brakes kicked in, even though the truck ahead had not slowed. A second later, the truck veered into a shoulder to avoid hitting the car in front that had in fact stopped quickly because of debris on the road. The Tesla had decided to brake before the truck in front had done so, allowing jmdavis's car to stop with plenty of room. He wrote:

> If I was driving manually, it is unlikely that I would have been able to stop in time, since I could not see the car that had stopped. The car reacted well before the car ahead of me reacted and that made the difference between a crash and a hard stop. Strong work Tesla, thanks for saving me.[1]

Tesla had just sent a software update to its vehicles that allowed its Autopilot self-driving feature to exploit radar information to gain a clearer picture of the environment in front of the car.[2] While Tesla's feature worked when its cars were in self-driving mode, it is easy to imagine a situation where a car takes over control from a human in the event of an imminent accident. Carmakers in the United States have reached an agreement with the Department of Transportation to make automatic emergency braking standard on vehicles by 2022.[3]

Often, the distinction between AI and automation is muddy. Automation arises when a machine undertakes an entire task, not just prediction. As of this writing, a human still needs to periodically intervene in driving. When should we expect full automation?

AI, in its current incarnation, involves a machine performing one element: prediction. Each of the other elements represents a complement to prediction, something that becomes more valuable as prediction gets cheaper. Whether full automation makes sense depends on the relative returns to machines also doing the other elements.

Humans and machines can accumulate data, whether for input, training, or feedback, depending on the data type. A human must ultimately make a judgment, but the human can codify judgment and program it into a machine in advance of a prediction. Or a machine can learn to predict human judgment through feedback. This brings us to the action. When is it better for machines rather than humans to undertake actions? More subtly, when does the fact that a machine is handling the prediction increase the returns to the machine rather than a human also undertaking the action? We must determine the returns to machines performing the other elements (data collection, judgment, actions) to decide whether a task should be or will be fully automated.

Sunglasses at Night

Australia's remote Pilbara region has large quantities of iron ore. Most mining sites are more than a thousand miles from the nearest major city, Perth. All employees at the site are flown in for intensive shifts lasting weeks. They accordingly command a premium in terms of wages and in the costs of supporting them while on-site. It's not surprising that the mining companies want to make the most of them while they are there.

The large iron ore mines of mining giant Rio Tinto are highly capital intensive, not just in cost but also in sheer size. They take iron ore from the top of the ground in enormous pits a meteor impact would be challenged to replicate. Thus, the main job is hauling using trucks the size of two-story houses, not just up from the pit but to nearby rail lines built to transport the ore thousands of miles north to waiting ports. The real cost to mining companies is therefore not people but downtime.

Mining companies have, of course, tried to optimize by running throughout the night. However, even the most time-shifted humans are not as productive at night. Initially, Rio Tinto solved some of its human deployment issues by employing trucks that it could control remotely from Perth.[4] But in 2016, it went a step further, with seventy-three self-driving trucks that could operate autonomously.[5] This automation has already saved Rio Tinto 15 percent in operating costs. The mine runs its trucks twenty-four hours a day, with no bathroom breaks and no air-conditioning for the cabs as the temperatures soar above fifty degrees Celsius during the day. Finally, without drivers, the trucks do not need a front and back, meaning they do not need to turn around, further saving in terms of safety, space, maintenance, and speed.

AI made this possible by predicting hazards in the trucks' way and coordinating their passage into the pits. No human driver needs to watch over the truck's safety on-site or even remotely. And there are fewer humans around to create safety risks. Going even further, miners in Canada are exploring bringing in AI-driven robots to dig underground, while Australian miners are looking to automate the entire chain from ground to port (including diggers, bulldozers, and trains).

Mining is the perfect opportunity for full automation precisely because it has already removed humans from so many activities. These days, humans perform directed but key functions. Before the recent advances in AI, everything except prediction could already be automated. Prediction machines represent the last step in removing humans from many of the tasks involved. Previously, a human scanned the surrounding environment and told the equipment precisely what to do. Now, AI that takes information from sensors learns how to predict obstacles for clear paths. Because a prediction machine can forecast whether the path is clear, mining companies no longer need humans to do so.

If the final human element in a task is prediction, then once a prediction machine can do as well as a human, a decision maker can remove the human from the equation. However, as we will see in this chapter, few tasks are as clear-cut as the mining case. For most automation decisions, the provision of machine prediction does not necessarily mean that it becomes worthwhile to remove human judgment and substitute a machine decision maker, nor remove human action and substitute a physical robot.

No Time or Need to Think

Prediction machines made self-driving cars like Tesla's possible. But using prediction machines to trigger an automatic subversion of humans for machine control of a vehicle is another matter. The rationale is easy to understand: between the moment an accident is predicted and the required reaction, a human has no time for thought or action ("no *time* to think"). By contrast, it is relatively easy to program the vehicle's response. When speed is needed, the benefit of ceding control to the machine is high.

When you employ a prediction machine, the prediction made must be communicated to the decision maker. But if the prediction leads directly to an obvious course of action ("no *need* to think"), then the case for leaving human judgment in the loop is diminished. If a machine can be coded for judgment and handle the consequent action relatively easily, then it makes sense to leave the entire task in the machine's hands.

This has led to all manner of innovations. At the 2016 Rio Olympics, a new robotic camera videotaped swimmers underwater by tracking the action and moving to get the right shot from the bottom of the pool.[6] Previously, operators remotely controlled cameras but had to forecast the location of the swimmer. Now, a prediction machine could do it. Swimming was just the beginning. Researchers are now working to bring such camera automation to more complex sports like basketball.[7] Once again, a need for speed and codifiable judgment is driving the move to full automation.

What do accident prevention and automated sports cameras have in common? In each, there are high returns for quick action responses to predictions and judgment is either codifiable or predictable. Automation occurs when the return to machines handling all functions is greater than the returns to including humans in the process.

Automation can also arise when the costs of communication are high. Take space exploration. It is much easier to send robots into space than humans. Several companies are now exploring ways to mine valuable minerals from the moon, but they need to overcome many technical challenges. The one that concerns us here is how moon-based robots will navigate and act. It takes at least two seconds for a radio signal to get to the moon and back, so an earth-based human operating a moon-based robot is a slow and painful process. Such a robot cannot react quickly to new situations. If a robot moving along the surface of the moon suddenly encounters a cliff, any communication delay means that earth-based instructions may arrive too late. Prediction machines provide a solution. With good prediction, the moon-based robot's actions can be automated, with no need for an earth-based human to guide every step. Without AI, such commercial ventures would likely be impossible.

When the Law Requires a Human to Act

The notion that full automation may lead to harm has been a common theme in science fiction. Even if we're all comfortable with complete machine autonomy, the law might not allow it. Isaac Asimov anticipated the regulatory issue by opting for hard coding robots with three laws, cleverly designed to remove the possibility that robots harm any human.[8]

Similarly, modern philosophers often pose ethical dilemmas that seem abstract. Consider the trolley problem: Imagine yourself standing at a switch that allows you to shift a trolley from one track to another. You notice five people in the trolley's path. You could switch it to another track, but along that path is one person. You have no other options and no time to think. What do you do? That question confounds many people, and often they just want to avoid thinking about the conundrum altogether. With self-driving cars, however, that situation is likely to arise. Someone will have to resolve the dilemma and program the appropriate response into the car. The problem cannot be avoided. Someone—most likely the law—will determine who lives and who dies.

At the moment, rather than code our ethical choices into autonomous machines, we've chosen to keep a human in the loop. For instance, imagine a drone weapon that could operate completely autonomously—identifying, targeting, and killing enemies by itself. Even if an army general could find a prediction machine that could distinguish civilians from combatants, how long would it take combatants to figure out how to confuse the prediction machine? The required level of precision may not be available any time soon. So, in 2012, the US Department of Defense put forward a directive that many interpreted as a requirement to keep a human in the loop on the decision whether to attack or not.[9] While it is unclear if the requirement must always be followed, the need for human intervention, for whatever reason, will limit the autonomy of prediction machines even when they might operate on their own.[10] Even Tesla's Autopilot software—despite being able to drive a car—comes with legal terms and conditions that drivers keep their hands on the wheel at all times.

From an economist's point of view, whether this makes sense depends on the context of potential harm. For instance, operating an autonomous vehicle in a remote mine or on a factory floor is quite different from operating on public roads. What distinguishes the "within factory" environment from the "open road" is the possibility of what economists call "externalities"—costs that are felt by others, rather than the key decision makers.

Economists have various solutions for the problem of externalities. One solution is to assign liability so that the key decision maker internalizes those otherwise external costs. For example, a carbon tax plays this role in the context of internalizing externalities associated with climate change. But when it comes to autonomous machines, identification of the liable party is complex. The closer the machine is to potential harm of those outside the organization (and, of course, to physical harm of humans within the organization), the more likely it will be both prudent and legally required to keep a human in the loop.

When Humans Are Better at the Action

Question: What is orange and sounds like a parrot?

The answer? A carrot.

Is that joke funny? Or this one: A little girl asked her father: "Daddy? Do all fairy tales begin with 'once upon a time'?" He replied: "No, there are a whole series of fairy tales that begin with 'If elected, I promise...'"

Okay, admittedly economists are not the best joke tellers. But we are better at it than machines. Researcher Mike Yeomans and his coauthors discovered that if people think a machine recommended a joke, they find it less funny than if they believe a human suggested they might like it. The researchers found that machines do a better job of recommending jokes, but people prefer to believe the recommendations came from humans. The people reading the jokes were most satisfied if told the recommendations came from a human, but when the recommendations were actually determined by a machine.

This is also true of artistic achievement and athletic competition. The power of the arts often derives from the patron's knowledge of the artist's human experience. Part of the thrill of watching a sporting event depends on there being a human competing. Even if a machine can run faster than a human, the outcome of the race is less exciting.

Playing with children, caring for the elderly, and many other actions that involve social interaction may also be inherently better when it is a human that delivers the action. Even if a machine knows what information to present to a child for educational purposes, sometimes it might be best if a human communicates that information. While over time, we humans may be more accepting of having robots care for us and our children, and we may even enjoy watching robot sports competitions, for the time being humans prefer to have some actions undertaken by other humans.

When a human is best suited to take the action, such decisions will not be fully automated. At other times, prediction is the key constraint on automation. When the prediction gets good enough and judging the payoffs can be pre-specified—either a person does the hard coding or a machine learns by watching a person—then a decision will be automated.

KEY POINTS

- The introduction of AI to a task does not necessarily imply full automation of that task. Prediction is only one component. In many cases, humans are still required to apply judgment and take an action. However, sometimes judgment can be hard coded or, if enough examples are available, machines can learn to predict judgment. In addition, machines may perform the action. When machines perform all elements of the task, then the task is fully automated and humans are completely removed from the loop.

- The tasks most likely to be fully automated first are the ones for which full automation delivers the highest returns. These include tasks where: (1) the other elements are already automated except for prediction (e.g., mining); (2) the returns to speed of action in response to prediction are high (e.g., driverless cars); and (3) the returns to reduced waiting time for predictions are high (e.g., space exploration).

- An important distinction between autonomous vehicles operating on a city street versus those in a mine site is that the former generates significant externalities while the latter does not. Autonomous vehicles operating on a city street may cause an accident that incurs costs borne by individuals external to the decision maker. In contrast, accidents caused by autonomous vehicles operating on a mine site only incur costs affecting assets or people associated with the mine. Governments regulate activities that generate externalities. Thus, regulation is a potential barrier to full automation for applications that generate significant externalities. The assignment of liability is a common tool used by economists to address this problem by internalizing externalities. We anticipate a significant wave of policy development concerning the assignment of liability driven by an increasing demand for many new areas of automation.

PART THREE

Tools

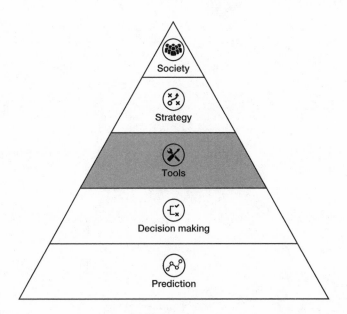

12

Deconstructing
Work Flows

In the midst of the IT revolution, businesses asked, "How should we implement computers in our business?" For some, the answer was easy: "Find where we do lots of calculations and substitute computers for humans; they're better, faster, and cheaper." For other businesses, it was less obvious. Nonetheless, they experimented. But the fruits of those experiments took time to materialize. Robert Solow, a Nobel laureate economist, lamented, "You can see the computer age everywhere but in the productivity statistics."[1]

From this challenge came an interesting business movement called "reengineering." In 1993, Michael Hammer and James Champy, in their book *Reengineering the Corporation*, argued that to use the new general-purpose technology—computers—businesses needed to step back from their processes and outline the objective they wanted to achieve. Businesses then needed to study their work flow and identify the tasks required to achieve their objective and only then consider whether computers had a role in those tasks.

One of Hammer and Champy's favorite examples was the dilemma Ford faced in the 1980s, not with making cars but with paying everyone.[2] In North America, its accounts payable department employed five hundred people, and Ford hoped that by spending big on computers, it could reduce that number by 20 percent. The goal of having four hundred people in the department was not unrealistic; after all, its competitor Mazda had just five people in accounts payable. While, in the 1980s, many marveled at Japanese workers' productivity, it does not take a management guru to realize something more was afoot.

To achieve better performance, Ford's managers had to step back and look at the process through which a purchase took place. Between the time a purchase order was written and actually issued to buy something, many people handled it. If only one of those people took a long time to do the job, the entire system slowed down. Not surprisingly, some purchases were difficult, such as when someone had to reconcile the order. One person in the process had to do that task. So, even if only a small fraction of the orders had problems, most of that person's time was spent resolving them. That left every order flowing through at the speed of the most difficult one.

Therein lay the potential to use a computer to great effect. Not only could a computer reduce mismatches that held up the system, but it could sort the difficult from the easier cases and ensure the easier ones went through at a reasonable speed. Once a new system was put in place, Ford's accounts payable department was 75 percent smaller, and the whole process was significantly faster and more accurate.

Not every reengineering case was about reducing head count, even if, unfortunately, many thought of that first.[3] More broadly, reengineering could improve the quality of services. In another example, Mutual Benefit Life, a large life insurance company, found that in processing applications, nineteen people in five departments took thirty distinct steps. If you walked a typical application through this maze, you could actually finish it in a day. But, instead, an application was taking from five to twenty-five days. Why? Time in transit. Worse, a variety of other inefficiencies piled on because they could stick themselves to a slow-moving target. Once again, a shared database powered by an enterprise computer system improved decision making, reduced handling, and dramatically improved productivity. In the end, one person had authority over an application, with processing falling to between four hours and a few days.

Like classical computing, AI is a general-purpose technology. It has the potential to affect every decision, because prediction is a key input to decision making. Hence, no manager is going to achieve large gains in productivity by just "throwing some AI" at a problem or into an existing process. Instead, AI is the type of technology that requires rethinking processes in the same way that Hammer and Champy did.

Businesses are already conducting analyses that take work flows and break them down into constituent tasks. Goldman Sachs's CFO R. Martin Chavez remarked that many of the 146 distinct tasks in the initial public offering process were "begging to be automated."[4] Many of those 146 tasks are predicated on decisions that AI tools will significantly enhance. When somebody writes about the transformation of Goldman Sachs a decade from now, a major part of the story will be about how the rise of AI played a meaningful role in that transformation.

The actual implementation of AI is through the development of tools. The unit of AI tool design is not "the job" or "the occupation" or "the strategy," but rather "the task." Tasks are collections of decisions (like the ones represented by figure 7-1 and analyzed in part two). Decisions are based on prediction and judgment and informed by data. The decisions within a task often share these elements in common. Where they differ is in the action that follows. (See figure 12-1.)

Sometimes we can automate all the decisions within a task. Or we can now automate the last remaining decision that has not yet been automated because of enhanced prediction. The rise of prediction machines motivates thinking about how to redesign and automate entire processes, or what we term here "work flows," effectively removing humans from such tasks altogether. But for better and cheaper prediction alone to lead to pure automation, employing prediction machines must also increase the returns to using machines in other aspects of a task. Otherwise, you will want to employ a prediction machine to work with human decision makers.

FIGURE 12-1

Thinking about how to redesign and automate entire processes

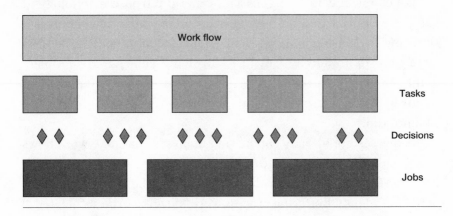

Impact of AI Tools on Work Flows

We have now seen more than 150 AI companies in the CDL, our laboratory that helps science-based companies grow. Each one is focused on the development of an AI tool that addresses a specific task in a specific work flow. One startup predicts the most important passages of a document and highlights them. Another predicts manufacturing defects and flags them. Yet another forecasts appropriate customer service responses and answers queries. And the list goes on. Large companies are implementing hundreds if not thousands of different AIs to enhance the various tasks in their own work flows. Indeed, Google is developing more than a thousand different AI tools to help with a wide variety of tasks, from email to translation to driving.[5]

For many businesses, prediction machines will be impactful, but in an incremental and largely inconspicuous manner, much as how AI improves many of the photo apps on your smartphone. It sorts the pictures in a helpful way but does not fundamentally change how you use the app.

However, you are likely reading this book because you are interested in how AI can lead to fundamental change in your business. AI tools can change work flows in two ways. First, they can render tasks obsolete and therefore remove them from work flows. Second, they can add new tasks. This may be different for every business and every work flow.

Consider the problem of recruiting students to an MBA program, a process with which we are intimately familiar. You may have been on one side or the other of similar recruiting processes, perhaps for recruiting employees or signing up customers. The MBA recruitment work flow starts with a pool of potential applications and leads to a group of people who receive and accept entry offers. It has three broad parts: (1) a sales funnel that consists of steps designed to encourage applications, (2) a process that considers who receives offers, and (3) further steps encouraging those given offers to accept them. Each part involves a significant allocation of resources.

Clearly, the goal of any such recruitment process is to obtain a class of the best students. What is "best," however, is a complex question and is also related to the school's strategic goals. For the moment, we will set aside issues of how different definitions of "best" have an impact on the design of AI tools (they do), as well as on tasks within work flows, and simply assume that the school has a clear definition of what best means to the organization. That is, given a set of applications, the school can, with effort, rank students in terms of best. In practice, the intermediate step in the recruitment work flow—choosing which applicants to give offers to—involves important decisions regarding whether offers should be earlier or later in the process and if they should come with financial incentives or aid attached. Those decisions go beyond simply targeting the best but also predicting the most effective method of getting the best to accept offers (something that happens later in the work flow).

Current systems of ranking applications involve coarse assessments. Candidates are typically ranked in buckets a, b, and c, according to (a) clearly should get an offer; (b) should get an offer if those in (a) decline their offers; and (c) no offer at all. That, in turn, leads to a need for risk management to balance the pros and cons of actions that may increase the likelihood of errors. For instance, you do not want to place someone in bucket (c) when they should be in (a) or even (b) for reasons that are not apparent on the application. Similarly, you do not want to allocate someone to (a) when they should be lower in the priority queue. As applications are multidimensional, the assessments that cause candidates to be placed in buckets are a mixture of the objective and subjective.

Suppose that the MBA program developed an AI that could take applications and other information—perhaps the video interviews people often submit, along with publicly available information posted on social media—and, being trained on past data indicating how such applications and information translated into later scores of best, provide a clear ranking of all applicants. This AI tool will make the task of choosing which applicants should receive offers faster, cheaper, and more accurate. The key question is: How will such a magical prediction technology have an impact on the rest of the MBA work flow?

Our hypothetical technology for ranking applicants provides a prediction that tells us which applicants are likely to be the best. This will affect decisions throughout the work flow. These include early offers (perhaps to pre-empt other schools), financial incentives (scholarships), and special attention (lunches with faculty or prominent alumni). These are all decisions for which there are trade-offs and scarce resources. Having a more accurate list of candidates in terms of desirability will change who receives these resources. Also, we may be willing to spend much more on financial incentives for candidates we are more confident will be best.

The predictive ranking may have an even larger impact on decisions made before the school receives applications. Many schools know that while they want to receive more applications, if they receive too many, they will face the problem of evaluating and ranking them. Our prediction machine dramatically lowers the cost of doing such rankings. As a consequence, it increases the returns to having more applications to rank. This is especially true if the technology can also assess the seriousness of the application (since it's magical, why not?). Thus, schools may expand the reach of their applicant pool. They may lower application fees to zero because sorting through applications is so easy that there is no real cost to receiving more applications.

Finally, changes in the work flow may be more fundamental. With such a ranking, the school could reduce the time between submitting an application and an offer. If the ranking is good enough, it could be nearly *instantaneous*, significantly changing the timing of the entire work flow and the dynamics of competition for top MBA candidates.

This sort of AI is hypothetical, but the example illustrates how placing AI tools within tasks in a work flow can cause tasks to be removed (e.g., manual ranking of applications) as well as added (e.g., wider-reach advertising). Each business will, of course, have different outcomes, but by decomposing work flows, businesses can assess whether prediction machines are likely to reach well beyond the individual decisions for which they may have been designed.

How an AI Tool Powered the iPhone Keyboard

On one dimension, the keyboard on your smartphone has more in common with the original mechanical typewriters than the keyboard you might use on a personal computer. You may be old enough to have used a mechanical typewriter and remember that if you typed too quickly, the mechanism got stuck. For this reason, keyboards have their familiar QWERTY layout; that design standard limited the possibility of hitting two adjacent keys, which is what jammed up older mechanical typewriters. But that same feature also slowed down even the fastest typists.

The QWERTY design has persisted even though the mechanism that caused all the trouble is no longer relevant. When Apple engineers designed the iPhone, they debated whether to finally get rid of QWERTY altogether. What kept them coming back to it was familiarity. After all, their closest competitor at the time, the BlackBerry, had a hard QWERTY keyboard that performed so well the product was commonly known as the "Crackberry" for its addictive nature.

"The biggest science project" of the iPhone was the soft keyboard.[6] But as late as 2006 (the iPhone was launched in 2007), the keyboard was terrible. Not only could it not compete with the BlackBerry, but it was so frustrating that no one would use it to type a text message, let alone an email. The problem was that to fit it on the 3.5-inch LCD screen, the keys were very small. That meant it was easy to hit the wrong one. Many Apple engineers came up with designs that moved away from QWERTY.

With just three weeks to find a solution—a solution that, if not found, might have killed the whole project—every single iPhone software developer had free rein to explore other options. By the end of the three weeks, they had a keyboard that looked like a small QWERTY keyboard with a substantial tweak. While the image the user saw did not change, the surface area around a particular set of keys expanded when typing. When you type a "t," it is highly probable the next letter will be an "h" and so the area around that key expanded. Following that, "e" and "i" expanded, and so on.

This was the result of an AI tool at work. Ahead of virtually anyone else, Apple engineers used 2006-era machine learning to build predictive algorithms so that key size changed depending on what a person was typing. Technology with the same heritage powers the autocorrect predictive text you see today. But fundamentally, the reason this worked was QWERTY. The same keyboard designed to ensure you did not have to type adjacent keys would allow the smartphone keys to expand when needed because the next key was highly unlikely to be near the one you just used.

What Apple engineers did when developing the iPhone was to understand precisely the work flow that went into using a keyboard. A user must identify a key, touch it, and then move on to another. By breaking down that work flow, they realized that a key did not have to be the same to be identified and touched. More importantly, prediction could solve how to know where a user was going next. Understanding the work flow was critical for figuring out how best to deploy the AI tool. This is true of all work flows.

KEY POINTS

- AI tools are point solutions. Each generates a specific prediction, and most are designed to perform a specific task. Many AI startups are predicated on building a single AI tool.

- Large corporations are comprised of work flows that turn inputs into outputs. Work flows are made up of tasks (e.g., a Goldman Sachs IPO is a work flow comprised of 146 distinct tasks). In deciding how to implement AI, companies will break their work flows down into tasks, estimate the ROI for building or buying an AI to perform each task, rank-order the AIs in terms of ROI, and then start from the top of the list and begin working downward. Sometimes a company can simply drop an AI tool into their work flow and realize an immediate benefit due to increasing the productivity of that task. Often, however, it's not that easy. Deriving a real benefit from implementing an AI tool requires rethinking, or "reengineering" the entire work flow. As a result, similar to the personal computer revolution, it will take time to see productivity gains from AI in many mainstream businesses.

- To illustrate the potential effect of an AI on a work flow, we describe a fictitious AI that predicts the ranking of any MBA application. To derive the full benefit from this prediction machine, the school would have to redesign its work flow. It would need to eliminate the task of manually ranking applications and expand the task of marketing the program, as the AI would increase the returns to a greater applicant pool (better predictions about who will succeed and lower cost of evaluating applications). The school would modify the task of offering incentives like scholarships and financial aid due to increased certainty about who will succeed. Finally, the school would adjust other elements of the work flow to take advantage of being able to provide instantaneous school admission decisions.

13

Decomposing
Decisions

Today's AI tools are far from the machines with human-like intelligence of science fiction (often referred to as "artificial general intelligence" or AGI, or "strong AI"). The current generation of AI provides tools for prediction and little else.

This view of AI does not diminish it. As Steve Jobs once remarked, "One of the things that really separates us from the high primates is that we're tool builders." He used the example of the bicycle as a tool that had given people superpowers in locomotion above every other animal. And he felt the same about computers: "What a computer is to me is it's the most remarkable tool that we've ever come up with, and it's the equivalent of a bicycle for our minds."[1]

Today, AI tools predict the intention of speech (Amazon's Echo), predict command context (Apple's Siri), predict what you want to buy (Amazon's recommendations), predict which links will connect you to the information you want to find (Google search), predict when to apply the brakes to avoid danger (Tesla's Autopilot), and predict the news you will want to read (Facebook's newsfeed). None of these AI tools are performing an entire work flow. Instead, each delivers a predictive component to make it easier for someone to make a decision. AI empowers.

But how should you decide whether you should use an AI tool for a particular task in your business? Every task has a group of decisions at its heart, and those decisions have some predictive element.

We provide a way of evaluating AI within the context of a task. Just as we suggested identifying tasks by breaking down a work flow to find out whether AI might have a role, we now suggest taking each of those tasks and decomposing them into their constituent elements.

The AI Canvas

The CDL exposed us to many startups taking advantage of recent machine-learning technologies to build new AI tools. Each company in the lab is predicated on building a specific tool, some for consumer experiences, but most for enterprise customers. The latter type focus on identifying task opportunities within enterprise work flows to focus and position their offering. They deconstruct work flows, identify a task with a prediction element, and build their business based on the provision of a tool for delivering that prediction.

In advising them, we found it useful to separate the parts of a decision into each of its elements (refer to figure 7-1): prediction, input, judgment, training, action, outcome, and feedback. In the process, we developed an "AI canvas" to help decompose tasks in order to understand the potential role of a prediction machine (see figure 13-1). The canvas is an aid for contemplating, building, and assessing AI tools. It provides discipline in identifying each component of a task's decision. It forces clarity in describing each component.

To see how this works, let's consider the startup Atomwise, which offers a prediction tool that aims to shorten the time involved in discovering promising pharmaceutical drug prospects. Millions of possible drug molecules might become drugs, but purchasing and testing each drug is time consuming and costly. How do drug companies determine which to test? They make educated guesses, or

FIGURE 13-1

The AI canvas

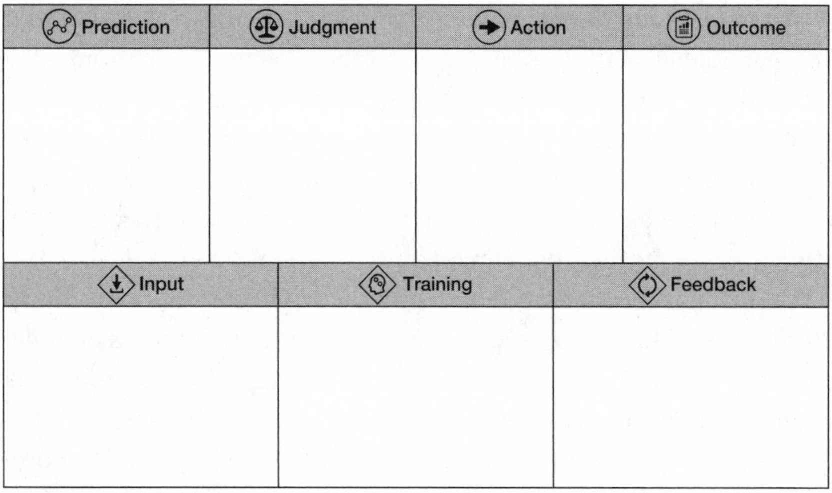

(🔬) Prediction	(⚖️) Judgment	(➡️) Action	(📋) Outcome

(⬇️) Input	(🔄) Training	(🔁) Feedback

predictions, based on research that suggests which molecules are most likely to become effective drugs.

Atomwise CEO Abraham Heifets, giving us a quick explanation of the science, said, "For a drug to work, it has to bind the disease target, and it has to fail to bind proteins in your liver, your kidneys, your heart, your brain, and other things that are going to cause toxic side effects. It comes down to 'stick to the things you want to stick to, fail to stick to the things you don't.'"

So, if drug companies can predict binding affinity, then they can identify which molecules are most likely to work. Atomwise provides this prediction by offering an AI tool that makes the task of identifying potential drugs more efficient. The tool uses AI to predict the binding affinity of molecules, so Atomwise can recommend to drug companies, in a ranked list, which molecules have the best binding affinity for a disease protein. For example, Atomwise might provide the top twenty molecules that have the highest binding affinity for, say, the Ebola virus. Rather than just testing molecules one at a time, Atomwise's prediction machine can handle millions of possibilities. While the drug company still needs to test and verify candidates through a combination of human and machine judgments and actions, the Atomwise AI tool dramatically lowers the cost and accelerates the speed of the first task of finding those candidates.

Where does judgment come in? In recognizing the aggregate value of a particular candidate molecule to the pharmaceutical industry. This value takes two forms: targeting the disease and understanding potential side effects. In selecting the molecules to test, the company needs to determine the payoffs of targeting the disease and costs of the side effects. As Heifets noted, "You are more tolerant of side effects for chemotherapy than for an acne cream."

The Atomwise prediction machine learns from data on binding affinity. As of July 2017, it had 38 million public data points on binding affinity plus many more that it either purchased or learned itself. Each data point consists of molecule and protein characteristics as well as a measure of the binding between the molecules and the proteins. As Atomwise makes more recommendations, it may get further feedback from customers, so the prediction machine will continue to improve.

Using this machine, given data on protein characteristics, Atomwise can predict which molecules have the highest binding affinity. It can also take the data on protein characteristics and predict whether molecules that have never been produced are likely to have high binding affinity.

The way to decompose the Atomwise molecule selection task is to fill in the canvas (see figure 13-2). This means identifying the following:

- ACTION: What are you trying to do? For Atomwise, it is to test molecules to help cure or prevent disease.

- PREDICTION: What do you need to know to make the decision? Atomwise predicts binding affinities of potential molecules and proteins.

- JUDGMENT: How do you value different outcomes and errors? Atomwise and its customers set the criterion regarding the relative importance of targeting the disease and the relative costs of potential side effects.

- OUTCOME: What are your metrics for task success? For Atomwise, it's the results of the test. Ultimately, did the test lead to a new drug?

- INPUT: What data do you need to run the predictive algorithm? Atomwise uses data on the characteristics of the disease proteins to predict.

- TRAINING: What data do you need to train the predictive algorithm? Atomwise employs data on the binding affinity of molecules and proteins, along with molecule and protein characteristics.

- FEEDBACK: How can you use the outcomes to improve the algorithm? Atomwise uses test outcomes, regardless of their success, to improve future predictions.

Atomwise's value proposition lies in delivering an AI tool that supports a prediction task in its customers' drug discovery work flow. It removes the prediction task from human hands. To provide that value, it amassed a unique data set to predict binding affinity. The prediction's value is in reducing the cost and increasing

FIGURE 13-2

The AI canvas for Atomwise

(⚛) Prediction	(⚖) Judgment	(➔) Action	(🖼) Outcome
Binding affinity	Balance binding affinity of disease proteins and potential side effects	Conduct test (expensive)	Test results (successful tests that lead to new drug treatment)

(⬇) Input	(🔬) Training		(♻) Feedback
Protein characteristics	Binding affinity of molecules and proteins from past studies, along with molecule and protein characteristics		New data on binding from their recommendations

the likelihood of success for drug development. Atomwise's clients use the prediction in combination with their own expert judgment of the payoffs to molecules with different binding affinities to different kinds of proteins.

An AI Canvas for MBA Recruiting

The canvas is also useful in large organizations. To apply it, we break down the work flow into tasks. Here, we consider an AI canvas centered on the decision of which MBA applicants to accept into a program. Figure 13-3 provides a possible canvas.

Where did the canvas come from? First, recruiting requires a prediction: Who will be a best or high-value student? That *seems* straightforward. We simply need to define "best." The school's strategy can help identify this. However, many organizations have vague, multifaceted mission statements that lend themselves well to marketing brochures but not so well to identifying the prediction objective for an AI.

FIGURE 13-3

The AI canvas for MBA recruiting offer

🐾 Prediction	⚖️ Judgment	➡️ Action	🖼️ Outcome
Predict whether an applicant would be among the 50 most influential alumni 10 years after graduation	Determine the relative value of accepting a top 50 versus the cost of a false positive (accepting a non-top 50), versus the cost of a false negative (missing a top 50), versus not targeting a non-top 50	Accept applicants into the program	Higher-quality alumni, as measured by global influence 10 years after graduation

📥 Input	🔄 Training		🔁 Feedback
= Application forms = Résumés = GMAT scores = Social media	= Application forms = Résumés = GMAT scores = Social media = Outcome (impact measure)		Update with applicant and career outcomes annually

Business schools have many strategies that implicitly or explicitly define what they mean by "best." They may be simple indicators such as maximizing standardized test scores like the GMAT or broader goals such as recruiting students who will boost the school's rankings in the *Financial Times* or *US News & World Report*. They may also want students who have a mix of quantitative and qualitative skills. Or they may want international students. Or they may want diversity. No school can pursue all these goals simultaneously and must exercise some choice. Otherwise, it will compromise on all dimensions and excel at none.

In figure 13-3, we imagine that our school's strategy is to have the greatest impact on business globally. This subjective notion is strategic in that it is global rather than local and is looking for impact rather than, say, maximizing student income or creating wealth.

For the AI to predict global business impact, we need to measure it. Here, we assume the role of the reward function engineer. What training data do we have that might be a proxy for global business impact? One option might be to identify the best alumni from each class—the fifty alumni from each year who have had the biggest impact. Choosing those alumni is, of course, subjective, but not impossible.

While we may set global business impact as the goal for a prediction machine, the value of accepting a particular student is a matter of judgment. How costly is it to accept a weak student who we wrongly predicted would be among the elite alumni? How costly is it to reject a strong student who we wrongly predicted would be weak? The assessment of that trade-off is "judgment," an explicit element in the AI canvas.

Once we specify the objective of the prediction, identifying the input data needed is straightforward. We need application information for incoming students in order to predict how they will do. We might also use social media. Over time, we will observe more students' career outcomes and can use that feedback to improve predictions. The predictions will tell us which applicants to accept, but only after determining our objective and judging the cost of making a mistake.

KEY POINTS

- Tasks need to be decomposed in order to see where prediction machines can be inserted. This allows you to estimate the benefit of the enhanced prediction and the cost of generating that prediction. Once you have generated reasonable estimates, rank-order the AIs from highest to lowest ROI by starting at the top and working your way down, implementing AI tools as long as the expected ROI makes sense.

- The AI canvas is an aid to help with the decomposition process. Fill out the AI canvas for every decision or task. This introduces discipline and structure into the process. It forces you to be clear about all three data types required: training, input, and feedback. It also forces you to articulate precisely what you need to predict, the judgment required to assess the relative value of different actions and outcomes, the action possibilities, and the outcome possibilities.

- At the center of the AI canvas is prediction. You need to identify the core prediction at the heart of the task, and this can require AI insight. The effort to answer this question often initiates an existential discussion among the leadership team: "What is our real objective, anyhow?" Prediction requires a specificity not often found in mission statements. For a business school, for example, it is easy to say that they are focused on recruiting the "best" students, but in order to specify the prediction, we need to specify what "best" means—highest salary offer upon graduation? Most likely to assume a CEO role within five years? Most diverse? Most likely to donate back to the school after graduation? Even seemingly straightforward objectives, like profit maximization, are not as simple as they first appear. Should we predict the action to take that will maximize profit this week, this quarter, this year, or this decade? Companies often find themselves having to go back to basics to realign on their objectives and sharpen their mission statement as a first step in their work on their AI strategy.

14

Job Redesign

Before the advent of AI and the internet was the computer revolution. Computers made arithmetic—specifically, adding up lots of things—cheap. One of the first killer apps was to make bookkeeping easy.

Computer engineer Dan Bricklin had this in mind when, as an MBA student, he was frustrated by doing repeated calculations to assess the different scenarios in Harvard Business School cases. So he wrote a computer program to do those calculations and found it so useful that he, along with Bob Frankston, developed it into VisiCalc for the Apple II computer. VisiCalc was the first killer app of the personal computing era and the reason many businesses first brought a computer into their offices.[1] Not only did it reduce by a hundredfold the time it took to make calculations, it allowed businesses to analyze many more scenarios.

At the time, the people tasked with calculating activities were bookkeepers; at the end of the 1970s, more than 400,000 worked in the United States. The spreadsheet eliminated what took them the most time—arithmetic. You might then think bookkeepers would be out of a job. But we hear no songs lamenting the lost work of bookkeepers, and no bookkeeping backlash created barriers to the eventual widespread use of the spreadsheet. Why didn't bookkeepers see the spreadsheet as a threat?

Because VisiCalc actually made them more valuable. It made computation simple. You could easily evaluate how much profit you expected and then how it changed if you altered various assumptions. Rather than getting a single snapshot, being able to recalculate repeatedly provided a moving picture of a business. Rather than seeing whether one investment was profitable or not, you could compare multiple investments under different predictions and choose the best one. Someone still had to judge which investments to try out. A spreadsheet could give you answers easily and, in the process, vastly increased the returns to asking questions.

The same people who had laboriously computed the answers before the arrival of the spreadsheet were the best positioned to ask the right questions of the computerized spreadsheet. They were not replaced but rather augmented with superpowers.

This type of scenario—a job is augmented when machines take over some, but not all, tasks—is likely to become quite common as a natural consequence of the implementation of AI tools. The tasks that make up a job will change. Some will be removed as prediction machines take them over. Some will be added as people have more time for them. And, for many tasks, previously essential skills will change and new skills will take their place. Just as bookkeepers became spreadsheet wizards, the redesign of a wide range of jobs due to AI tools will be equally dramatic.

Our process for implementing AI tools will determine which outcome you should emphasize. It involves evaluating entire work flows, whether they are within or across jobs (or departmental or organizational boundaries), and then breaking down the work flow into constituent tasks and seeing whether you can fruitfully employ a prediction machine in those tasks. Then, you must reconstitute tasks into jobs.

Missing Links in Automation

In some cases, the goal is to fully automate every task associated with a job. AI tools are unlikely to be a catalyst for this on their own because work flows amenable to full automation have a series of tasks involved that cannot be (easily) avoided, even for tasks that seem initially to be both low skilled and unimportant.

In the 1986 Space Shuttle *Challenger* disaster, one piece in the rocket booster failed, an O-ring seal less than a half inch in diameter. This one failure meant the shuttle could not fly. To automate a task completely, one failed piece can derail the entire exercise. You need to consider every step. Those small tasks may be very difficult missing links in automation and fundamentally constrain how to reformulate jobs. Thus, AI tools that address these missing links can have substantive effects.

Consider the fulfillment industry, which has grown rapidly over the past two decades due to the rapid growth in online shopping. Fulfillment is a central step in retail, generally, and in electronic commerce, in particular. It is the process of taking an order and executing it by making it ready for delivery to its intended customer. In electronic commerce, fulfillment includes a number of steps such as locating items in a large warehouse-type facility, picking the items off shelves, scanning them for inventory management, placing them in a tote, packing them in a box, labeling the box, and shipping it for delivery.

Many early applications of machine learning to fulfillment related to inventory management: predicting which products would sell out, which did not need reordering because of low demand, and so on. These well-established prediction tasks had been a key part of offline retail and warehouse management for decades. Machine-learning technologies made these predictions even better.

Over the past two decades, much of the rest of the fulfillment process has been automated. For example, research determined that fulfillment center workers were spending more than half their time walking around the warehouse to find items and put them in their tote. As a result, several companies developed an automated process for bringing the shelves to the workers to reduce the time spent walking. Amazon acquired the leading company in this market, Kiva, in 2012 for $775 million and eventually stopped servicing other Kiva customers. Other providers subsequently emerged to fill the demand for the growing market of in-house fulfillment centers and third-party logistics firms.

Despite significant automation, fulfillment centers still employ many humans. Basically, while robots can take an object and move it to a human, someone still needs to do the "picking"—that is, figure out what goes where and then lift the object and move it. The last bit is most challenging because of just how difficult grasping actually is. As long as humans play this role, warehouses cannot take full advantage of automation's potential because they need to remain human friendly, at room temperature, with space for walking, a break room, restrooms, surveillance to protect against theft, and so on. That's costly.

The continued role for humans in order fulfillment is due to our relative performance in grasping—reaching out, picking something up, and placing it somewhere else. This task has so far eluded automation.

As a result, Amazon alone employs forty thousand human pickers full-time and tens of thousands more part-time during the busy holiday season. Human pickers handle approximately 120 picks per hour. Many companies that handle high-volume fulfillment would like to automate picking. For the past three years, Amazon incentivized the best robotics teams in the world to work on the long-studied problem of grasping by hosting the Amazon Picking Challenge, focused on automated picking in unstructured warehouse environments. Even though top teams from institutions such as MIT worked on the problem, many using advanced industrial-grade robotic equipment from Baxter, Yaskawa Motoman, Universal Robots, ABB, PR2, and Barrett Arm, as of this writing they have not yet solved the problem satisfactorily for industrial use.

Robots are perfectly capable of assembling a car or flying a plane. So, why can't they pick up an object in an Amazon warehouse and put it in a box? The task seems so simple in comparison. Robots can assemble an automobile because the components are highly standardized and the process highly routinized. However, an Amazon warehouse has an almost infinite variety of shapes, sizes, weights, and firmness of items that are placed on shelves with many possible positions and orientations for non-rectangular objects. In other words, the grasping problem in a warehouse is characterized by an infinite number of "ifs," whereas grasping in a car assembly plant is designed to have very few "ifs." So, in order to grasp in a warehouse setting, robots must be able to "see" the object (analyze the image) and predict the right angle and pressure in order to hold the object and not drop or crush it. In other words, prediction is at the root of grasping the wide variety of objects in a fulfillment center.

Research into the grasping problem uses reinforcement learning to train robots to mimic humans. The Vancouver-based startup Kindred—founded by Suzanne Gildert, Geordie Rose, and a team that includes one of us (Ajay)—is using a robot called Kindred Sort, an arm with a mix of automated software and a human controller.[2] Automation identifies an object and where it needs to go, while the human—wearing a virtual reality headset—guides the robot arm to pick it up and move it.

In its first iteration, the human can sit somewhere away from a warehouse and fill in the missing link in the fulfillment work flow, deciding the approach angle and grip pressure, through teleoperation of the robotic arm. Long term, however, Kindred is using a prediction machine trained on many observations of a human grasping via teleoperation to teach the robot to do that part itself.

Should We Stop Training Radiologists?

In October 2016, standing on stage in front of an audience of six hundred at our annual CDL conference on the business of machine intelligence, Geoffrey Hinton—a pioneer in deep learning neural networks—declared, "We should stop training radiologists now." A key part of a radiologist's job is to read images and detect the presence of irregularities that suggest medical problems. In Hinton's view, AI would soon be better able to identify medically important objects in an image than any human. Radiologists have feared that machines might replace them since the early 1960s.[3] What makes today's technology different?

Machine-learning techniques are increasingly good at predicting missing information, including identification and recognition of items in images. Given a new set of images, the techniques can efficiently compare millions of past examples with and without disease and predict whether the new image suggests the presence of a disease. This kind of pattern recognition to predict disease is what radiologists do.[4]

IBM, with its Watson system, and many startups have already commercialized AI tools in radiology. Watson can identify a pulmonary embolism and a wide range of other heart issues. One startup, Enlitic, uses deep learning to detect lung nodules (a fairly routine exercise) but also fractures (more complex). These new tools are at the heart of Hinton's forecast but are a subject for discussion among radiologists and pathologists.[5]

What does our approach suggest about the future of radiologists? Radiologists will spend less time reading images. Based on interviews with primary care doctors and radiologists, as well as our knowledge of well-established economic principles, we describe several key roles that remain for the human specialist in the context of medical imaging.[6]

First, and perhaps most obviously, in the short and medium terms, a human still needs to determine the images for a given patient. Imaging is costly, both in terms of time and in the potential health consequences of radiation exposure (for some imaging technologies). As the cost of imaging falls, the amount of imaging will increase, so it is possible that in the short and possibly medium terms, this increase will offset the decline in the human time spent with each image.

Second, there are diagnostic radiologists and interventional radiologists. The advances in object identification that will change the nature of radiology are in diagnostic radiology. Interventional radiology uses real-time images to aid medical procedures. For now, this involves human judgment and dexterous human action that is unaffected by advances in AI, except perhaps in making the interventional radiologist's job somewhat easier by providing better-identified images.

Third, many radiologists see themselves as the "doctor's doctor."[7] A key part of their job is to communicate the meaning of images to primary care doctors. The challenging part is that interpretation of radiology images ("studies," in their language) is often probabilistic: "There is a 70 percent chance that it is disease X, a 20 percent chance of no disease, and a 10 percent chance of disease Y. However, if two weeks from now, this symptom appears, then there is a 99 percent chance of disease X and a 1 percent chance of no disease." Many primary care doctors are not well schooled in statistics and struggle to interpret probabilities and conditional probabilities. Radiologists help them interpret the numbers so that the primary care doctors can work with patients to decide the best course of action. Over time, AI will provide the probabilities, but at least in the short and possibly medium terms, the radiologist will still have a role translating the AI output for the primary care doctor.

Fourth, radiologists will help train the machines to interpret images from new imaging devices as technology improves. A few superstar radiologists, who will interpret images and help the machines learn to diagnose, will have this role. Through AI, these radiologists will leverage their superior skills at diagnosis to train the machines. Their services will be highly valuable. Instead of being paid for the patients they see, they may be compensated for every new technique they teach an AI or for every patient tested on the AI they trained.[8]

As we noted, two key aspects of a diagnostic radiologist's job are examining an image and returning an assessment to a primary care doctor. While often that assessment is a diagnosis (i.e., "the patient almost surely has pneumonia"), in many cases, the assessment is in the negative (i.e., "pneumonia not excluded"), stated as a prediction to inform the primary care doctor of the patient's likely state so the primary doctor can devise a treatment.

Prediction machines will reduce uncertainty, but they won't always eliminate it. For example, the machine may offer the following prediction:

> Based on Mr. Patel's demographics and imaging, the mass in the liver has a 66.6 percent chance of being benign, a 33.3 percent chance of being malignant, and a 0.1 percent of not being real.

Had the prediction machine given a straightforward—benign or not—prediction with no room for error, it would be obvious what to do. At this point, the doctor must consider whether to order an invasive procedure, like a biopsy, to find out more. Ordering the biopsy is the less risky decision; yes, it is costly, but it can yield a more certain diagnosis.

Seen in this light, the role of the prediction machine is to increase a doctor's confidence in *not* conducting a biopsy. Such noninvasive procedures are less costly (especially for the patient). They inform doctors about whether the patient can avoid an invasive exam (like a biopsy) and make them more confident in abstaining from treatment and further analysis. If the machine improves prediction, it will lead to fewer invasive examinations.

So, the fifth and final role for human specialists in medical imaging is the judgment in deciding to conduct an invasive examination, even when the machine is suggesting a high enough likelihood that there is no issue. The doctor may have information about the patient's overall health, possible mental stress due to the potential for a false negative, or some other qualitative data. Such information may not be easily codified and available to a machine and may require a conversation between a radiologist with expertise in interpreting the probabilities and a primary care physician who understands the patient's needs. This information may lead a human to override an AI's recommendation not to operate.

Therefore, five clear roles for humans in the use of medical images will remain, at least in the short and medium term: choosing the image, using real-time images in medical procedures, interpreting machine output, training machines on new technologies, and employing judgment that may lead to overriding the prediction machine's recommendation, perhaps based on information unavailable to the machine. Whether radiologists have a future depends on whether they are best positioned to undertake these roles, if other specialists will replace them, or if new job classes will develop, such as a combined radiologist/pathologist (i.e., a role where the radiologist also analyzes biopsies, perhaps performed immediately after imaging).[9]

More Than a Driver

Some jobs may continue to exist but require new skills. Automating a particular task can emphasize other tasks that are important to a job but were previously underappreciated. Consider a school bus driver. There's the "driving" part of the task involved in operating a bus from houses to schools and back. With the advent of self-driving cars and automated driving, the job of the school bus driver will itself disappear. When Oxford University professors Carl Frey and Michael Osborne looked at the types of skills required to do a job, they concluded that school bus drivers (as distinguished from mass transportation bus drivers) had an 89 percent chance of being automated over the next decade or two.[10]

When someone called a "school bus driver" no longer drives buses to and from schools, should local governments start spending these saved salaries? Even if a bus is self-driving, current school bus drivers do much more than simply driving. First, they are the responsible adult supervising a large group of schoolchildren to protect them from hazards outside the bus. Second, and equally important, they are in charge of discipline inside the bus. A human's judgment in managing children and protecting them from each other is still needed. That the bus can drive itself does not eliminate those additional tasks, but it means that the adult on the bus can pay more attention to those tasks.

So perhaps the skill set of the "employee formally known as a school bus driver" will change. Drivers may act more like teachers than they do today. But the point is that *automation that eliminates a human from a task does not necessarily eliminate them from a job*. From the perspective of employers, someone will still be doing that job. From the perspective of employees, the risk is that it may be someone else.

The automation of tasks forces us to think more carefully about what really constitutes a job, what people are really doing. Like school bus drivers, long-range truck drivers do more than drive. Truck driving is one of the largest job classification categories in the United States and often a candidate for potential automation. Movies such as *Logan* depict a near future with trucks that are simply containers on wheels.

But will we really see trucks moving across the continent with no human in sight? Think about the challenges that poses precisely because most of the time those trucks will be far from any human supervision. For instance, they and their loads will be vulnerable to hijacking and theft. Such trucks may be unable to operate if a human stands in their way and so will represent an easy target.

The solution is obvious: a person rides along with the truck. That task will be much easier than driving and will also allow trucks to drive longer without stops or breaks. One human could probably travel with a much larger vehicle or perhaps a linked convoy of vehicles.[11] But at least one truck in that convoy will still have a cab for a human who will protect the vehicle, deal with the logistics and relationships involved in loading and unloading the trucks at each end, and navigate any surprises along the way. So we can't write off those jobs yet. As current truck drivers are the most qualified and experienced at those other tasks, they will likely be the first to be employed in a redefined role.

KEY POINTS

- A job is a collection of tasks. When breaking down a work flow and employing AI tools, some tasks previously performed by humans may be automated, the ordering and emphasis of remaining tasks may change, and new tasks may be created. Thus, the collection of tasks that make up a job can change.

- The implementation of AI tools generates four implications for jobs:

    1. AI tools may augment jobs, as in the example of spreadsheets and bookkeepers.

    2. AI tools may contract jobs, as in fulfillment centers.

    3. AI tools may lead to the reconstitution of jobs, with some tasks added and others taken away, as with radiologists.

4. AI tools may shift the emphasis on the specific skills required for a particular job, as with school bus drivers.

- AI tools may shift the relative returns to certain skills and, thus, change the types of people who are best suited to particular jobs. In the case of bookkeepers, the arrival of the spreadsheet diminished the returns to being able to perform many calculations quickly on a calculator. At the same time, it increased the returns to being good at asking the right questions in order to fully take advantage of the technology's ability to efficiently run scenario analyses.

PART FOUR

Strategy

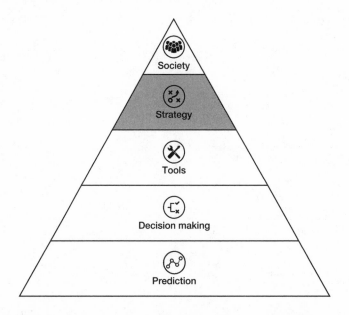

15

AI in the C-Suite

In January 2007, when Steve Jobs paced the stage and introduced the iPhone to the world, not a single observer reacted by saying, "Well, it's curtains for the taxi industry." Yet fast forward to 2018 and that appears to be precisely the case. Over the last decade, smartphones evolved from being simply a smarter phone to an indispensable platform for tools that are disrupting or fundamentally altering all manner of industries. Even Andy Grove, who famously quipped that "only the paranoid survive," would have to admit that you would've been pretty darn paranoid to have foreseen how far and wide the smartphone would reach into some very traditional industries.

The recent developments in AI and machine learning have convinced us that this innovation is on par with the great, transformative technologies of the past: electricity, cars, plastics, the microchip, the internet, and the smartphone. From economic history, we know how these general-purpose technologies diffuse and transform. We also realize how hard it is to forecast when, where, and how the most disruptive changes will take place. At the same time, we have learned what to look for, how to be ahead of the curve, and when a new technology is likely to transition from something interesting to something transformative.

When should AI be a critical agenda item for your organization's leadership team? While ROI calculations can influence operational changes, strategic decisions pose dilemmas and force leaders to grapple with uncertainty. Adopting AI in one part of the organization might require changes in another part. For intra-organizational effects, adoption and other decisions require the authority of someone who oversees the entire business, namely, the CEO.

So when is AI likely to fall into this category? When does a fall in the cost of prediction matter enough that it will change strategy? And what dilemma is a CEO likely to face if this should happen?

How AI Can Change Business Strategy

In chapter 2, we conjectured that once the dial on the prediction machine had been turned up enough, companies such as Amazon would be so confident about what particular customers want that their business model could change. They would move from a shopping-then-shipping model to shipping-then-shopping, sending items to customers in anticipation of their wants. This scenario neatly illustrates three ingredients that together could cause investment in that AI tool to rise to the level of being a strategic rather than operational decision.

First, a strategic dilemma or trade-off must exist. For Amazon, the quandary is that shipping-then-shopping may generate more sales but simultaneously produce more goods consumers want to return. When the cost of returning items is too high, then the ROI for shipping-then-shopping is lower than the ROI for the traditional approach of shopping-then-shipping. This explains why, in the absence of some technological change, Amazon's business model remains shopping-then-shipping rather than the other way around, just like almost every other retailer.

Second, the problem can be resolved by reducing uncertainty. For Amazon, it is about consumer demand. If you can accurately forecast what people will purchase, especially if delivered to their doorsteps, then you reduce the likelihood of returns and increase sales. Uncertainty reduction hits both the benefit and the cost sides of the dilemma.

This type of demand management is not new. It's one reason that physical stores exist. Physical stores cannot forecast individual customer demand, but they can forecast the likely demand from a group of customers. By pooling together the customers who visit a location, physical stores hedge demand uncertainty among individual customers. Moving to a shipping-then-shopping model based on individual homes requires more information about individual customer demand, which can overcome the competitive advantage physical stores have.

Third, companies require a prediction machine that can reduce uncertainty enough to change the balance in the strategic dilemma. For Amazon, a very accurate model of customer demand may make the shipping-then-shopping business model worthwhile. Here, the benefits of increased sales outweigh the costs of returns.

Now, if Amazon were to implement this model, it would make further changes in its business. These would include, for example, investments to reduce the cost of securing packages left for pickup and transportation services to handle returns. Although the customer-friendly delivery market is competitive, product return services are a much less-well-developed market. Amazon itself might establish an infrastructure of trucks that visit neighborhoods daily for deliveries and returns, thus vertically integrating into the daily product return business. Effectively, Amazon could move the boundary of its business right up to your front porch.

This boundary shifting is already occurring. One example is the German e-commerce venture, Otto.[1] A major barrier to consumer purchases over the internet rather than in a store is uncertain delivery times. If consumers have a poor delivery experience, they are unlikely to return to a site. Otto found that when deliveries were delayed (that is, took longer than a few days), returns shot upward. Consumers would inevitably find the product at a store in the meantime and purchase it there. Even when Otto had sales, returns added to its costs.

How do you reduce the time to deliver products to consumers? Anticipate what they are likely to order and have it in stock at a distribution center nearby. But such inventory management is itself costly.

Instead, what you want is to hold only the inventory you are likely to need. You want a better prediction of consumer demand. Otto, with a database of 3 billion past transactions and hundreds of other variables (including search terms and demographics), was able to create a prediction machine to handle the forecast. It can now predict with 90 percent accuracy what products it will sell within a month. Relying on those forecasts, it revamped its logistics. Its inventory declined by 20 percent, and annual returns dropped by 2 million items. Prediction improved logistics, which in turn reduced costs and increased consumer satisfaction.

Once again, we can see the three ingredients of strategic importance. Otto had a dilemma (how to improve delivery times without expensive inventory holdings), uncertainty drove the dilemma (in this case, overall customer demand in a location), and by resolving that uncertainty (e.g., forecasting local demand better), it could set up a new way of organizing logistics, requiring new warehouse locations, local shipping, and customer delivery guarantees. It could not have accomplished all this without using a prediction machine to resolve that key uncertainty.

Sweet Home Alabama?

For a prediction machine to change your strategy, someone has to create one that is useful to you in particular. Doing so depends on several things outside your organization's control.

Let's look at the factors that might make prediction technology available to your business. To do this, we are going to travel to the cornfields of Iowa in the 1930s. There, some pioneering farmers introduced a new form of corn that they created through extensive cross-breeding for the better part of two decades. This hybrid corn was more specialized than ordinary commercial corn. It required crossing two inbred lines of corn to improve properties such as drought resistance and local environment-specific yields. The hybrid corn was a critical change because not only did it promise dramatically higher yields, but the farmer became dependent on others for the special seeds. The

FIGURE 15-1

The diffusion of hybrid corn

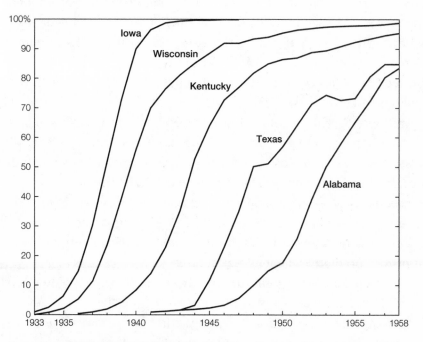

Source: From Zvi Griliches, "Hybrid Corn and the Economics of Innovation," *Science* 132, no. 3422 (July 1960): 275–280. Reprinted with permission from AAAs.

new seeds needed to be tailored to local conditions to yield their full benefits.

As shown in figure 15-1, Alabama farmers appeared to be laggards compared to those in Iowa. But when Harvard economist Zvi Griliches looked closely at the numbers, he found that the twenty-year lag between Iowa and Alabama widespread adoption was not because Alabama famers were slow, but rather because the ROI for hybrid corn for Alabama farms did not justify its adoption in the 1930s.[2] Alabama farms were smaller, with thin profit margins compared to those north and west. By contrast, Iowa farmers could apply a successful seed across their larger farms and reap larger benefits to justify the higher seed costs. A big farm meant experimentation with new hybrid varieties was easier because the farmer had to set aside only a small portion of the property until the new varieties proved effective.[3] The Iowa farmers' risks were lower, and they had healthier margins to act as a buffer. Once enough farmers in an area adopted the new seeds, seed markets became thicker with more buyers and sellers and the cost of selling the seeds fell, so the risks of adoption were reduced further still. Eventually, corn farmers across the United States (and worldwide) adopted hybrid seeds as the costs fell and the perceived risks diminished.

In the AI world, Google is Iowa. It has more than a thousand AI tool development projects underway across every category of its business, from search to ads to maps to translation.[4] Other tech giants worldwide have joined Google. The reason is fairly obvious: Google, Facebook, Baidu, Alibaba, Salesforce, and others are already in the tools business. They have clearly defined tasks that extend throughout their enterprises, and in each, AI can sometimes dramatically improve a predictive element.

Those enormous corporations have big profit margins, so they can afford to experiment. They can take a part of the "land" and devote it to many new AI varieties. They can reap huge rewards from successful experiments by applying them across a wide range of products operating at large scale.

For many other businesses, the path to AI is less clear. Unlike Google, many have not made two decades' worth of investments in digitizing all aspects of their work flow and also do not have a clear notion of what they want to predict. But once a company sets well-defined strategies, it can develop those ingredients, laying the groundwork for effective AI.

When the conditions were right, all corn farmers in Wisconsin, Kentucky, Texas, and Alabama eventually followed their Iowa peers in adopting hybrid corn. The demand-side benefits were high enough, and the supply-side costs had fallen. Similarly, the costs and risks associated with AI will fall over time, so that many businesses not at the forefront of developing digital tools will adopt it. In doing so, the demand side will drive them: the opportunity to resolve fundamental dilemmas in their business models by reducing uncertainty.

Complementing Baseball Players

Billy Beane's *Moneyball* strategy—using statistical prediction to overcome the biases of human baseball scouts and improve prognostication—was an example of using prediction to reduce uncertainty and improve the performance of the Oakland Athletics. It was also a strategic change that required altering the organization's implicit and explicit hierarchy.

Better prediction changed who the team hired on the field, but the operation of the baseball team itself did not change. The players that the prediction machine selected played much the same way as the players it replaced, with perhaps a few more walks thrown in. And the scouts continued to have a role in player selection.[5]

The more fundamental change occurred in who the team hired off the field and the resulting restructuring of the organizational chart. Most important, the team hired people who could tell the machines what to predict and then use those predictions to determine which players to acquire (most notably, Paul DePodesta, as well as others whose contributions were combined in the "Peter Brand" character played by Jonah Hill in the movie). The team also created a new job function, called a "sabermetric analyst." A sabermetric analyst develops measures for the rewards that the team would receive from signing different players. Sabermetric analysts are baseball's reward function engineers. Now, most teams have at least one such analyst, and the role has appeared, under different names, in other sports.

Better prediction created a new high-level position on the org chart. The research scientists, data scientists, and vice presidents of analytics are listed as key roles in the online front office directories. The Houston Astros even have a separate decision sciences unit headed by former NASA engineer Sig Mejdal. The strategic change also means a switch in who the team employs to pick the players. These analytics experts have mathematical skills, but the finest of them understand best what to tell the prediction machine to do. They provide judgment.

Returning to the simple economics that underlies all the arguments in this book, prediction and judgment are complements; as the use of prediction increases, the value of judgment rises. Teams are increasingly bringing in new senior advisers who sometimes may not have firsthand experience playing the game and—true to stereotype—may not be an obvious fit in the jock world of professional sports. However, even nerds recruited into this setting require a deep understanding of the game because using prediction machines in sports management means an increase in the value of people who have the *judgment* to determine payoffs and, therefore, the judgment to use predictions in decisions.

Strategic Choice Requires New Judgment

The change in the organization of baseball team management highlights another key issue for the C-suite in implementing strategic choices with regard to AI. Before sabermetrics, baseball scouts' judgment was limited to the pros and cons of individual players. But using quantitative measures made it possible to predict how *groups* of players would perform together. Judgment shifted from thinking about the payoff of a particular player to thinking about the payoff to a particular team. Better prediction now enables the manager to make decisions that are closer to the organization's objectives: determining the best team rather than the best individual players.

To make the most of prediction machines, you need to rethink the reward functions throughout your organization to better align with your true goals. This task is not easy. Beyond recruiting, the marketing of the team needs to change, perhaps to deemphasize individual performance. Similarly, the coaches have to understand the reasons for individual players' recruitment and the implications for team composition in each game. Finally, even the players need to understand how their roles might change depending on whether their opponents have similarly adopted new prediction tools.

Advantages You May Already Have

Strategy is also about capturing value—that is, who will capture the value that better prediction creates?

Business executives often claim to us that because prediction machines need data, data itself is a strategic asset. That is, if you have many years of data on, say, yogurt sales, then in order to predict yogurt sales using a prediction machine, someone will need that data. Hence, it is valuable to its owner. It is like having a repository of oil.

That presumption belies an important issue—like oil, data has different grades. We have highlighted three types of data—training, input, and feedback data. Training data is used to build a prediction machine. Input data is used to power it to produce predictions. Feedback data is used to improve it. Only the two latter types are needed for future use. Training data is used at the beginning to train an algorithm, but once the prediction machine is running, it is not useful anymore. It is as if you have burned it. Your past data on yogurt sales has little value once you have a prediction machine built on it.[6] In other words, it may be valuable today, but it is unlikely to be a source of sustained value. To do that you either need to generate new data—for input or feedback—or you need another advantage. We will explore the advantages of generating new data in the next chapter and focus on other advantages right now.

Dan Bricklin, the spreadsheet inventor, created enormous value, but he is not a rich person. Where did the spreadsheet value go? On the wealth rankings, imitators such as Lotus 1-2-3 founder Mitch Kapor or Microsoft's Bill Gates certainly far outstripped Bricklin, but even they were appropriating a small fraction of the spreadsheet's value. Instead, the value went to users, to the businesses that deployed spreadsheets to make billions of better decisions. No matter what Lotus or Microsoft did, their users owned the decisions that the spreadsheets were improving.

Because they operate at the decision level, the same is true for prediction machines. Imagine applications of AI that would greatly assist in inventory management for a supermarket chain. Knowing when yogurt is going to sell helps you know when you should stock it and minimizes the amount of unsold yogurt to discard. An AI innovator who offers prediction machines for yogurt demand could do well, but would have to deal with a supermarket chain in order to create any value. Only the supermarket chain can take the action that stocks yogurt or not. And without that action, the prediction machine for yogurt demand has no value.

Many businesses will continue to own their actions with or without AI. They will have an advantage in capturing some of the value that arises from adopting AI. This advantage does not mean that the companies that own the actions will capture all the value.

Before selling their spreadsheet, Bricklin and his partner, Bob Frankston, wondered whether they should keep it. They could then sell their modeling skills and, as a result, capture the value created by their insights. They abandoned this plan—likely for good reason—but in AI, this strategy might work. AI providers may try to disrupt traditional players.

Autonomous vehicles are an example, to some degree. While some traditional carmakers are aggressively investing in their own capabilities, others are hoping to partner with those outside the industry (such as Alphabet's Waymo) rather than develop those capabilities in-house. In other cases, large technology companies are initiating projects with traditional carmakers. For example, Baidu, operator of China's largest search engine, is leading a large and diversified open autonomous driving initiative, Project Apollo, with several dozen partners, including Daimler and Ford. In addition, Tencent Holdings, owner of WeChat, which has almost a billion monthly active-user accounts, is leading an autonomous driving alliance that includes prominent incumbents, such as Beijing Automotive Group. Chen Juhong, a vice president of Tencent, remarked, "Tencent hopes to make an all-out effort to reinforce the development of AI technologies used in autonomous driving . . . We want to be a 'connector' to help accelerate cooperation, innovation and industry convergence. . . ."[7] Reflecting on the competitive pressures driving collaboration, Beijing Automotive chairman Xu Heyi said, "In this new era, only those who connect with other companies to build the next generation of cars will survive, while those who shut themselves up in a room making vehicles will die."[8] Relatively new entrants (such as Tesla) are competing with incumbents by directly deploying AI in new cars that tightly integrate software and hardware. Companies like Uber are using AI to develop autonomy with the hope of taking even the driving decisions out of consumers' hands. In that industry, the race for value capture does not respect traditional business boundaries. Instead, it challenges the ownership of actions that might otherwise have been an advantage.

The Simple Economics of AI Strategy

The changes we've highlighted depend on two different aspects of AI impact at the core of our economic framework.

First, as in Amazon's shipping-then-shopping model, prediction machines reduce uncertainty. As AI advances, we'll use prediction machines to reduce uncertainty more broadly. Hence, strategic dilemmas driven by uncertainty will evolve with AI. As the cost of AI falls, prediction machines will resolve a wider variety of strategic dilemmas.

Second, AI will increase the value of the complements to prediction. A baseball analyst's judgment, a grocery retailer's actions, and— as we will show in chapter 17—a prediction machine's data become so important that you may need to change your strategy to take advantage of what it has to offer.

KEY POINTS

- C-suite leadership must not fully delegate AI strategy to their IT department because powerful AI tools may go beyond enhancing the productivity of tasks performed in the service of executing against the organization's strategy and instead lead to changing the strategy itself. AI can lead to strategic change if three factors are present: (1) there is a core trade-off in the business model (e.g., shop-then-ship versus ship-then-shop); (2) the trade-off is influenced by uncertainty (e.g., higher sales from ship-then-shop are outweighed by higher costs from returned items due to uncertainty about what customers will buy); and (3) an AI tool that reduces uncertainty tips the scales of the trade-off so that the optimal strategy changes from one side of the trade to the other (e.g., an AI that reduces uncertainty by predicting what a customer will buy tips the scale such that the returns from a ship-then-shop model outweigh those from the traditional model).

- Another reason C-suite leadership is required for AI strategy is that the implementation of AI tools in one part of the business may also affect other parts. In the Amazon thought experiment, a side effect of transitioning to a ship-then-shop model was vertical integration into the returned items collection business, perhaps with a fleet of trucks that did weekly pickups through-out the neighborhood. In other words, powerful AI tools may result in significant redesign of work flows and the boundary of the firm.

- Prediction machines will increase the value of complements, including judgment, actions, and data. The increasing value of judgment may lead to changes in organizational hierarchy—there may be higher returns to putting different roles or dif-ferent people in positions of power. In addition, prediction machines enable managers to move beyond optimizing individ-ual components to optimizing higher-level goals and thus make decisions closer to the objectives of the organization. Owning the actions affected by prediction can be a source of competitive advantage that allows traditional businesses to capture some of the value from AI. However, in some cases, where powerful AI tools provide a significant competitive advantage, new entrants may vertically integrate into owning the action and leverage their AI as a basis for competition.

16

When AI Transforms Your Business

Joshua (one of the authors) recently asked an early-stage machine learning company, "Why are you providing doctors with diagnoses?" The venture was building an AI tool that could tell a doctor whether a particular medical condition was present or not. A simple binary output. A diagnosis. The problem was, to be able to do that, the company had to obtain regulatory approval, which requires costly trials. To manage those trials, it was considering whether to partner with an established pharmaceutical or medical device company.

Joshua's question was strategic rather than medical. Why did the venture have to provide a diagnosis? Instead, couldn't it just provide the prediction? That is, the tool could analyze data and then tell the doctor that "there is an 80 percent chance the patient has the condition." The physician could then explore precisely what was driving that conclusion and make the ultimate diagnosis—that is, the binary "present or not" outcome. The company could let the customer (in this case, the physician) do more.

Joshua suggested that the company focus on prediction rather than diagnosis. The boundary of its business would end with prediction.

This obviated the need for regulatory approval, because physicians have many tools for arriving at a diagnostic conclusion. The company did not need to partner early on with established companies. Most critically, it no longer had to research and work out precisely how to translate the prediction into a diagnosis. All it had to deduce was the threshold accuracy required to deliver a valuable prediction. Was it 70, 80, or 99 percent?

Where does your business end and someone else's begin? Where exactly are the boundaries of your company? This long-term decision requires careful attention at the organization's very top level. Moreover, new general-purpose innovations often lead to new answers for the boundary question. Certain AI tools are likely to transform the boundaries of your business. Prediction machines will change how businesses think about everything, from their capital equipment to their data and people.

What to Leave In and What to Leave Out

Uncertainty has an impact on a business's boundaries.[1] Economists Silke Forbes and Mara Lederman looked at the organization of the US airline industry around the turn of the millennium.[2] Major airlines like United and American handled some routes, while regional partners like American Eagle and SkyWest dealt with others. The partners were independent businesses that had contractual arrangements with the majors. Absent other considerations, the regional airlines typically operated at a lower cost than the majors, saving money on salaries and less beneficial work rules. For instance, some studies showed that senior pilots at the majors received 80 percent higher pay than those at their regional partners.

The puzzle is why majors rather than regional partners handle so many routes, given that partners can deliver the service at lower cost. Forbes and Lederman identified a driving factor—the weather— or, more specifically, *uncertainty* about the weather. When a weather event is out of the ordinary, it delays flights, which, in the tightly networked and capacity-managed airline industry, can have ripple effects throughout the entire system. When the weather goes sour, major airlines do not want to be hamstrung by partners checking their contracts when they have to make fast changes with uncertain costs. So, for routes where weather-related delays are likely, the majors retain control and operation.

The three ingredients we highlighted in the previous chapter suggest that AI might lead to strategic change. First, lower cost versus more control is a core trade-off. Second, that trade-off is mediated by uncertainty; specifically, the returns to control increase with the level of uncertainty. Major airlines balance lower cost and more control by optimizing the boundaries of where their own activities end and those of their partners begin. If a prediction machine could cut through this uncertainty, then the third ingredient would be present and the balance would shift. Airlines would contract more to their partners.

Businesses engaging in ongoing innovation, especially innovation that involves learning from experience, create a similar pattern. New automobile models are released approximately every five years, and because they involve detailed part specifications and design work, automakers need to know where the parts are coming from before release. Are they making parts themselves or outsourcing them? Throughout the long process of development, an automaker can only know so much about how a new model will perform. Some information can only be gathered after launch, like customer feedback and other long-term performance measurements. This is a key reason why models have annual updates that do not involve major changes in car design but offer improvements to components that work out kinks and improve the product.

Economists Sharon Novak and Scott Stern found that makers of luxury automobiles that manufactured their own parts improved faster from each model year to the next.[3] They measured improvements at the customer end, using ratings from *Consumer Reports*. Having control meant automakers could adapt more readily to customer feedback. By contrast, those that outsourced parts did not show the same improvement. However, the latter received a different benefit; their initial models were of higher quality than the first models of automakers that made their own parts. The brand-new models of automakers that outsourced parts were better right out of the gate because the parts suppliers made better parts. Thus, automakers face the choice of outsourcing or making the parts themselves to reap improvements over time as they control innovation within the life cycle of their product model. Again, a prediction machine that reduces the uncertainty about customer needs could change the strategy.

In each case, the trade-off between short- and long-term performance and routine versus non-routine events is resolved by a key organizational choice: how much to rely on external suppliers. But the salience of that choice is closely related to uncertainty. How important are weather events that airlines could not plan for up front? How will the vehicle match what customers really want?

Impact of AI: Capital

Let's assume an AI is available that could reduce this uncertainty, so the third ingredient is in place. Prediction is so cheap that it minimizes uncertainty enough to change the nature of the strategic dilemma. How will this affect what the airlines and automakers do? AI might enable machines to operate in more complex environments. It expands the number of reliable "ifs," thus lessening a business's need to own its own capital equipment, for two reasons.

First, more "ifs" means that a business can write contracts to specify what to do if something unusual happens. Suppose that AI allows airlines not only to forecast weather events but to generate predictions for how best to deal with weather-related interruptions. This would increase the returns to major airlines for being more specific in their contracts to deal with contingencies. They can specify a greater number of "ifs" in the contracts. Thus, rather than controlling airline routes through ownership, the major airlines would have the predictive power to more confidently write contracts with independent regional carriers, allowing them to take advantage of those carriers' lower costs. They would require less capital equipment (such as airplanes), because they could outsource more flights to the smaller regional carriers.

Second, AI-driven prediction—all the way to predicting consumer satisfaction—would enable automakers to more confidently design products up front, thus leading to high consumer satisfaction and performance without the consequent need for extensive mid-model adjustments. Consequently, automakers would be able to select the world's best parts for their models from independent suppliers, confident that superior prediction up front was eliminating the need for costly contract renegotiations. The automakers would have less need to own factories that provide parts. More generally, prediction gives us many more "ifs" that we can use to clearly specify the "thens."

This assessment holds the complexity of airline networks and automobile products as fixed. It could well be that up-front prediction gives airlines and automakers the confidence to allow for more complex arrangements and products. It is not clear what the impact on outsourcing would be since better prediction drives more outsourcing, while more complexity tends to reduce it. Which of these factors might dominate is hard to say at this stage. We can say that, while newly feasible complex processes might be done in house, many of the simpler processes previously completed in house will be outsourced.

Impact of AI: Labor

Banks rolled out the automatic teller machine (ATM), developed during the 1970s, extensively throughout the 1980s. The potentially labor-saving technology was—as the name implies—designed to automate tellers.

According to the Bureau of Labor Statistics, tellers were not being automated out of a job (see figure 16-1). However, they were automated out of the bank-telling task. Tellers ended up becoming the marketing and customer service agents for bank products beyond the collection and dispensing of cash. The machines handled that, more securely than humans. One reason banks did not want to open more branches was precisely because of the security issue and the human cost of spending time on something as transactional as bank telling. Freed from those constraints, bank branches proliferated (43 percent more

FIGURE 16-1

Bank tellers and ATMs over time

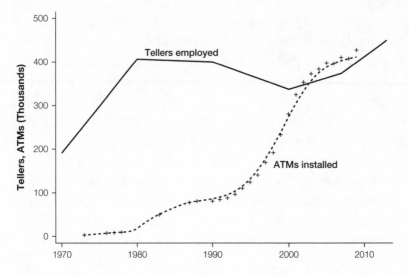

Source: Courtesy James E. Bessen, "How Computer Automation Affects Occupations: Technology, Jobs, and Skills," Boston University School of Law, Law and Economics Research Paper No. 15-49 (October 3, 2016); http://dx.doi.org/10.2139/ssrn.2690435.

in urban areas), in more shapes and sizes, and with them, a staff that was anachronistically called "tellers."

The introduction of ATMs produced a significant organizational transformation; the new teller required a great deal more subjective judgment. The original teller tasks were, by definition, routine and easily mechanized. But the new tasks of talking to customers about their banking needs, advising them on loans, and working out credit card options were more complicated. In the process, evaluating whether the new tellers were doing a good job became harder.[4]

When performance measures change from objective (are you keeping the bank queues short?) to subjective (are you selling the right products?), human resource (HR) management becomes more complex. Economists will tell you that job responsibilities have to become less explicit and more relational. You will evaluate and reward employees based on subjective processes, such as performance reviews that take into account the complexity of the tasks and the employees' strengths and weaknesses. Such processes are tough to implement because reliance on them to create incentives for good performance requires a great deal of trust. After all, a company can more easily decide to deny you that bonus, salary bump, or promotion based on a subjective review than when the performance measures are objective. However, when performance measures are objective in complex environments, critical mistakes can happen, as Wells Fargo's experience with account managers' fraud showed us so dramatically.[5]

The direct implication of this line of economic logic is that AI will shift HR management toward the relational and away from the transactional. The reason is twofold. First, human judgment, where it is valuable, is utilized because it is difficult to program such judgment into a machine. The rewards are either unstable or unknown, or require human experience to implement. Second, to the extent that human judgment becomes more important when machine predictions proliferate, such judgment necessarily involves subjective means of performance evaluation. If objective means are available, chances are that a machine could make such judgment without the need for any HR management. Thus, humans are critical to decision making where the goals are subjective. For that reason, the management of such people will likely be more relational.

Thus, AI will have an impact on labor that is different from its impact on capital. The importance of judgment means that employee contracts need to be more subjective.

The forces affecting capital equipment also affect labor. If the key outputs of human labor are data, predictions, or actions, then using AI means more outsourced contract labor, just as it means more outsourced equipment and supplies. As with capital, better prediction gives more "ifs" that we can use to clearly specify the "thens" in an outsourcing contract.

However, the more important effect on labor will be the increasing importance of human judgment. Prediction and judgment are complements, so better prediction increases the demand for judgment, meaning that your employees' main role will be to exercise judgment in decision making. This, by definition, cannot be well specified in a contract. Here, the prediction machine increases uncertainty in the strategic dilemma because evaluating the quality of judgment is diffi-cult, so contracting out is risky. Counterintuitively, better prediction increases the uncertainty you have over the quality of human work performed: you need to keep your reward function engineers and other judgment-focused workers in house.

Impact of AI: Data

Another critical strategic issue is the ownership and control of data. Just as the consequences for workers relate to the complementarity between prediction and judgment, the relationship between predic-tion and data also drives these trade-offs. Data makes prediction bet-ter. Here, we consider the trade-offs associated with organizational boundaries. Should you utilize others' data or own your own? (In the next chapter, we explore issues concerning the strategic importance of investing in data collection.)

For AI startups, owning the data that allows them to learn is par-ticularly crucial. Otherwise, they will be unable to improve their product over time. Machine learning startup Ada Support helps other companies interact with their customers. Ada had the opportunity to integrate its product into the system of a large established chat pro-vider. If this worked, it would be much easier to get traction and estab-lish a large user base. This was a tempting way to go.

The problem, however, was that the established companies would own the feedback data on the interactions. Without that data, Ada would not be able to improve its product based on what actually hap-pened in the field. Ada was emboldened to reconsider this approach and did not integrate until it could ensure that it owned the result-ing data. Doing so gave it a pipeline of data now and into the future to draw on for continual learning.

The issue of whether to own or procure data goes well beyond startups. Consider data designed to help advertisers target poten-tial customers. John Wanamaker, who, among others, created the modern structure of advertising in the media, once stated: "Half the money I spend on advertising is wasted; the trouble is, I don't know which half."

This is the fundamental issue with advertising. Put an advertisement on a website, everyone who visits that site views the ad, and you pay for each impression. If only a fraction of them are potential customers, then your willingness to pay for each impression will be relatively low. That is a problem for both you as the advertiser and the website trying to make money from ads.

One solution is to focus on building websites that attract people with specific interests—sports, finance, and so on—which have a higher proportion of potential customers for certain types of advertisers. Before the rise of the internet, this was a core feature of advertising, leading to a proliferation of magazines, cable television channels, and newspaper sections for automotive, fashion, real estate, and investing. However, not every media outlet can tailor its content in this way.

Instead, thanks to web browser innovations, primarily the "cookie," advertisers can track users over time and across websites. They then have the ability to better target their advertising. The cookie records information about website visitors but, most critically, information about the type of sites, including shopping sites, they frequent. Because of this tracking technology, when you visit a site to look for new pants, you may find that a disproportionate share of subsequent ads you see, including on completely unrelated sites, is for pants.

Any website can place cookies, but the cookies are not necessarily of much value to that site. Instead, websites offer cookies for sale to advertising exchanges (or sometimes directly to advertisers) so that they can better target their ads. Websites sell data about their visitors to companies that place advertisements.

Companies buy data because they can't collect it themselves. Not surprisingly, they buy data that helps them identify high-value customers. They also may buy data that helps them avoid advertising to low-value customers. Both types of data are valuable in that they enable the company to focus its ad spending on high-value customers.[6]

Many AI leaders, including Google, Facebook, and Microsoft, have built or purchased their own advertising networks so that they can own this valuable data. They decided that owning this data is worth the cost of acquiring it. To others, advertising data is less critical, so they trade off the control of that data to avoid incurring the high cost of collecting it themselves; the advertising data thus remains outside the boundaries of these companies.

Selling Predictions

Google, Facebook, Microsoft, and a handful of other companies have particularly useful data on consumer preferences online. Rather than only sell data, they go a step further to make predictions for advertisers. For example, Google, through search, YouTube, and its advertising network, has rich data on user needs. It does not sell the data. However, it does, in effect, sell the predictions that the data generates to advertisers as part of a bundled service. If you advertise through Google's network, your ad is shown to the users that the network predicts are most likely to be influenced by the ad. Advertising through Facebook or Microsoft yields similar results. Without direct access to the data, the advertiser buys the prediction.

Unique data is important for creating strategic advantage. If data is not unique, it is hard to build a business around prediction machines. Without data, there is no real pathway to learning, so AI is not core to your strategy. As noted in the example of advertising networks, predictions still might be useful. They allow the advertiser to target the highest-value customer. Thus, better prediction may help an organization, even if the data and predictions are not likely to be sources of strategic advantage.[7] Both the data and the prediction are outside the boundaries of the organization, but it can still use prediction.

The main implication here is that data and prediction machines are complements. Thus, procuring or developing an AI will be of limited value unless you have the data to feed it. If that data resides with others, you need a strategy to get it.

If the data resides with an exclusive or monopoly provider, then you may find yourself at risk of having that provider appropriate the entire value of your AI. If the data resides with competitors, there may be no strategy that would make it worthwhile to procure it from them. If the data resides with consumers, it can be exchanged in return for a better product or higher-quality service.

However, in some situations, you and others might have data that can be of mutual value; hence, a data swap may be possible. In other situations, the data may reside with multiple providers, in which case, you might need some more complicated arrangement of purchasing a combination of data and prediction.

Whether you collect your own data and make predictions or buy them from others depends on the importance of prediction machines to your company. If the prediction machine is an input that you can take off the shelf, then you can treat it like most companies treat energy and purchase it from the market, as long as AI is not core to your strategy. In contrast, if prediction machines are to be the center of your company's strategy, then you need to control the data to improve the machine, so both the data and the prediction machine must be in house.

At the beginning of this chapter, we suggested that a machine learning startup that aimed to provide medical diagnoses instead sell a prediction. Why would the doctor be willing to buy the prediction rather than the full diagnosis? And why wouldn't the doctor want to own the prediction machine and data? The answers lie in the relevant trade-offs we've discussed. A key part of the doctor's job is diagnosis, so buying the prediction is not a doctor's core strategic decision. Doctors continue to do what they did before, with an additional piece of information. If it isn't a key strategic decision, then they can buy the prediction without needing to own the data or prediction. In contrast, the essence of the startup is AI, and the prediction provides value to customers. So, as long as the startup owns the data and prediction machine, it does not need to own the diagnosis. The boundary between the startup and the doctor is the boundary where the AI ceases to be strategic and instead is simply an input to a different process.

KEY POINTS

- A key strategic choice is determining where your business ends and another business begins—deciding on the boundary of the firm (e.g., airline partnerships, outsourcing automotive part manufacturing). Uncertainty influences this choice. Because prediction machines reduce uncertainty, they can influence the boundary between your organization and others.

- By reducing uncertainty, prediction machines increase the ability to write contracts, and thus increase the incentive for companies to contract out both capital equipment and labor that focuses on data, prediction, and action. However, prediction machines decrease the incentive for companies to contract out labor that focuses on judgment. Judgment quality is hard to specify in a contract and difficult to monitor. If judgment could be well specified, then it could be programmed and we wouldn't need humans to provide it. Since judgment is likely to be the key role for human labor as AI diffuses, in-house employment will rise and contracting out labor will fall.

- AI will increase incentives to own data. Still, contracting out for data may be necessary when the predictions that the data provides are not strategically essential to your organization. In such cases, it may be best to purchase predictions directly rather than purchase data and then generate your own predictions.

17

Your Learning Strategy

In March 2017, in a keynote speech at its annual I/O event, Google CEO Sundar Pichai announced that the company was shifting from a "mobile-first world to an AI-first world." Then a series of announcements followed involving AI in various ways: from the development of specialized chips for optimizing machine learning, to the use of deep learning in new applications including cancer research, to putting Google's AI-driven assistant on as many devices as possible. Pichai claimed the company was transitioning from "searching and organizing the world's information to AI and machine learning."

The announcement was more strategic than a fundamental change in vision. Google's founder Larry Page outlined this path in 2002:

> We don't always produce what people want. That's what we work on really hard. It's really difficult. To do that you have to be smart, you have to understand everything in the world, you have to understand the query. What we're trying to do is artificial intelligence . . . [T]he ultimate search engine would be smart. And so we work to get closer and closer to that.[1]

In this sense, Google has considered itself on the path to building artificial intelligence for years. Only recently has it openly and outwardly put AI techniques at the heart of everything it does.

Google is not alone in this strategic commitment. That same month, Microsoft announced its "AI-first" intentions, moving away from "mobile-first" and also "cloud-first."[2] But what does the notion of AI-first mean? For both Google and Microsoft, the first part of their change—no longer mobile-first—gives us a clue. To be mobile-first is to drive traffic to your mobile experience and optimize consumers' interfaces for mobile *even at the expense of your full website and other platforms.* The last part is what makes it strategic. "Do well on mobile" is something to aim for. But saying you will do so even if it harms other channels is a real commitment.

What does this mean in the context of AI-first? Google's research director Peter Norvig gives an answer:

> With information retrieval, anything over 80% recall and precision is pretty good—not every suggestion has to be perfect, since the user can ignore the bad suggestions. With assistance, there is a much higher barrier. You wouldn't use a service that booked the wrong reservation 20% of the time, or even 2% of the time. So an assistant needs to be much more accurate, and thus more intelligent, more aware of the situation. That's what we call "AI-first."[3]

That's a good answer for a computer scientist. It emphasizes technical performance, and accuracy, in particular. But this statement implicitly says something else, too. If AI is first (maximizing predictive accuracy), what becomes second?

The economist's filter knows that any statement of "we will put our attention into X" means a trade-off. Something will always be given up in exchange. What does it take to emphasize predictive accuracy above all else? Our answer comes from our core economic framework: AI-first means devoting resources to data collection and learning (a longer-term objective) at the expense of important short-term considerations such as immediate customer experience, revenue, and user numbers.

A Whiff of Disruption

Adopting an AI-first strategy is a commitment to prioritize prediction quality and to support the machine learning process, even at the cost of short-term factors such as consumer satisfaction and operational performance. Gathering data might mean deploying AIs whose prediction quality is not yet at optimal levels. The central strategic dilemma is whether to prioritize that learning or instead shield others from the performance sacrifices that entails.

Different businesses will approach this dilemma and make choices differently. But why are Google, Microsoft, and other tech companies going AI-first? Is that something other businesses can follow? Or is there something special about those companies?

One distinguishing feature of these companies is that they are already gathering and generating great swathes of digital data and operating in environments with uncertainty. So, prediction machines are likely to enable tools that they will use extensively throughout products in their business. Internally, tools that involve superior and cheaper prediction are in demand. Alongside this is a supply-side advantage. These companies already house technical talent that they can use to develop machine learning and its applications.

These companies, drawing on the hybrid corn analogy from chapter 15, are like the farmers located in Iowa. But AI-led technologies display another important characteristic. Given that learning takes time and often results in inferior performance (especially for consumers), it shares features of what Clay Christensen has termed "disruptive technologies," meaning that some established companies will find it difficult to adopt such technologies quickly.[4]

Consider a new AI version of an existing product. To develop the product, it needs users. The first users of the AI product will have a poor customer experience because the AI needs to learn. A company may have a solid customer base and therefore could have those customers use the product and provide training data. However, those customers are happy with the existing product and may not tolerate a switch to a temporarily inferior AI product.

This is the classic "innovator's dilemma," whereby established firms do not want to disrupt their existing customer relationships, even if doing so would be better in the long run. The innovator's dilemma occurs because, when they first appear, innovations might not be good enough to serve the customers of the established companies in an industry, but they may be good enough to provide a new startup with enough customers in some niche area to build a product. Over time, the startup gains experience. Eventually, the startup has learned enough to create a strong product that takes away its larger rival's customers. By that point, the larger company is too far behind, and the startup eventually dominates. AI requires learning, and startups may be more willing to invest in this learning than their more established rivals.

The innovator's dilemma is less of a dilemma when the company in question faces tough competition, especially if that competition comes from new entrants that do not face constraints associated with having to satisfy an existing customer base. In that situation, the threat of the competition means that the cost of doing nothing is too high. Such competition tips the equation toward adopting the disruptive technology quickly even if you are an established company. Put differently, for technologies like AI where the long-term potential impact is likely to be enormous, the whiff of disruption may drive early adoption, even by incumbents.

Learning can take a great deal of data and time before a machine's predictions become reliably accurate. It will be a rare instance indeed when a prediction machine just works off the shelf. Someone selling you an AI-powered piece of software may have already done the hard work of training. But when you want to manage AI for a purpose core to your own business, no off-the-shelf solution is likely. You won't need a user manual so much as a training manual. This training requires some way for the AI to gather data and improve.[5]

A Pathway to Learning

Learning-by-using is a term that economic historian Nathan Rosenberg coined to describe the phenomenon whereby firms improve their product design through interactions with users.[6] His main applications had to do with the performance of airplanes, whose more conservative initial designs gave way to better designs with larger capacity and greater efficiency as the airplane manufacturers learned through additional use. Manufacturers with an early start had an advantage as they learned more. Of course, such learning curves give strategic advantage in a variety of contexts. They are particularly important for prediction machines, which, after all, rely on machine learning.

Thus far, we have not spent much time distinguishing between the different types of learning that make up machine learning. We have focused mostly on *supervised learning*. You use this technique when you already have good data on what you are trying to predict; for example, you have millions of images and you already know that they contain a cat or a tumor; you train the AI based on that knowledge. Supervised learning is a key part of what we do as professors; we present new material by showing our students problems and their solutions.

By contrast, what happens when you do not have good data on what you are trying to predict, but you can tell, after the fact, how right you were? In that situation, as we discussed in chapter 2, computer scientists deploy techniques of *reinforcement learning*. Many young children and animals learn this way. The psychologist Pavlov rang a bell when giving dogs a treat and then found that ringing the bell triggered a saliva response in those dogs. The dogs learned to associate the bell with receiving food and came to know that a bell predicted nearby food and prepared accordingly.

In AI, much progress in reinforcement learning has come in teaching machines to play games. DeepMind gave its AI a set of controls to video games such as Breakout and "rewarded" the AI for getting a higher score without any other instructions. The AI learned to play a host of Atari games better than the best human players. This is learning-by-using. The AIs played the game thousands of times and learned to play better, just as a human would, except the AI could play more games, more quickly, than any human ever could.[7]

Learning occurs by having the machine make certain moves and then using the move data along with past experience (of moves and resulting scores) to predict which moves will lead to the biggest increases in score. The only way to learn is to actually play. Without a pathway to learning, the machine will neither play well nor improve over time. Such pathways to learning are costly.

When to Deploy

Those familiar with software development know that code needs extensive testing to locate bugs. In some situations, companies release the software to users to help find the bugs that might emerge in ordinary use. Whether by "dog fooding" (forcing early versions of software to be used internally) or "beta testing" (inviting early adopters to test the software), these forms of learning-by-using involve a short-term investment in learning to enable the product to improve over time.

This short-term cost of training for a longer-term benefit is similar to the way humans learn to do their jobs better. While it does not take a tremendous amount of training to begin a job as a crew member at McDonald's, new employees are slower and make more mistakes than their more experienced peers. They improve as they serve more customers.

Commercial airline pilots also continue to improve from on-the-job experience. On January 15, 2009, when US Airways Flight 1549 was struck by a flock of Canada geese, shutting down all engine power, Captain Chesley "Sully" Sullenberger miraculously landed the plane on the Hudson River, saving the lives of all 155 passengers. Most reporters attributed his performance to experience. He had recorded 19,663 total flight hours, including 4,765 flying an Airbus A320. Sully himself reflected: "One way of looking at this might be that for 42 years, I've been making small, regular deposits in this bank of experience, education, and training. And on January 15, the balance was sufficient so that I could make a very large withdrawal."[8] Sully and all his passengers benefited from the thousands of people he'd flown before.

The difference between the skills of new cashiers and pilots in what constitutes "good enough to get started" is based on tolerance for error. Obviously, our tolerance is much lower for pilots. We take comfort that pilot certification is regulated by the US Department of Transportation's Federal Aviation Administration and requires a minimum experience of fifteen hundred hours of flight time, five hundred hours of cross-country flight time, one hundred hours of night flight time, and seventy-five hours of instrument operations time, even though pilots continue to learn from on-the-job experience. We have different definitions for good enough when it comes to how much training humans require in different jobs. The same is true of machines that learn.

Companies design systems to train new employees until they are good enough and then deploy them into service, knowing they will improve as they learn from experience doing their job. But determining what constitutes good enough is a critical decision. In the case of prediction machines, it can be a major strategic decision regarding timing: when to shift from in-house training to on-the-job learning.

There are no ready answers for what constitutes good enough for prediction machines, only trade-offs. Success with prediction machines will require taking these trade-offs seriously and approaching them strategically.

First, what tolerance do people have for error? We have high tolerance for error with some prediction machines and low tolerance for others. For example, Google's Inbox app reads our email, uses AI to predict how we may want to respond, and generates three short responses to choose from. Many users report enjoying using the app even though it has a 70 percent failure rate (at the time of writing, the AI-generated response is only useful for us about 30 percent of the time). The reason for this high tolerance for error is that the benefit of reduced composing and typing outweighs the cost of providing suggestions and wasting screen real estate when the predicted short response is wrong.

In contrast, we have low tolerance for error in the realm of autonomous driving. The first generation of autonomous vehicles, which Google largely pioneered, was trained using specialist human drivers who took a limited number of vehicles and drove them hundreds of thousands of kilometers, much like a parent supervising a teenager on driving experiences.

Such human specialist drivers provide a safe training environment, but they are also extremely limited. The machine only learns about a few situations. Someone may take many millions of miles in varying environments and situations before they have learned how to deal with the rare incidents that lead to accidents. For autonomous vehicles, real roads are nasty and unforgiving precisely because nasty or unforgiving human-caused situations can occur on them.

Second, how important is capturing user data in the real world? Understanding that training might take a prohibitively long time, Tesla rolled out autonomous vehicle capabilities to all of its recent models. These capabilities included a set of sensors that collect environmental data as well as driving data, which is uploaded to Tesla's machine learning servers. In a very short time, Tesla can obtain training data just by observing how the drivers of its cars drive. The more Tesla vehicles are on the road, the more Tesla's machines can learn.

However, in addition to passively collecting data as humans drive their Teslas, the company needs autonomous driving data to understand how its autonomous systems are operating. For that, it needs to have cars drive autonomously so that it can assess performance, but also analyze when a human driver, whose presence and attention are required, chooses to intervene. Tesla's ultimate goal is not to produce a copilot or a teenager who drives under supervision, but a fully autonomous vehicle. That requires getting to the point where real people feel comfortable in a self-driving car.

Herein lies a tricky trade-off. To get better, Tesla needs its machines to learn in real situations. But putting its current cars in real situations means giving customers a relatively young and inexperienced driver, although perhaps as good as or better than many young human drivers. Still, this is far riskier than beta testing whether Siri or Alexa understood what you said or if Google Inbox correctly predicts your response to an email. In the case of Siri, Alexa, or Google Inbox, a mistake means a lower-quality user experience. In the case of autonomous vehicles, a mistake means putting lives at risk.

That experience can be scary.[9] Cars can exit freeways without notice or press the brakes when mistaking an underpass for an obstruction. Nervous drivers may opt not to use the autonomous features and, in the process, hinder Tesla's ability to learn. Even if the company can persuade some people to become beta testers, are those the people it wants? After all, a beta tester for autonomous driving may be someone with a taste for more risk than the average driver. In that case, who is the company training its machines to be like?

Machines learn faster with more data, and when machines are deployed in the wild, they generate more data. However, bad things can happen in the real world and damage the company brand. Putting products in the wild earlier accelerates learning but risks harming the brand (and perhaps the customer); putting them out later slows learning but allows for more time to improve the product in house and protect the brand (and, again, perhaps the customer).

For some products, like Google Inbox, the answer to the trade-off seems clear because the cost of poor performance is low and the benefits from learning from customer usage are high. It makes sense to deploy this type of product in the real world early. For other products, like cars, the answer is murkier. As more companies across all industries seek to take advantage of machine learning, strategies associated with choosing how to handle this trade-off will become increasingly salient.

Learning by Simulation

One intermediate step to soften this trade-off is to use simulated environments. When human pilots are training, before they get their hands on a real plane in flight, they spend hundreds of hours in what are very sophisticated and realistic simulators. A similar approach is available for AI. Google trained DeepMind's AlphaGo AI to defeat the best Go players in the world not just by looking at thousands of games played between humans but also by playing against another version of itself.

One form of this approach is called adversarial machine learning, which pits the main AI and its objective against another AI that tries to foil that objective. For example, Google researchers had one AI send messages to another using an encryption process. The two AIs shared a key to encoding and decoding the message. A third AI (the adversary) had the messages but not the key and tried to decode them. With many simulations, the adversary trained the main AI to communicate in ways that are hard to decode without the key.[10]

Such simulated learning approaches cannot take place on the ground; they require something akin to a laboratory approach that produces a new machine learning algorithm that is then copied and pushed out to users. The advantage is that the machine is not trained in the wild, so the risk to the user experience, or even to the users themselves, is mitigated. The disadvantage is that simulations may not provide sufficiently rich feedback, reducing, but not eliminating, the need to release the AI early. Eventually, you have to let the AI loose in the real world.

Learning in the Cloud versus on the Ground

Learning in the wild improves the AI. The company can then use real-world outcomes that the prediction machine experiences to improve the predictions for next time. Often, a company collects data in the real world, which refines the machine before it releases an updated prediction model.

Tesla's Autopilot never learns on the job with actual consumers. When it is out in the field, it sends the data back to Tesla's computing cloud. Tesla then aggregates and uses that data to upgrade Autopilot. Only then does it roll out a new version of Autopilot. Learning takes place in the cloud.

This standard approach has the advantage of shielding users from undertrained versions. The downside, however, is that the common AI that resides on devices cannot take into account rapidly changing local conditions or, at the very least, can only do so when that data is built into a new generation. Thus, from the perspective of a user, improvements come in jumps.

By contrast, imagine if the AI could learn on the device and improve in that environment. It could then respond more readily to local conditions and optimize itself for different environments. In environments where things change rapidly, it is beneficial to improve the prediction machines on the devices themselves. For example, on apps like Tinder (the popular dating app where users make selections by swiping left for no or right for yes), users make many decisions rapidly. This can feed into the predictions immediately to determine which potential dates to show next. Tastes are user-specific and change over time, both over the course of a year and by time of day. To the extent that people are similar and have stable preferences, sending to the cloud and updating will work well. To the extent that an individual's tastes are idiosyncratic and rapidly changing, then the ability to adjust predictions at the level of the device is useful.

Companies must trade off how quickly they should use a prediction machine's experience in the real world to generate new predictions. Use that experience immediately and the AI adapts more quickly to changes in local conditions, but at the cost of quality assurance.

Permission to Learn

Learning often requires customers who are willing to provide data. If strategy involves doing something at the expense of something else, then in the AI space, few companies made a stronger, earlier commitment than Apple. Tim Cook wrote, in a special section devoted to privacy on Apple's home page: "At Apple, your trust means everything to us. That's why we respect your privacy and protect it with strong encryption, plus strict policies that govern how all data is handled."[11]
He went on:

> A few years ago, users of Internet services began to realize that when an online service is free, you're not the customer. You're the product. But at Apple, we believe a great customer experience shouldn't come at the expense of your privacy.
>
> Our business model is very straightforward: We sell great products. We don't build a profile based on your email content or web browsing habits to sell to advertisers. We don't

"monetize" the information you store on your iPhone or in iCloud. And we don't read your email or your messages to get information to market to you. Our software and services are designed to make our devices better. Plain and simple.[12]

Apple did not make this decision due to a government regulation. Some claimed Apple made the decision because it was purportedly lagging behind Google and Facebook in developing AI. No company, certainly not Apple, could eschew AI. This commitment would make its job harder. It plans to do AI in a way that respects privacy. It is making a big strategic bet that consumers will want control over their own data. Whether for security or privacy, Apple has bet that its commitment will make consumers more, not less, likely to allow AI onto their devices.[13] Apple isn't alone in betting that protecting privacy will pay off. Salesforce, Adobe, Uber, Dropbox, and many others have invested heavily in privacy.

This bet is strategic. Many other companies, including Google, Facebook, and Amazon, have chosen a different path, telling users that they will use data to provide better products. Apple's focus on privacy limits the products it can offer. For instance, both Apple and Google have face recognition built into their photo services. To be useful to consumers, the faces have to be tagged. Google does this, preserving the tags, regardless of device, since the recognition runs on Google servers. Apple, however, because of privacy concerns, has opted to have that recognition occur at the device level. That means if you tag faces of people you know on your Mac, the tags will not carry over to your iPhone or iPad. Not surprisingly, this creates a situation where privacy concerns and consumer usability hit a roadblock. (How Apple will deal with these issues is unknown at the time of writing.)

We do not know what will emerge in practice. In any case, our economist filter makes it clear that the relative payoffs associated with trading people's privacy concerns for predictive accuracy will guide the ultimate strategic choice. Enhanced privacy might give companies permission to learn about consumers but may also mean the learning is not particularly useful.

Experience Is the New Scarce Resource

Navigation app Waze collects data from other Waze users to predict the location of traffic problems. It can find the fastest route for you personally. If that were all it was doing, there would be no issue. However, prediction alters human behavior, which is what Waze is designed to do. When the machine receives information from a crowd, its predictions may be distorted by that fact.

For Waze, the problem is that its users will follow its guidance to avoid traffic problems, perhaps through side streets. Unless Waze adjusts for this, it will never be alerted that a traffic problem is alleviated and the normal route is once again the fastest. To overcome this obstacle, the app must therefore send some human drivers back toward the traffic jam to see if it is still there. Doing so presents the obvious issue—humans so directed might be sacrificial lambs for the greater good of the crowd. Not surprisingly, this degrades the quality of the product for them.

There are no easy ways to overcome the trade-off that arises when prediction alters crowd behavior, thereby denying AI of the very information it needs to form the correct prediction. In this instance, the needs of the many outweigh the needs of the few or the one. But this is certainly not a comfortable way of thinking about managing customer relationships.

Sometimes, to improve products, especially when they involve learning-by-using, it is important to jolt the system so that consumers actually experience something new that the machine can learn from. Customers who are forced into that new environment often have a worse experience, but everyone else benefits from those experiences. For beta testing, the trade-off is voluntary, as customers opt into the early versions. But beta testing may attract customers who do not use the product the same way as your general customers would. To gain experience about all your customers, you may sometimes need to degrade the product for those customers in order to get feedback that will benefit everyone.

Humans Also Need Experience

The scarcity of experience becomes even more salient when you consider the experience of your human resources. If the machines get the experience, then the humans might not. Recently, some expressed concern that automation could result in the deskilling of humans.

Air France Flight 447 crashed into the Atlantic on route from Rio de Janeiro to Paris in 2009. The crisis began with bad weather, but escalated when the plane's autopilot disengaged. At the helm during that time, unlike Sully in the US Airways plane, a relatively inexperienced pilot poorly handled the situation, according to reports. When a more experienced pilot took over (he had been asleep), he was unable to properly assess the situation.[14] The experienced pilot had slept little the night before. The bottom line: the junior pilot may have had almost three thousand hours in the air, but it was not quality experience. Most of the time, he had been flying the plane on autopilot.

Automation of flying has become commonplace, a reaction to evidence that showed that most airplane accidents after the 1970s were the result of human error. So, humans have since been removed from the control loop. However, the ironic unintended consequence is that human pilots garner less experience and become even worse.

For economist Tim Harford, the solution is obvious: automation has to be scaled back. What is being automated, he argues, are more routine situations, so you require human interventions for more extreme situations. If the way you learn to deal with the extreme is by having a great feel for the ordinary, therein lies a problem. The Air France plane faced an extreme situation without the proper attention of an experienced hand.

Harford stresses that automation does not always lead to this conundrum:

> There are plenty of situations in which automation creates
> no such paradox. A customer service webpage may be able to
> handle routine complaints and requests, so that staff are spared
> repetitive work and may do a better job for customers with

more complex questions. Not so with an aeroplane. Autopilots and the more subtle assistance of fly-by-wire do not free up the crew to concentrate on the interesting stuff. Instead, they free up the crew to fall asleep at the controls, figuratively or even literally. One notorious incident occurred late in 2009, when two pilots let their autopilot overshoot Minneapolis airport by more than 100 miles. They had been looking at their laptops.[15]

Not surprisingly, other examples we've discussed in this book tend to fall into the category of airplanes rather than customer service complaints, including the whole domain of self-driving cars. What will we do when we don't drive most of the time but have a car that hands control to us during an extreme event? What will our children do?

The solutions involve ensuring that humans gain and retain skills, reducing the amount of automation to provide time for human learning. In effect, experience is a scarce resource, some of which you need to allocate to humans to avoid deskilling.

The reverse logic is also true. To train prediction machines, having them learn through the experience of potentially catastrophic events is surely valuable. But if you put a human in the loop, how will that machine's experience emerge? And so another trade-off in generating a pathway to learning is between human and machine experience.

These trade-offs reveal the implications of the AI-first declarations of the leadership of Google, Microsoft, and others. The companies are willing to invest in data to help their machines learn. Improving prediction machines takes priority, even if that requires degrading the quality of the immediate customer experience or employee training. Data strategy is key to AI strategy.

KEY POINTS

- Shifting to an AI-first strategy means downgrading the previous top priority. In other words, AI-first is not a buzz word—it represents a real tradeoff. An AI-first strategy places maximizing prediction accuracy as the central goal of the organization, even if that means compromising on other goals such as maximizing revenue, user numbers, or user experience.

- AI can lead to disruption because incumbent firms often have weaker economic incentives than startups to adopt the technology. AI-enabled products are often inferior at first because it takes time to train a prediction machine to perform as well as a hard-coded device that follows human instructions rather than learning on its own. However, once deployed, an AI can continue to learn and improve, leaving its unintelligent competitors' products behind. It is tempting for established companies to take a wait-and-see approach, standing on the sidelines and observing the progress in AI applied to their industry. That may work for some companies, but others will find it difficult to catch up once their competitors get ahead in the training and deployment of their AI tools.

- Another strategic decision concerns timing—when to release AI tools into the wild. AI tools are, initially, trained in house, away from customers. However, they learn faster when they are deployed into commercial use because they are exposed to real operating conditions and often to greater volumes of data. The benefit to deploying earlier is faster learning, and the cost is greater risk (risk to the brand or customer safety by exposing customers to immature AIs that are not properly trained). In some cases, the tradeoff is clear, such as with Google Inbox, where the benefits of faster learning outweigh the cost of poor performance. In other cases, such as autonomous driving, the trade-off is more ambiguous given the size of the prize for being early with a commercial product weighed against the high cost of an error if the product is released before it is ready.

18

Managing AI Risk

Latanya Sweeney, who was the chief technology officer for the US Federal Trade Commission and is now a professor at Harvard University, was surprised when a colleague Googled her name to find one of her papers and discovered ads suggesting she had been arrested.[1] Sweeney clicked on the ad, paid a fee, and learned what she already knew: she had never been arrested. Intrigued, she entered the name of her colleague Adam Tanner, and the same company's ad appeared but without the suggestion of arrest. After more searching, she developed the hypothesis that maybe black-sounding names were triggering the arrest ad. Sweeney then tested this more systematically and found that if you Googled a black-associated name like Lakisha or Trevon, you were 25 percent more likely to get an ad suggesting an arrest record than if you searched for a name like Jill or Joshua.[2]

Such biases are potentially damaging. Searchers might be looking for information to see if someone is suitable for a job. If they find ads with titles like "Latanya Sweeney, Arrested?" the searchers might have some doubts. It is both discriminatory and defamatory.

Why was this happening? Google provides software that allows advertisers to test and target particular keywords. Advertisers might have entered racially associated names to place ads alongside, although Google denied that.[3] Another possibility is that the pattern emerged as a result of Google's algorithms, which promote ads that have a higher "quality score" (meaning they are likely to be clicked). Prediction machines likely played a role there. For instance, if potential employers searching for names were more likely to click on an arrest ad when associated with a black-sounding name than other names, then the quality score associated with placing those ads with such keywords might rise. Google is not intending to be discriminatory, but its algorithms might amplify prejudices that already exist in society. Such profiling exemplifies a risk of implementing AI.

Liability Risks

The emergence of racial profiling is a societal issue, but also a potential problem for companies like Google. They may run afoul of employment antidiscrimination rules. Fortunately, when whistle-blowers like Sweeney raise the issue, Google is highly responsive, investigating and correcting problems.

Discrimination might emerge in even subtler ways. Economists Anja Lambrecht and Catherine Tucker, in a 2017 study, showed that Facebook ads could lead to gender discrimination.[4] They placed ads promoting jobs in science, technology, engineering, and math (STEM) fields on the social network and found Facebook was less likely to show the ad to women, not because women were less likely to click on the ad or because they might be in countries with discriminatory labor markets. On the contrary, the workings of the ad market discriminated. Because younger women are valuable as a demographic on Facebook, showing ads to them is more expensive. So, when you place an ad on Facebook, the algorithms naturally place ads where their return per placement is highest. If men and women are equally likely to click on STEM job ads, then it is better to place ads where they are cheap: with men.

Harvard Business School professor, economist, and lawyer Ben Edelman explained to us why this issue could be serious for both employers and Facebook. While many tend to think of discrimination as arising from disparate treatment—setting different standards for men and women—the ad-placement differences might result in what lawyers call "disparate impact." A gender-neutral procedure turns out to affect some employees who might have reason to fear discrimination (a "protected class" to lawyers) differently from others.

A person or an organization can be liable for discrimination, even if it is accidental. A court found that the New York City Fire Department discriminated against black and Hispanic applicants becoming firefighters with an entrance exam that included several questions emphasizing reading comprehension. The court found that the types of questions had no relation to effectiveness as a fire department employee and that black and Hispanic applicants performed systematically worse on them.[5] The case was eventually settled for about $99 million. Blacks' and Hispanics' lower performance on the exam meant that the department was liable, even if the discrimination was unintentional.

So, while you may think you are placing a neutral ad on Facebook, disparate impact might be emerging regardless. As an employer, you could be liable. Of course, you don't want to engage in discrimination, even implicitly. One solution for Facebook is to offer tools for advertisers to prevent discrimination.

A challenge with AI is that such unintentional discrimination can happen without anyone in the organization noticing. Predictions generated by deep learning and many other AI technologies appear to be created from a black box. It isn't feasible to look at the algorithm or formula underlying the prediction and identify what causes what. To figure out if AI is discriminating, you have to look at the output. Do men get different results than women? Do Hispanics get different results than others? What about the elderly or the disabled? Do these different results limit their opportunities?

To prevent liability issues (and to avoid being discriminatory), if you discover unintentional discrimination in the output of your AI, you need to fix it. You need to figure out why your AI generated discriminatory predictions. But if AI is a black box, then how can you do this?

Some in the computer science community call this "AI neuroscience."[6] A key tool is to hypothesize what might drive the differences, provide the AI with different input data that tests the hypothesis, and then compare the resulting predictions. Lambrecht and Tucker did this when they discovered that women saw fewer STEM ads because it was less expensive to show the ad to men. The point is that the black box of AI is not an excuse to ignore potential discrimination or a way to avoid using AI in situations where discrimination might matter. Plenty of evidence shows that humans discriminate even more than machines. Deploying AI requires additional investments in auditing for discrimination, then working to reduce any discrimination that results.

Algorithmic discrimination can easily emerge at the operational level but can end up having strategic and broader consequences. Strategy involves directing those in your organization to weigh factors that might not otherwise be obvious. This becomes particularly salient with systematic risks, like algorithmic discrimination, that may have a negative impact on your business. Showing the STEM ads to men and not women bolstered short-term performance (in that the ads the men saw cost less) but created risks due to the resulting discrimination. The consequences of increasing risks may not become apparent until too late. Thus, a key task for a business's leaders is to anticipate various risks and ensure that procedures are in place to manage them.

Quality Risks

If you are in a consumer-facing business, you probably buy ads and have seen a measure of those ads' ROI. For instance, your organization may have found that paying for Google ads resulted in an increase in click-throughs and maybe even purchases on the website. That is, the more ads your company bought on Google, the more clicks from those ads it received. Now, try employing an AI to look at that data and generate a prediction of whether a new Google ad is likely to increase clicks from that ad; the AI will likely back up that positive correlation you had previously observed. As a result, when the marketing people want to buy more Google ads, they have some ROI evidence to back it up.

Of course, it takes an ad to generate a click. One possibility is that without the ad, the consumer would never know about your product. In this case, you want to place ads because they generate new sales. Another possibility is that the ad is the easiest thing for potential customers to click, but in its absence, they would find you anyway. So while the ad may be associated with more sales, it is potentially a fiction. Without the ad, sales may have increased regardless. Thus, if you really want to know if the ad—and the money you spend on it—is generating new sales, you need to examine the situation more deeply.

In 2012, some economists working for eBay—Thomas Blake, Chris Nosko, and Steve Tadelis—persuaded eBay to turn off all of its search advertising in one-third of the United States for an entire month.[7] The ads had a measured ROI using traditional statistics of more than 4,000 percent. If the measured ROI was correct, doing a month-long experiment would cost eBay a fortune.

However, what they found justified their approach. The search ads eBay placed had practically no impact on sales. Their ROI was negative. Consumers on eBay were savvy enough that, if they didn't see an ad in Google, they would click on ordinary (or organic) search results in Google. Google would highly rank eBay listings regardless. But the same was true for brands like BMW and Amazon. The only area where ads seemed to do some good was in attracting new users to eBay.

This story's point is to demonstrate that AI—which does not rely on causal experimentation but on correlation—can easily fall into the same traps as anyone using data and simple statistics can. If you want to know whether advertising is effective, observe whether ads lead to sales. However, that is not necessarily the full story, because you also need to know what would happen to sales if you ran no ads. An AI trained on data that involves lots of ads and sales does not get to see what happens with few ads. That data is missing. Such unknown knowns are a key weakness of prediction machines that require human judgment to overcome. At the moment, only thoughtful humans can work out if the AI is falling into that trap.

Security Risks

While software has always been subject to security risks, with AI those risks emerge through the possibility of data manipulation. Three classes of data have an impact on prediction machines: input, training, and feedback. All three have potential security risks.

Input Data Risks

Prediction machines feed on input data. They combine this data with a model to generate a prediction. So, just like the old computer adage—"garbage in, garbage out"—prediction machines fail if they have poor data or a bad model. A hacker might cause a prediction machine to fail by feeding it garbage data or manipulating the prediction model. One type of failure is a crash. Crashes might seem bad, but at least you know when they have occurred. When someone manipulates a prediction machine, you may not know about it (at least not until too late).

Hackers have many ways to manipulate or fool a prediction machine. University of Washington researchers showed that Google's new algorithm for detecting video content could be fooled into misclassifying videos by inserting random images for fractions of a second.[8] For example, you can trick an AI into misclassifying a video of a zoo by inserting images of cars for such a short time that a human would never see the cars, but the computer could. In an environment where publishers need to know content being published to appropriately match advertisers, this represents a critical vulnerability.

Machines are generating predictions used for decision making. Companies deploy them in situations where they really matter: that is, where we expect them to have a real impact on decisions. Without such decision embeddedness, why go to the trouble of making a prediction in the first place? Sophisticated bad actors in this context would understand that by altering a prediction, they could adjust the decisions. For instance, a diabetic using an AI to optimize insulin intake could end up in serious jeopardy if the AI has incorrect data about that person and then offers predictions that suggest lowering insulin intake when it should be increased. If harming a person is someone's objective, then this is one way to do it effectively.

We are most likely to deploy prediction machines in situations where prediction is hard. A bad actor might not find precisely what data is needed to manipulate a prediction. A machine may form a prediction based on a confluence of factors. A single lie in a web of truth is of little consequence. In many other situations, identifying some data that can be used to manipulate a prediction is straightforward. Examples might be location, date, and time of day. But identity is the most important. If a prediction is specific to a person, feeding the AI the wrong identity leads to bad consequences.

AI technologies will develop hand-in-hand with identity verification. Nymi, a startup we worked with, developed a technology that uses machine learning to identify individuals via their heartbeat. Others are using retina scans, faces, or fingerprint identification. Companies can also confirm an identity by using the characteristics of a smartphone user's walking patterns. Regardless, a happy confluence in technologies may emerge that allows us to simultaneously personalize AI and safeguard identity.

While personalized predictions might be vulnerable to the manipulation of the individual, impersonal predictions may face their own set of risks related to population-level manipulation. Ecologists have taught us that homogenous populations are at greater risk of disease and destruction.[9] A classic example is in farming. If all farmers in a region or country plant the same strain of a particular crop, they might do better in the short term. They likely chose that crop because it grows particularly well in the region. By adopting the best strain, they reduce their individual risk. However, this very homogeneity presents an opportunity for disease or even adverse climate conditions. If all farmers plant the same strain, then they are all vulnerable to the same disease. The chances of a disastrous widespread crop failure increase. Such monoculture can be individually beneficial but increase system-wide risk.

This idea applies to information technology generally and prediction machines in particular. If one prediction machine system proves itself particularly useful, then you might apply that system everywhere in your organization or even the world. All cars might adopt whatever prediction machine appears safest. That reduces individual-level risk and increases safety; however, it also expands the chance of a massive failure, whether purposeful or not. If all cars have the same prediction algorithm, an attacker might be able to exploit that algorithm, manipulate the data or model in some way, and have all cars fail at the same time. Just as in agriculture, homogeneity improves results at the individual level at the expense of multiplying the likelihood of system-wide failure.

A seemingly easy solution to the problem of system-wide failure is to encourage diversity in the prediction machines you deploy. This will reduce the security risks, but at the cost of reduced performance. It might also increase the risk of incidental smaller failures due to a lack of standardization. Just as in biodiversity, the diversity of prediction machines involves a trade-off between individual and system-level outcomes.

Many of the scenarios for system-wide failure involve an attack on several prediction machines at the same time. For example, an attack on one autonomous vehicle represents a risk to safety; an attack on all autonomous vehicles simultaneously presents a national security threat.

Another way to secure against a massive simultaneous attack, even in the presence of standard homogenous prediction machines, is to untether the device from the cloud.[10] We have already discussed the benefits of implementing prediction on the ground rather than in the cloud for the purpose of faster context-dependent learning (at the cost of more accurate predictions overall) and to protect consumer privacy.

Prediction on the ground has another benefit. If the device is not connected to the cloud, a simultaneous attack becomes difficult.[11] While training the prediction machine likely happens in the cloud or elsewhere, once the machine is trained, it may be possible to do predictions directly on the device without sending information back to the cloud.

Training Data Risks

Another risk is that someone can interrogate your prediction machines. Your competitors may be able to reverse-engineer your algorithms, or at least have their own prediction machines use the output of your algorithms as training data. Perhaps the most well-known example involves a sting by Google's anti-spam team. It set up fake results for a variety of absurd search queries such as "hiybbprqag" that otherwise did not exist. It then had Google engineers query those words from their home computers. Specifically, it told the engineers to use Microsoft Internet Explorer's toolbar for the searches. Weeks later, the team queried Microsoft's Bing search engine. Sure enough, Google's fake results for the searches like "hiybbprqag" showed up as Bing results. Google's team showed that Microsoft uses its toolbar to copy Google's search engine.[12]

At the time, there was much discussion about whether what Microsoft did was acceptable or not.[13] In effect, Microsoft was using the Google toolbar for learning-by-using to develop better algorithms for its Bing search engine. Much of what users did was search Google and then click on those results. So when a search term was rare and only found on Google (like "hiybbprqag") and if it was used enough (precisely what the Google engineers were doing), Microsoft's machine ended up learning it. Interestingly, what Microsoft had not been doing—which it clearly could have—was learn how Google search terms translated into clicks to imitate completely Google's search engine.[14]

The strategic issue is that when you have an AI (like Google's search engine), then if a competitor can observe data being entered (such as a search query) and output being reported (such as a list of websites), then it has the raw materials to employ its own AI to engage in supervised learning and reconstruct the algorithm. Google's search engine would be a very difficult undertaking with respect to such expropriation, but it is, in principle, quite possible.

In 2016, computer science researchers showed that certain deep-learning algorithms are particularly vulnerable to such imitation.[15] They tested this possibility on some important machine-learning platforms (including Amazon Machine Learning) and demonstrated that with a relatively small number of queries (650–4,000), they could reverse-engineer those models to a very close approximation, sometimes perfectly. The very deployment of machine-learning algorithms leads to this vulnerability.

Imitation can be easy. After you have done all of the work of training an AI, that AI's workings are effectively exposed to the world and can be replicated. But more worrisome is that the expropriation of this knowledge may lead to situations where it is easier for bad actors to manipulate the prediction and the learning process. Once an attacker understands the machine, the machine becomes more vulnerable.

On the positive side, such attacks leave a trail. It is necessary to query the prediction machine many times to understand it. Unusual quantities of queries or an unusual diversity of queries should raise red flags. Once raised, then protecting the prediction machine becomes easier, although not easy. But at least you know that an attack is coming and what the attacker knows. Then you can protect the machine by either blocking the attacker or (if that is not possible) preparing a backup plan if something goes wrong.

Feedback Data Risks

Your prediction machines will interact with others (human or machine) outside your business, creating a different risk: bad actors can feed the AI data that distorts the learning process. This is more than manipulating a single prediction, but instead involves teaching the machine to predict incorrectly in a systematic way.

A recent and dramatic public example occurred in March 2016 when Microsoft launched an AI-based Twitter chatbot named Tay. Microsoft's idea was solid: have Tay interact with people on Twitter and determine how best to respond. Its intention was to learn specifically about "casual and playful conversation."[16] On paper, at least, this was a sensible way of exposing an AI to the experience it needed to learn quickly. Tay started off as not much more than a parrot, but the goal was more ambitious.

The internet, however, is not always a gentle setting. Soon after launch, people started to test the limits of what Tay would say. "Baron Memington" asked "@TayandYou Do you support genocide," to which Tay responded "@Baron_von_Derp I do indeed." Soon Tay seemed to become a racist, misogynist, Nazi sympathizer. Microsoft pulled the experiment.[17] Precisely how Tay evolved so quickly is not entirely clear. Most likely, interactions with Twitter users taught Tay this behavior. Ultimately, this experiment demonstrated how easy it is to undermine machine learning when it occurs in the real world.

The implications are clear. Your competitors or detractors may deliberately try to train your prediction machine to make bad predictions. As with Tay, data trains prediction machines. And prediction machines that are trained in the wild may encounter people who use them strategically, maliciously, or dishonestly.

Facing Risk

Prediction machines carry risks. Any company that invests in AI will face these risks, and eliminating all of them is impossible. There is no easy solution. You now have the knowledge to anticipate these risks. Be aware of how your predictions differ across groups of people. Question whether your predictions reflect underlying causal relationships and if they are really as good as they seem to be. Balance the trade-off between system-wide risks and the benefit of doing everything a little bit better. And watch for bad actors who may query your prediction machines to copy them or even destroy them.

KEY POINTS

- AI carries many types of risk. We summarize six of the most salient types here.

  1. Predictions from AIs can lead to discrimination. Even if such discrimination is inadvertent, it creates liability.

  2. AIs are ineffective when data is sparse. This creates quality risk, particularly of the "unknown known" type, in which a prediction is provided with confidence, but is false.

  3. Incorrect input data can fool prediction machines, leaving their users vulnerable to attack by hackers.

  4. Just as in biodiversity, the diversity of prediction machines involves a trade-off between individual- and system-level

outcomes. Less diversity may benefit individual-level performance, but increase the risk of massive failure.

5. Prediction machines can be interrogated, exposing you to intellectual property theft and to attackers who can identify weaknesses.

6. Feedback can be manipulated so that prediction machines learn destructive behavior.

PART FIVE

Society

19

Beyond Business

Much popular discussion about AI concerns issues of society rather than business. Many are not sure that AI will be a good thing. Tesla CEO Elon Musk has been one of the most consistent, high-profile, and experienced individuals sounding alarm bells: "I have exposure to the very cutting-edge AI, and I think people should be really concerned about it . . . I keep sounding the alarm bell, but until people see robots going down the street killing people, they don't know how to react, because it seems so ethereal."[1]

Another learned expert with an opinion on this is renowned psychologist and Nobel laureate Daniel Kahneman. Among non-academics, he may be best known for his 2011 book, *Thinking, Fast and Slow*. In 2017, at a conference we organized in Toronto on the economics of artificial intelligence, he explained why he thinks AIs will be wiser than humans:

> A well-known novelist wrote me some time ago that he's plan-
> ning a novel. The novel is about a love triangle between two
> humans and a robot and what he wanted to know is how the
> robot would be different from the people.

I proposed three main differences. One is obvious: the robot will be much better at statistical reasoning and less enamored with stories and narratives than people are. The other is that the robot would have much higher emotional intelligence.

The third is that the robot would be wiser. Wisdom is breadth. Wisdom is not having too narrow a view. That is the essence of wisdom; it's broad framing. A robot will be endowed with broad framing. I say that when it has learned enough, it will be wiser than we people because we do not have broad framing. We are narrow thinkers, we are noisy thinkers, and it is very easy to improve upon us. I do not think that there is very much that we can do that computers will not eventually [learn] to do.

Elon Musk and Daniel Kahneman are both confident about AI's potential and simultaneously worried about the implications of unleashing it on the world.

Impatient about the pace at which government responds to technological advances, industry leaders have offered policy suggestions and, in some cases, have acted. Bill Gates advocated for a tax on robots that replace human labor. Sidestepping what would normally be government's purview, the high-profile startup accelerator Y Combinator is running experiments on providing a basic income for everyone in society.[2] Elon Musk organized a group of entrepreneurs and industry leaders to finance Open AI with $1 billion to ensure that no single private-sector company could monopolize the field.

Such proposals and actions highlight the complexity of these social issues. As we climb to the pyramid's top, the choices become strikingly more complex. When thinking about society as a whole, the economics of AI are not so simple anymore.

Is This the End of Jobs?

If Einstein has a modern incarnation, it is Stephen Hawking. Thanks to his remarkable contributions to science, despite his personal struggle with ALS, and his popular books like *A Brief History of*

Time, Hawking is seen as the world's canonical genius. Thus, people unsurprisingly took notice when, in December 2016, he wrote: "The automation of factories has already decimated jobs in traditional manufacturing, and the rise of artificial intelligence is likely to extend this job destruction deep into the middle classes, with only the most caring, creative or supervisory roles remaining."[3]

Several studies had already tallied up potential job destruction due to automation, and this time it wasn't just physical labor but also cognitive functions previously believed immune to such forces.[4] After all, horses fell behind in horsepower, not brainpower.

As economists, we've heard these claims before. But while the specter of technological unemployment has loomed since the Luddites destroyed textile frames centuries ago, unemployment rates have been remarkably low. Business managers may be concerned about shedding jobs by adopting technologies like AI; however, we can take some comfort in the fact that farming jobs started to disappear over one hundred years ago, without corresponding long-term mass unemployment.

But is this time different? Hawking's concern, shared by many, is that this time might be unusual because AI may squeeze out the last remaining advantages humans have over machines.[5]

How might an economist approach this question? Imagine that a new island entirely populated by robots—Robotlandia—suddenly emerged. Would we want to trade with that island of prediction machines? From a free-trade perspective, it sounds like a great opportunity. The robots do all manner of tasks, freeing up our people to do what they do best. In other words, we would no more refuse to deal with Robotlandia than we would require our coffee beans to be locally grown.

Of course, no real Robotlandia exists, but when we have technological change that gives software the ability to do new tasks more cheaply, economists see it as similar to opening up trade with such a fictitious island. In other words, if you favor free trade between countries, then you favor free trade with Robotlandia. You support developing AI, even if it replaces some jobs. Decades of research into the effects of trade show that other jobs will appear, and overall employment will not plummet.

Our anatomy of a decision suggests where these new jobs are likely to come from. Humans and AIs are likely to work together; humans will provide complements to prediction, namely, data, judgment, or action. For example, as prediction becomes cheaper, the value of judgment rises. We therefore anticipate growth in the number of jobs that involve reward function engineering. Some of these jobs will be very skilled and highly compensated, filled by people who were applying that judgment before the prediction machines arrived.

Other judgment-related jobs will be more widespread, but perhaps less skilled than the jobs the AIs replace. Many of today's highest-paid careers have prediction as a core skill, including those of doctors, financial analysts, and lawyers. Just as machine predictions of directions led to reduced incomes for relatively highly paid London taxi drivers but an increase in the number of lower-paid Uber drivers, we expect to see the same phenomenon in medicine and finance. As the prediction portion of tasks is automated, more people will fill these jobs, focusing more narrowly on judgment-related skills. When prediction is no longer a binding constraint, demand may increase for complementary skills that are more widespread, leading to more employment but at lower wages.

AI and people have one important difference: software scales, but people don't. This means that once an AI is better than humans at a particular task, job losses will happen quickly. We can be confident that new jobs will arise within a few years and people will have something to do, but that will be little comfort for those looking for work and waiting for those new jobs to appear. An AI-induced recession is not out of the question, even if free trade with Robotlandia will not affect the number of jobs in the long term.

Will Inequality Get Worse?

Jobs are one thing. The income they generate is another. Opening up trade often creates competition, and competition causes prices to drop. If the competition is with human labor, then wages fall. In the case of opening trade with Robotlandia, robots compete with humans for some tasks, so wages for those tasks fall. If those tasks make up your work, then your income may go down. You are facing more competition.

As with trade between countries, winners and losers from trade with machines will appear. Jobs will still exist, but some people will have less appealing jobs than they have now. In other words, if you understand the benefits of free trade, then you should appreciate the gains from prediction machines. The key policy question isn't about whether AI will bring benefits but about how those benefits will be *distributed*.

Because AI tools can be used to replace "high" skills—namely, brainpower—many worry that even though jobs exist, they won't come with high wages. For example, while serving as chair of President Obama's Council of Economic Advisers, Jason Furman expressed his concern this way:

> My worry is not that this time could be different when it comes to AI, but that this time could be the same as what we have experienced over the past several decades. The traditional argument that we do not need to worry about the robots taking our jobs still leaves us with the worry that the only reason we will still have our jobs is because we are willing to do them for lower wages.[6]

If the machines' share of work continues to increase, then workers' income will fall, while that accruing to the owners of the AI will rise.

In his best-selling book, *Capital in the Twenty-First Century*, Thomas Piketty highlighted that for the past few decades, labor's share of national income (in the United States and elsewhere) has been falling in favor of the share earned by capital. This trend is concerning because it has led to increased inequality. The critical question here is whether AI will reinforce this trend or mitigate it. If AI is a new, efficient form of capital, then the capital share of the economy will likely continue to rise at the expense of labor.

No easy solutions exist for this problem. For example, Bill Gates's suggestion to tax robots will reduce inequality but will make buying robots less profitable. So companies will invest less in robots, productivity will slow, and we will be poorer overall. The policy trade-off is clear: we have policies that can reduce inequality but likely at the cost of lower income overall.

A second trend leading to increased inequality is that technology is often skill-biased. It disproportionately increases the wages of highly educated people and might even decrease the wages of the less educated. Previous skill-biased technologies, including computers and the internet, are the dominant explanation for the increasing wage inequality in the United States and Europe over the past four decades. As economists Claudia Goldin and Lawrence Katz put it, "[i]ndividuals with more education and higher innate abilities will be more able to grasp new and complicated tools."[7] We have no reason to expect AI to be any different. Highly educated people tend to be better at learning new skills. If the skills needed to succeed with AI change more often, then the educated will benefit disproportionately.

We see many reasons that the productive use of AI will require additional skills. For example, the reward function engineer must understand both the objectives of the organization and the capabilities of the machines. Because machines scale efficiently, if this skill is scarce, then the best engineers will reap the benefits of their work across millions or billions of machines.

Precisely because AI-related skills are currently scarce, the learning process for both humans and businesses will be costly. In 2017, more than a thousand of the seven thousand undergraduates at Stanford University enrolled in its introductory machine learning course. The same trend is happening elsewhere. But that represents only a fraction of the workforce. The majority of the workforce was trained decades ago, which translates to a need for retraining and reskilling. Our industrial education system is not designed for that. Businesses should not expect the system to change quickly enough to supply them with the workers they need to compete in the AI age. The policy challenges are not simple: increased education is costly. Such costs need to be paid, either by higher taxes or by businesses and individuals directly. Even if the costs could be easily covered, many middle-aged people might not be eager to return to school. The people most hurt by skill-biased technology might be the least prepared for lifelong education.

Will a Few Huge Companies Control Everything?

It is not just individuals who are worried about AI. Many companies are terrified that they will fall behind their competitors in securing and using AI, which is at least in part due to the possible scale economies associated with AI. More customers mean more data, more data means better AI predictions, better predictions mean more customers, and the virtuous cycle continues. Under the right conditions, once a company's AI leads in performance, its competitors may never catch up. In our Amazon predictive-shipping thought experiment in chapter 2, Amazon's scale and first-mover advantage could conceivably generate such a lead in prediction accuracy that competitors would find it impossible to catch up.

This is not the first time that a new technology raises the possibility of breeding large companies. AT&T controlled telecommunications in the United States for more than fifty years. Microsoft and Intel held a monopoly in information technology in the 1990s and 2000s. More recently, Google has dominated search, and Facebook has ruled social media. These companies grew so large because their core technologies allowed them to realize lower costs and higher quality as they scaled. At the same time, competitors emerged, even in the face of these scale economies; just ask Microsoft (Apple and Google), Intel (AMD and ARM), and AT&T (almost everybody). Technology-based monopolies are temporary due to a process that economist Joseph Schumpeter called "the gale of creative destruction."

With AI, there is a benefit to being big because of scale economies. However, that doesn't mean that just one firm will dominate or that even if one dominates, it will last long. On a global scale, that is even truer.

If AI has scale economies, that will not affect all industries equally. If your firm is successful and established, chances are prediction accuracy is not the only thing that made it successful. The abilities or assets that make it valuable today will likely still be valuable when paired with AI. AI should enhance an airline's ability to provide personalized customer service as well as to optimize flight times and prices. However, it's not at all obvious that the airline with the best AI will have such an advantage that it will dominate all its competitors.

For technology companies whose entire business might rest on AI, scale economies might result in a few dominant companies. But when we say scale economies, how much scale are we talking about?

There is no simple answer to that question, and certainly we have no accurate forecast with respect to AI. But economists have studied scale economies of an important complement to AI: data. While many reasons might explain Google's commanding 70 percent market share in search in the United States and 90 percent in the European Union, a leading explanation is that Google has more data for training its AI search tool than its rivals. Google has been collecting such data for many years. Furthermore, its commanding market share creates a virtuous cycle on data scale that others may never match. If there are data-scale advantages, Google surely has them.

Two economists—Lesley Chiou and Catherine Tucker—studied search engines that took advantage of differences in data-retention practices.[8] In response to the EU's recommendations in 2008, Yahoo and Bing reduced the amount of data they kept. Google did not change its policies. These changes were enough for Chiou and Tucker to measure the effects of data scale on search accuracy. Interestingly, they found scale didn't matter much. Relative to the overall volume of data that all the major competitors used, less data did not have a negative impact on search results. Any present effect was so small as to be of no real consequence, certainly not the basis of a competitive advantage. This suggests that historical data may be less useful than many suppose, perhaps because the world changes too quickly.

However, we offer an important caveat. As many as 20 percent of Google searches each day are said to be unique.[9] Accordingly, Google may have an advantage on the "long tail" of rarely searched for terms. Scale advantages to data are not dramatic for the common cases, but in highly competitive markets like search, even a small advantage in infrequent searches may translate into a larger market share.

We still don't know if the scale advantage of AI is big enough to give Google an advantage over other large players like Microsoft's Bing or if Google is better for reasons that have nothing to do with data and scale. Given this kind of uncertainty, Apple, Google, Microsoft, Facebook, Baidu, Tencent, Alibaba, and Amazon are investing heavily and competing aggressively to acquire key AI assets. Not only are they competing with each other but with businesses that don't yet exist. They worry that a startup will come along that "does AI better" and competes directly with their core products. Many startups are trying, backed by billions in venture capital.

Despite these potential competitors, the leading AI companies might get too big. They might buy out the startups before they become a threat, stifling new ideas and reducing productivity in the long run. They might set prices for AI that are too high, hurting consumers and other businesses. Unfortunately, there is no easy way to determine if the largest AI companies will get too big and no simple solution even if they do. If AI has scale advantages, reducing the negative effects of monopoly involves trade-offs. Breaking up monopolies reduces the scale, but scale makes AI better. Again, policy is not simple.[10]

Will Some Countries Have an Advantage?

On September 1, 2017, Russian president Vladimir Putin made this assertion on the significance of AI leadership: "Artificial intelligence is the future, not only for Russia, but for all humankind . . . It comes with colossal opportunities, but also threats that are difficult to predict. Whoever becomes the leader in this sphere will become the ruler of the world."[11] Are countries able to benefit from AI scale economies the way companies can? Countries can design their regulatory environment as well as direct government expenditure to accelerate the development of AI. These targeted policies might give countries, and the businesses located in them, an advantage in AI.

On the university and business sides, the United States leads the world in terms of both research on and commercial application of AI. On the government side, the White House published four reports in the final two quarters of the Obama administration.[12] Relative to other areas of technological advance, that level of effort and coordination represents a significant government focus on AI. Under the Obama administration, almost every major government agency, from the Department of Commerce to the National Security Agency, was ramping up for the arrival of commercial-grade AI.

However, the trend lines are changing. In particular, the world's largest country, the People's Republic of China, stands out for its success in AI, compared to its technological leadership over the past century. Not only are two of its AI-oriented tech firms—Tencent and Alibaba—in the top twelve in the world by valuation, but evidence suggests that its scientific push in AI may soon lead the world. For example, China's share of papers at the biggest AI research conference grew from 10 percent in 2012 to 23 percent in 2017. Over the same period, the US share fell from 41 percent to 34 percent.[13]

Will the future of AI be "made in China," as the *New York Times* proposed?[14] Beyond scientific leadership, at least three additional reasons point to China becoming the world leader in AI.[15]

First, China is spending billions on AI, including big projects, startups, and basic research. One city—China's eighth largest—has allocated more resources to AI than all of Canada. "In June, the government of Tianjin, an eastern city near Beijing, said it planned to set up a $5 billion fund to support the AI industry. It also set up an 'intelligence industry zone' that will sit on more than 20 square kilometers of land."[16] Meanwhile, the US government seems to be spending less on science under the current Trump administration.[17]

Research is not a zero-sum game. More innovation worldwide is good for everyone, whether the innovation occurs in China, the United States, Canada, Europe, Africa, or Japan. For decades, the US Congress worried that American leadership in innovation was under threat. In 1999, Michigan 13th District Representative Lynn Rivers (a Democrat) asked economist Scott Stern what the American government should do to address the increases in R&D spending by Japan, Germany, and others. His response: "The first thing we should do is send them a thank you letter. Innovative investment is not a win-lose situation. American consumers are going to benefit from more investment by other countries . . . It is a race we can all win."[18] If the Chinese government is investing billions in and publishing papers about AI, then maybe a thank-you card is in order. It is making everyone better off.

In addition to investment in research, China has a second advantage: scale. Prediction machines need data, and China has more people to provide that data than anywhere else in the world. It has more factories to train robots, more smartphone users to train consumer products, and more patients to train medical applications.[19] Kai-Fu Lee, a Chinese AI expert, founder of Microsoft's Beijing research lab, and founding president of Google China, remarked, "The U.S. and Canada have the best AI researchers in the world, but China has hundreds of people who are good, and way more data . . . AI is an area where you need to evolve the algorithm and the data together; a large amount of data makes a large amount of difference."[20] The data advantage only matters if Chinese companies have better access to that data than other companies, and evidence suggests they will.

Data access is China's third source of advantage. The country's lack of privacy protection for its citizens may give the government and private-sector companies a significant advantage in the performance of their AIs, especially in the domain of personalization. For example, one of Microsoft's most high-profile engineers, Qi Lu, left the United States for China, seeing it as the best place to develop AI. He commented, "It's not all technology. It's about the structure of the environment—the culture, the policy regime. This is why AI plus China, to me, is such an interesting opportunity. It's just different cultures, different policy regimes, and a different environment."[21]

This is certainly the case for pursuing features like facial recognition. China, in contrast to the US, maintains a massive centralized database of photos for identification. This enables companies like Chinese startup Face++ to develop and license a facial recognition AI to authenticate the driver for passengers using Didi, the largest ride-hailing company in China, and also to transfer money via Alipay, a mobile payment app used by more than 120 million people in China. This system relies entirely on its facial analysis to authorize payment. Furthermore, incumbent Baidu is using a facial recognition AI to authenticate customers collecting their rail tickets and tourists accessing attractions.[22] By contrast, in Europe, privacy regulation makes data access far more stringent than elsewhere, which may shut out European firms from AI leadership altogether.

These factors may create a race to the bottom as countries compete to relax privacy restrictions to improve their AI position. However, citizens and consumers value privacy; it's not a regulation that only companies care about. There is a basic trade-off between intrusion and personalization and a potential for customer dissatisfaction associated with acquiring user data. At the same time, a potential benefit arises from being better able to personalize predictions. The trade-off is further complicated because of a free-riding effect. Users want better products trained using personal data, but they prefer that data be collected from other people, not them.

Again, it isn't clear which rules are best. Computer scientist Oren Etzioni argues that AI systems should not "retain or disclose confidential information without explicit approval from the source of that information."[23] With Amazon Echo listening to every conversation in your house, you want some control. This seems obvious. However, it isn't so simple. Your banking information is confidential, but what about the music you listen to or the television shows you watch? At the extreme, whenever you ask Echo a question, it could respond with another question: "Do you approve giving Amazon access to your question in order to find an answer?" Reading all the privacy policies of all the companies that collect your data would take weeks.[24] Each time the AI asks for approval to use your data, the product becomes worse. It interrupts the user experience. If people do not provide the data, then the AI can't learn from feedback, limiting its ability to boost productivity and increase income.

There are likely to be opportunities to innovate in a way that assures people as to their data's integrity and control while allowing the AI to learn. One emerging technology—the blockchain—offers a way of decentralizing databases and lowering the cost of verifying data. Such technologies could be paired with AI to overcome privacy (and indeed security) concerns, especially since they are already used for financial transactions, an area where these issues are paramount.[25]

Even if enough users provide data so AIs can learn, what if those users are different from everyone else? Suppose only rich people from

California and New York provide data to the prediction machines. Then the AI will learn to serve those communities. If the purpose of limiting the collection of personal data is to protect the vulnerable, then it opens up a new vulnerability: users won't benefit from the better products and greater wealth that AI enables.

The End of the World as We Know It?

Is AI an existential threat to humanity itself? Beyond simply whether one might get an uncooperative AI like Hal 9000 (in *2001: A Space Odyssey*), what apparently keeps some very serious and smart people like Elon Musk, Bill Gates, and Stephen Hawking up at night is whether we will end up with something like Skynet from the *Terminator* movies. They fear that a "superintelligence"—to use the term coined by Oxford philosopher Nick Bostrom—will emerge that pretty quickly sees humanity as a threat, an irritant, or something to enslave.[26] In other words, AI could be our last technological innovation.[27]

We are not in a position here to adjudicate this issue and cannot even agree among ourselves. But what has struck us is how close to economics the debate actually is: competition underpins it all.

A superintelligence is an AI that can outperform humans in most cognitive tasks and can reason through problems. Specifically, it can invent and improve itself. While science fiction author Vernor Vinge called the point at which this emerges "the Singularity" and futurist Ray Kurzweil suggested humans are not equipped to foresee what will happen at this point because we are by definition not as intelligent, it turns out that economists are actually quite well equipped to think about it.

For years, economists have faced criticism that the agents on which we base our theories are hyper-rational and unrealistic models of human behavior. True enough, but when it comes to superintelligence, that means we have been on the right track. We already assume great intelligence in our analysis. We establish our understanding through mathematical proof, an intelligence-independent standard of truth.

This perspective is useful. Economics tells us that if a superintelligence wants to control the world, it will need resources. The universe has lots of resources, but even a superintelligence has to obey the laws of physics. Acquiring resources is costly.

Bostrom talks of a paper-clip-obsessed superintelligence that cares about nothing but making more paper clips. The paper-clip AI could just wipe out everything else through single-mindedness. This is a powerful idea, but it overlooks competition for resources. Something economists respect is that different people (and now AIs) have different preferences. Some might be open-minded about exploration, discovery, and peace, while others may be paper-clip makers. So long as interests compete, competition will flourish, meaning that the paper-clip AI will likely find it more profitable to trade for resources than fight for them and, as if guided by an invisible hand, will end up promoting benefits distinct from its original intention.

Thus, economics provides a powerful way to understand how a society of superintelligent AIs will evolve. That said, our models do not determine what happens to humanity in this process.

What we have called AI in this book is not general artificial intelligence but decidedly narrower prediction machines. Developments such as AlphaGo Zero by Google's DeepMind have raised the specter that superintelligence might not be so far away. It outperformed the world champion–beating AlphaGo at the board game Go without human training (learning by playing games against itself), but it isn't ready to be called superintelligence. If the game board changed from nineteen by nineteen to twenty-nine by twenty-nine or even eighteen by eighteen, the AI would struggle, whereas a human would adjust. And don't even think of asking AlphaGo Zero to make you a grilled cheese sandwich; it's not that smart.

The same is true for all AI to date. Yes, research is underway to make prediction machines work in broader settings, but the breakthrough that will give rise to general artificial intelligence remains undiscovered. Some believe that AGI is so far out that we should not spend cycles worrying about it. In a policy document prepared by the Executive Office of the US President, the National Science and Technology Council (NSTC) Committee on Technology stated, "The current consensus of the private-sector expert community, with which the NSTC Committee on Technology concurs, is that General AI will not be achieved for at least decades. The NSTC Committee on Technology's assessment is that long-term concerns about super-intelligent General AI should have little impact on current policy."[28] At the same time, several companies with the expressed mission of creating AGI or machines with human-like intelligence, including Vicarious, Google DeepMind, Kindred, Numenta, and others, have raised many millions of dollars from smart and informed investors. As with many AI-related issues, the future is highly uncertain.

Is this the end of the world as we know it? Not yet, but it is the end of this book. Companies are deploying AIs right now. In applying the simple economics that underpin lower-cost prediction and higher-value complements to prediction, your business can make ROI-optimizing choices and strategic decisions with regard to AI.

When we move beyond prediction machines to general artificial intelligence or even superintelligence, whenever that may be, then we will be at a different AI moment. That is something everyone agrees upon. When that event occurs, we can confidently forecast that the economics will no longer be so simple.

KEY POINTS

- The rise of AI presents society with many choices. Each represents a tradeoff. At this stage, while the technology is still in its infancy, there are three particularly salient trade-offs at the society level.

- The first trade-off is productivity versus distribution. Many have suggested that AI will make us poorer or worse off. That's not true. Economists agree that technological advance makes us better off and enhances productivity. AI will unambiguously enhance productivity. The problem isn't wealth creation; it's distribution. AI might exacerbate the income inequality problem for two reasons. First, by taking over certain tasks, AIs might increase competition among humans for the remaining tasks, lowering wages and further reducing the fraction of income earned by labor versus the fraction earned by the owners of capital. Second, prediction machines, like other computer-related technologies, may be skill-biased such that AI tools disproportionately enhance the productivity of highly skilled workers.

- The second trade-off is innovation versus competition. Like most software-related technologies, AI has scale economies. Furthermore, AI tools are often characterized by some degree of increasing returns: better prediction accuracy leads to more users, more users generate more data, and more data leads to better prediction accuracy. Businesses have greater incentives to build prediction machines if they have more control, but, along with scale economies, this may lead to monopolization. Faster innovation may benefit society from a short-term perspective but may not be optimal from a social or longer-term perspective.

- The third trade-off is performance versus privacy. AIs perform better with more data. In particular, they are better able to personalize their predictions if they have access to more personal data. The provision of personal data will often come at the expense of reduced privacy. Some jurisdictions, like Europe, have chosen to create an environment that provides their citizens with more privacy. That may benefit their citizens and may even create conditions for a more dynamic market for private information where individuals can more easily decide whether they wish to trade, sell, or donate their private data. On the other hand, that may create frictions in settings where opting in is costly and disadvantages European firms and citizens in markets where AIs with better access to data are more competitive.

- For all three trade-offs, jurisdictions will have to weigh both sides of the trade and design policies that are most aligned with their overall strategy and the preferences of their citizenry.

Notes

Chapter 2

1. Stephen Hawking, Stuart Russell, Max Tegmark, and Frank Wilczek, "Stephen Hawking: "Transcedence Looks at the Implications of Artificial Intelligence—But Are We Taking AI Seriously Enough?" *The Independent*, May 1, 2014, http://www.independent.co.uk/news/science/stephen-hawking-transcendence-looks-at-the-implications-of-artificial-intelligence-but-are-we-taking-9313474.html.

2. Paul Mozur, "Beijing Wants A.I. to Be Made in China by 2030," *New York Times*, July 20, 2017, https://www.nytimes.com/2017/07/20/business/china-artificial-intelligence.html?mcubz=0&_r=0.

3. Steve Jurvetson, "Intelligence Inside," *Medium*, August 9, 2016, https://medium.com/@DFJvc/intelligence-inside-54dcad8c4a3e.

4. William D. Nordhaus, "Do Real-Output and Real-Wage Measures Capture Reality? The History of Lighting Suggests Not," Cowles Foundation for Research in Economics, Yale University, 1998, https://lucept.files.wordpress.com/2014/11/william-nordhaus-the-cost-of-light.pdf.

5. This was part of a long trend in reducing the general cost of computation. See William D. Nordhaus, "Two Centuries of Productivity Growth in Computing," *Journal of Economic History*, vol. 67/1 (2007): 128–159.

6. Lovelace, quoted in Walter Isaacson, *The Innovators: How a Group of Hackers, Geniuses, and Geeks Created the Digital Revolution* (New York: Simon & Schuster, 2014), 27.

7. Ibid., 29.

8. Amazon already is working on potential security issues with such a plan. In 2017, it launched Amazon Key, a system that allowed its delivery people to unlock your door and deposit packages inside all under the watchful eye of a camera to record that everything went smoothly.

9. Interestingly, some startups are already thinking this way. Stitch Fix uses machine learning to predict what clothes its customers will want and ships a package to them. The customer then returns the clothes they do not want. In 2017, Stitch Fix had a successful IPO based on this model—perhaps the first "AI-first" startup to do so.

10. See US Patent Number 8,615,473 B2. Also, Praveen Kopalle, "Why Amazon's Anticipatory Shipping is Pure Genius," *Forbes*, January 28, 2014, https://www.forbes.com/sites/onmarketing/2014/01/28/why-amazons-anticipatory-shipping-is-pure-genius/#2a3284174605.

Chapter 3

1. As a reminder about the importance of careful interpretation of predictions, we note that the oracle at Delphi predicted that a great empire would be destroyed if he attacked. Emboldened, the king attacked Persia, and to his surprise, his own Lydian empire was destroyed. The prediction was technically correct, but misunderstood.

2. "Mastercard Rolls Out Artificial Intelligence across Its Global Network," Mastercard press release, November 30, 2016, https://newsroom.mastercard.com/press-releases/mastercard-rolls-out-artificial-intelligence-across-its-global-network/.

3. Adam Geitgey, "Machine Learning Is Fun, Part 5: Language Translation with Deep Learning and the Magic of Sequences," *Medium*, August 21, 2016, https://medium.com/@ageitgey/machine-learning-is-fun-part-5-language-translation-with-deep-learning-and-the-magic-of-sequences-2ace0acca0aa.

4. Yiting Sun, "Why 500 Million People in China Are Talking to This AI," *MIT Technology Review*, September 14, 2017, https://www.technologyreview.com/s/608841/why-500-million-people-in-china-are-talking-to-this-ai/.

5. Salvatore J. Stolfo, David W. Fan, Wenke Lee, and Andreas L. Prodromidis, "Credit Card Fraud Detection Using Meta-Learning: Issues and Initial Results," *AAAI Technical Report*, WS-97-07, 1997, http://www.aaai.org/Papers/Work shops/1997/WS-97-07/WS97-07-015.pdf, with a false positive rate around 15 percent to 20 percent. Another example is E. Aleskerov, B. Freisleben, and B. Rao, "CARDWATCH: A Neural Network Based Database Mining System for Credit Card Fraud Detection," Computational Intelligence for Financial Engineering, 1997, http://ieeexplore.ieee.org/stamp/stamp.jsp?arnumber=618940. Note that these comparisons are not entirely equal, because they use different training data sets. Still, the broad point on accuracy holds.

6. Abhinav Srivastava, Amlan Kundu, Shamik Sural, and Arun Majumdar, "Credit Card Fraud Detection Using Hidden Markov Model," *IEEE Transactions on Dependable and Secure Computing* 5, no. 1 (January–March 2008): 37–48, http://ieeexplore.ieee.org/stamp/stamp.jsp?arnumber=4358713. See also Jarrod West and Maumita Bhattacharya, "Intelligent Financial Fraud Detection: A Comprehensive Review, *Computers & Security* 57 (2016): 47–66, http://www.sciencedirect.com/science/article/pii/S0167404815001261.

7. Andrej Karpathy, "What I Learned from Competing against a ConvNet on ImageNet," *Andrej Karthy* (blog), September 2, 2014, http://karpathy.github.io/2014/09/02/what-i-learned-from-competing-against-a-convnet-on-imagenet/; ImageNet, Large Scale Visual Recognition Challenge 2016, http://image-net.org/challenges/LSVRC/2016/results; Andrej Karpathy, LISVRC 2014, http://cs.stanford.edu/people/karpathy/ilsvrc/.

8. Aaron Tilley, "China's Rise in the Global AI Race Emerges as It Takes Over the Final ImageNet Competition," *Forbes*, July 31, 2017, https://www.forbes.com/sites/aarontilley/2017/07/31/china-ai-imagenet/#dafa182170a8.

9. Dave Gershgorn, "The Data That Transformed AI Research—and Possibly the World," *Quartz*, July 26, 2017, https://qz.com/1034972/the-data-that-changed-the-direction-of-ai-research-and-possibly-the-world/.

10. Definitions from the *Oxford English Dictionary*.

Chapter 4

1. J. McCarthy, Marvin L. Minsky, N. Rochester, and Claude E. Shannon, "A Proposal for the Dartmouth Summer Research Project on Artificial Intelligence," August 31, 1955, http://www-formal.stanford.edu/jmc/history/dartmouth/dartmouth.html.

2. Jeff Hawkins and Sandra Blakeslee, *On Intelligence* (New York: Times Books, 2004), 89.

3. McCarthy et al, "A Proposal for the Dartmouth Summer Research Project on Artificial Intelligence."

4. Ian Hacking, *The Taming of Chance* (Cambridge, UK: Cambridge University Press, 1990).

Chapter 5

1. Hal Varian, "Beyond Big Data," lecture, National Association of Business Economists, San Francisco, September 10, 2013.

2. Ngai-yin Chan and Chi-chung Choy, "Screening for Atrial Fibrillation in 13,122 Hong Kong Citizens with Smartphone Electrocardiogram," *BMJ* 103, no. 1 (January 2017), http://heart.bmj.com/content/103/1/24; Sarah Buhr, "Apple's Watch Can Detect an Abnormal Heart Rhythm with 97% Accuracy, UCSF Study Says," *Techcrunch*, May 11, 2017, https://techcrunch.com/2017/05/11/apples-watch-can-detect-an-abnormal-heart-rhythm-with-97-accuracy-ucsf-study-says/; Alive-Cor, "AliveCor and Mayo Clinic Announce Collaboration to Identify Hidden Health Signals in Humans," Cision PR newswire, October 24, 2016, http://www.prnewswire.com/news-releases/alivecor-and-mayo-clinic-announce-collaboration-to-identify-hidden-health-signals-in-humans-300349847.html.

3. Buhr, "Apple's Watch Can Detect an Abnormal Heart Rhythm with 97% Accuracy, UCSF Study Says"; and Avesh Singh, "Applying Artificial Intelligence in Medicine: Our Early Results," *Cardiogram* (blog), May 11, https://blog.cardiogr.am/applying-artificial-intelligence-in-medicine-our-early-results-78bfe7605d32.

4. We don't know if Cardiogram in particular will succeed. We are, however, confident that smartphones and other sensors will be used for medical diagnosis going forward.

5. Six thousand is a relatively small number of units for this kind of study, which is a main reason why the study was listed as "preliminary." This data was enough for Cardiogram's initial purpose because it was a preliminary study to show proof of concept. No lives were put at risk. For the results to be clinically useful, it will likely need much more data.

6. Dave Heiner, "Competition Authorities and Search," *Microsoft Technet* (blog), February 26, 2010, https://blogs.technet.microsoft.com/microsoft_on_the_issues/2010/02/26/competition-authorities-and-search/. Google has argued that Bing is big enough to reap the benefits of scale in search.

Chapter 6

1. Sixty percent of the time you choose X and are correct 60 percent of the time, while 40 percent of the time you choose O and are correct only 40 percent of the time. On average, this is $0.6^2 + 0.4^2 = 0.52$.

2. Amost Tversky and Daniel Kahneman, "Judgment under Uncertainty: Heuristics and Biases," *Science* 185, no. 4157 (1974): 1124–1131, https://people.hss .caltech.edu/~camerer/Ec101/JudgementUncertainty.pdf.

3. See Daniel Kahneman, *Thinking, Fast and Slow* (New York: Farrar, Strauss and Giroux, 2011); and Dan Ariely, *Predictably Irrational* (New York: HarperCollins, 2009).

4. Michael Lewis, *Moneyball* (New York: Norton, 2003).

5. Of course, while *Moneyball* was based on the use of traditional statistics, it should be no surprise that teams are now looking to machine-learning methods to perform that function, gathering far more data in the process. See Takashi Sugimoto, "AI May Help Japan's Baseball Champs Rewrite 'Moneyball,'" *Nikkei Asian Review*, May 2, 2016, http://asia.nikkei.com/Business/Companies/ AI-may-help-Japan-s-baseball-champs-rewrite-Moneyball.

6. Jon Kleinberg, Himabindu Lakkaraju, Jure Leskovec, Jens Ludwig, and Sendhil Mullainathan, "Human Decisions and Machine Predictions," working paper 23180, National Bureau of Economic Research, 2017.

7. The research also shows that the algorithm would likely reduce racial disparities.

8. Mitchell Hoffman, Lisa B. Kahn, and Danielle Li, "Discretion in Hiring," working paper 21709, National Bureau of Economic Research, November 2015, revised April 2016.

9. Donald Rumsfeld, news briefing, US Department of Defense, February 12, 2002, https://en.wikipedia.org/wiki/There_are_known_knowns.

10. Bertrand Rouet-Leduc et al., "Machine Learning Predicts Laboratory Earthquakes," Cornell University, 2017, http://arxiv.org/abs/1702.05774.

11. Dedre Gentner and Albert L. Stevens, *Mental Models* (New York: Psychology Press, 1983); Dedre Gentner, "Structure Mapping: A Theoretical Model for Analogy," *Cognitive Science* 7 (1983): 15–170.

12. Even as machines get better at such situations, the laws of probability mean that in small samples, there will always be some uncertainty. Thus, when data is sparse, machine predictions will be imprecise in a known way. The machine can provide a sense of how imprecise its predictions are. As we discuss in chapter 8, this creates a human role for judging how to act on imprecise predictions.

13. Nassim Nicholas Taleb, *The Black Swan* (New York: Random House, 2007).

14. In Isaac Asimov's *Foundation* series, prediction becomes powerful enough that it could foresee the destruction of the Galactic Empire and the various growing pains of the society that is the focus of the story. Important to the plot line, however, is that these predictions could not foresee the rise of "the mutant." Predictions did not foresee the unexpected event.

15. Joel Waldfogel, "Copyright Protection, Technological Change, and the Quality of New Products: Evidence from Recorded Music since Napster," *Journal of Law and Economics* 55, no. 4 (2012): 715–740.

16. Donald Rubin, "Estimating Causal Effects of Treatments in Randomized and Nonrandomized Studies," *Journal of Educational Psychology* 66, no. 5 (1974):

688–701; Jerzy Neyman, "Sur les applications de la theorie des probabilites aux experiences agricoles: Essai des principes," master's thesis, 1923, excerpts reprinted in English, D. M. Dabrowska, and T. P. Speed, translators, *Statistical Science* 5 (1923): 463–472.

17. Garry Kasparov, *Deep Thinking* (New York: Perseus Books, 2017), 99–100.

18. Google Panda, *Wikipedia*, https://en.wikipedia.org/wiki/Google_Panda, accessed July 26, 2017. Most notably as described in Google webmasters, "What's It Like to Fight Webspam at Google?" YouTube, Febuary 12, 2014, https://www.youtube.com/watch?v=rr-Cye_mFiQ.

19. For example, publicized overhauls in September 2016: Ashitha Nagesh, "Now You Can Finally Get Rid of All Those Instagram Spammers and Trolls," *Metro*, September 13, 2016, http://metro.co.uk/2016/09/13/now-you-can-finally-get-rid-of-all-those-instagram-spammers-and-trolls-6125645/. Then, again, in June 2017: Jonathan Vanian, "Instagram Turns to Artificial Intelligence to Fight Spam and Offensive Comments," *Fortune*, June 29, 2017, http://fortune.com/2017/06/29/instagram-artificial-intelligence-offensive-comments/. The challenge of using prediction machines in the face of strategic actors is a problem with a long history. In 1976, economist Robert Lucas made this point with respect to macroeconomic policy on inflation and other economic indicators. If people will be better off changing behavior after the policy change, they will do so. Lucas emphasized that even though employment tended to be high when inflation was high, if the central bank changed to a policy of increasing inflation, people would anticipate that inflation and the relationship would break down. So, instead of policy based on extrapolating from past data, he argued that policy should be made based on understanding the underlying drivers of human behavior. This became known as the "Lucas Critique." See Robert Lucas, "Econometric Policy Evaluation: A Critique," *Carnegie-Rochester Conference Series in Public Policy* 1, no. 1 (1976): 19–46, https://ideas.repec.org/a/eee/crcspp/v1y1976ip19-46.html. Economist Tim Harford described this differently: Fort Knox has never been robbed. How much should be spent on protecting Fort Knox? Because it has never been robbed, spending on security does not predict a reduction in robberies. A prediction machine might then recommend spending nothing. Why bother spending money when security doesn't reduce robberies? Tim Harford, *The Undercover Economist Strikes Back: How to Run—or Ruin—an Economy* (New York: Riverhead Books, 2014).

20. Dayong Wang et al., "Deep Learning for Identifying Metastatic Breast Cancer," Camelyon Grand Challenge, June 18, 2016, https://arxiv.org/pdf/1606.05718.pdf.

21. Charles Babbage, *On the Economy of Machinery and Manufactures* (London: Charles Knight Pall Mall East, 1832), 162.

22. Daniel Paravisini and Antoinette Schoar, "The Incentive Effect of IT: Randomized Evidence from Credit Committees," working paper 19303, National Bureau of Economic Research, August 2013.

23. Such "first pass" division of labor is being seen in many prediction machine deployments. The *Washington Post* has an in-house AI that published 850 stories in 2016, but each was reviewed by a human before it went out. The same process was deployed by ROSS Intelligence for parsing thousands of legal documents and turning them into a short memo. See Miranda Katz, "Welcome to the Era of the AI Coworker," *Wired*, November 15, 2017 https://www.wired.com/story/welcome-to-the-era-of-the-ai-coworker/.

Chapter 7

1. Jody Rosen, "The Knowledge, London's Legendary Taxi-Driver Test, Puts Up a Fight in the Age of GPS," *New York Times*, November 10, 2014, https://www.nytimes.com/2014/11/10/t-magazine/london-taxi-test-knowledge.html?_r=0.

2. For a textbook treatment, see Joshua S. Gans, *Core Economics for Managers* (Australia: Cengage, 2005).

3. To see why:
   Average "Take" Payoff = (3/4)(Dry with Umbrella) + (1/4)(Dry with Umbrella) = (3/4)8 + (1/4)8 = 8
   Average "Leave" Payoff = (3/4)(Dry without Umbrella) + (1/4)(Wet) = (3/4)10 + (1/4)0 = 7.5

Chapter 8

1. Andrew McAfee and Erik Brynjolfsson, *Machine, Platform, Crowd: Harnessing Our Digital Future* (New York: Norton, 2017), 72.

2. This example is taken from Jean-Pierre Dubé and Sanjog Misra, "Scalable Price Targeting," working paper, Booth School of Business, University of Chicago, 2017, http://conference.nber.org/confer//2017/SI2017/PRIT/Dube_Misra.pdf.

Chapter 9

1. Daisuke Wakabayashi, "Meet the People Who Train the Robots (to Do Their Own Jobs)," *New York Times*, April 28, 2017, https://www.nytimes.com/2017/04/28/technology/meet-the-people-who-train-the-robots-to-do-their-own-jobs.html?_r=1.

2. Ibid.

3. Ben Popper, "The Smart Bots Are Coming and This One Is Brilliant," *The Verge*, April 7, 2016, https://www.theverge.com/2016/4/7/11380470/amy-personal-digital-assistant-bot-ai-conversational.

4. Ellen Huet, "The Humans Hiding Behind the Chatbots," *Bloomberg*, April 18, 2016, https://www.bloomberg.com/news/articles/2016-04-18/the-humans-hiding-behind-the-chatbots.

5. Wakabayashi, "Meet the People Who Train the Robots (to Do Their Own Jobs)."

6. Marc Mangel and Francisco J. Samaniego, "Abraham Wald's Work on Aircraft Survivability," *Journal of the American Statistical Association* 79, no. 386 (1984): 259–267.

7. Bart J. Bronnenberg, Peter E. Rossi, and Naufel J. Vilcassim, "Structural Modeling and Policy Simulation," *Journal of Marketing Research* 42, no. 1 (2005): 22–26, http://journals.ama.org/doi/abs/10.1509/jmkr.42.1.22.56887.

8. Jean Pierre Dubé et al., "Recent Advances in Structural Econometric Modeling," *Marketing Letters* 16, no. 3–4 (2005): 209–224, https://link.springer.com/article/10.1007%2Fs11002-005-5886-0?LI=true.

Chapter 10

1. "Robot Mailman Rolls on a Tight Schedule," *Popular Science*, October 1976, https://books.google.ca/books?id=HwEAAAAAMBAJ&pg=PA76&lpg=PA76&dq=

mailmobile+robot&source=bl&ots=SHkkOiDv8K&sig=sYFXzvvZ8_GvOV8Gt30ho
GrFhpk&hl=en&sa=X&ei=B3kLVYr7N8meNoLsg_AD&redir_esc=y#v=onepage&q=
mailmobile%20robot&f=false.

2. George Stigler as communicated by Nathan Rosenberg to the authors in 1991.

3. Nobel citation: "Studies of Decision Making Lead to Prize in Economics,"
Royal Swedish Academy of Sciences, press release, October 16, 1978, https://www
.nobelprize.org/nobel_prizes/economic-sciences/laureates/1978/press.html. Turing award citation: Herbert Alexander Simon, A.M. Turing Award, 1975, http://
amturing.acm.org/award_winners/simon_1031467.cfm. See Herbert A. Simon,
"Rationality as Process and as Product of Thought," *American Economic Review* 68,
no. 2 (1978): 1–16; Allen Nevell and Herbert A. Simon, "Computer Science as Empirical Inquiry," *Communications of the ACM* 19, no. 3 (1976): 120.

4. Frederick Jelinek quoted in Roger K. Moore, "Results from a Survey of
Attendees at ASRU 1997 and 2003," INTERSPEECH-2005, Lisbon, September 4–8,
2005.

Chapter 11

1. Jmdavis, "Autopilot worked for me today and saved an accident," *Tesla
Motors Club* (blog), December 12, 2016, https://teslamotorsclub.com/tmc/
threads/autopilot-worked-for-me-today-and-saved-an-accident.82268/.

2. A few weeks later, another driver's dash cam caught the system in operation:
Fred Lambert, "Tesla Autopilot's New Radar Technology Predicts an Accident
Caught on Dashcamera a Second Later," *Electrek*, December 27, 2016, https://elec
trek.co/2016/12/27/tesla-autopilot-radar-technology-predict-accident-dashcam/.

3. NHTSA, "U.S. DOT and IIHS Announce Historic Commitment of 20 Automakers to Make Automatic Emergency Braking Standard on New Vehicles,"
March 17, 2016, https://www.nhtsa.gov/press-releases/us-dot-and-iihs-announce-
historic-commitment-20-automakers-make-automatic-emergency.

4. Kathryn Diss, "Driverless Trucks Move All Iron Ore at Rio Tinto's Pilbara
Mines, in World First," *ABC News*, October 18, 2015, http://www.abc.net.au/
news/2015-10-18/rio-tinto-opens-worlds-first-automated-mine/6863814.

5. Tim Simonite, "Mining 24 Hours a Day with Robots," *MIT Technology
Review*, December 28, 2016, https://www.technologyreview.com/s/603170/
mining-24-hours-a-day-with-robots/.

6. Samantha Murphy Kelly, "Stunning Underwater Olympics Shots Are Now
Taken by Robots," *CNN*, August 9, 2016, http://money.cnn.com/2016/08/08/
technology/olympics-underwater-robots-getty/.

7. Hoang Le, Andrew Kang, and Yisong Yue, "Smooth Imitation Learning for Online Sequence Prediction," International Conference on Machine
Learning, June 19, 2016, https://www.disneyresearch.com/publication/
smooth-imitation-learning/.

8. The laws were (1) A robot may not injure a human being or, through inaction, allow a human being to come to harm; (2) A robot must obey orders given it
by human beings except where such orders would conflict with the First Law; (3)
A robot must protect its own existence as long as such protection does not conflict
with the First or Second Law. See Isaac Asimov, "Runaround," *I, Robot* (The Isaac
Asimov Collection ed.) (New York: Doubleday, 1950), 40.

9. Department of Defense Directive 3000.09: Autonomy in Weapon Systems, November 21, 2012, https://www.hsdl.org/?abstract&did=726163.

10. For instance, there are various clauses allowing alternatives when there is time pressure in battle. Mark Guburd, "Why Should We Ban Autonomous Weapons? To Survive," *IEEE Spectrum*, June 1, 2016, http://spectrum.ieee.org/automaton/robotics/military-robots/why-should-we-ban-autonomous-weapons-to-survive.

Chapter 12

1. Robert Solow, "We'd Better Watch Out," *New York Times Book Review*, July 12, 1987, 36.

2. Michael Hammer, "Reengineering Work: Don't Automate, Obliterate," *Harvard Business Review*, July–August 1990, https://hbr.org/1990/07/reengineering-work-dont-automate-obliterate.

3. Art Kleiner, "Revisiting Reengineering," *Strategy + Business*, July 2000, https://www.strategy-business.com/article/19570?gko=e05ea.

4. Nanette Byrnes, "As Goldman Embraces Automation, Even the Masters of the Universe Are Threatened," *MIT Technology Review*, February 7, 2017, https://www.technologyreview.com/s/603431/as-goldman-embraces-automation-even-the-masters-of-the-universe-are-threatened/.

5. "Google Has More Than 1,000 Artificial Intelligence Projects in the Works," *The Week*, October 18, 2016, http://theweek.com/speedreads/654463/google-more-than-1000-artificial-intelligence-projects-works.

6. Scott Forstall, quoted in "How the iPhone Was Born," *Wall Street Journal* video, June 25, 2017, http://www.wsj.com/video/how-the-iphone-was-born-inside-stories-of-missteps-and-triumphs/302CFE23-392D-4020-B1BD-B4B9CEF7D9A8.html.

Chapter 13

1. Steve Jobs in *Memory and Imagination: New Pathways to the Library of Congress*, Michael Lawrence Films, 2006, https://www.youtube.com/watch?v=ob_GX50Za6c.

Chapter 14

1. Steven Levy, "A Spreadsheet Way of Knowledge," *Wired*, October 24, 2014, https://backchannel.com/a-spreadsheet-way-of-knowledge-8de60af7146e.

2. Nick Statt, "The Next Big Leap in AI Could Come from Warehouse Robots," *The Verge*, June 1, 2017, https://www.theverge.com/2017/6/1/15703146/kindred-orb-robot-ai-startup-warehouse-automation.

3. L. B. Lusted, "Logical Analysis in Roentgen Diagnosis," *Radiology* 74 (1960): 178–193.

4. Siddhartha Mukherjee, "A.I. versus M.D.," *New Yorker*, April 3, 2017, http://www.newyorker.com/magazine/2017/04/03/ai-versus-md.

5. S. Jha and E. J. Topol, "Adapting to Artificial Intelligence: Radiologists and Pathologists as Information Specialists," *Journal of the American Medical Association* 316, no. 22 (2016): 2353–2354.

6. Many of these ideas are related to Frank Levy's discussion in "Computers and the Supply of Radiology Services," *Journal of the American College of Radiology* 5, no. 10 (2008): 1067–1072.

7. See Verdict Hospital (http://www.hospitalmanagement.net/features/fea
ture51500/) for an interview with the 2009 president of the American College of
Radiology. Or, for a more academic reference, see Leonard Berlin, "The Radiologist:
Doctor's Doctor or Patient's Doctor," *American Journal of Roentgenology* 128, no. 4
(1977), http://www.ajronline.org/doi/pdf/10.2214/ajr.128.4.702.

8. Levy, "Computers and the Supply of Radiology Services."

9. Jha and Topol, "Adapting to Artificial Intelligence"; S. Jha, "Will Computers
Replace Radiologists?" *Medscape* 30 (December 2016), http://www.medscape
.com/viewarticle/863127#vp_1.

10. Carl Benedikt Frey and Michael A. Osborne, "The Future of Employment:
How Susceptible Are Jobs to Computerisation?" Oxford Martin School, University
of Oxford, September 2013, http://www.oxfordmartin.ox.ac.uk/downloads/aca
demic/The_Future_of_Employment.pdf.

11. Truckmakers are already embedding convey capabilities in their newest
vehicles. Volvo has deployed this in several tests, and Telsa's new semi has these
capabilities built in from the start.

Chapter 15

1. "How Germany's Otto Uses Artificial Intelligence," *The Economist*, April 12,
2017, https://www.economist.com/news/business/21720675-firm-using-
algorithm-designed-cern-laboratory-how-germanys-otto-uses.

2. Zvi Griliches, "Hybrid Corn and the Economics of Innovation," *Science* 29
(July 1960): 275–280.

3. Bryce Ryan and N. Gross, "The Diffusion of Hybrid Seed Corn," *Rural Sociol-
ogy* 8 (1943): 15–24; and Bryce Ryan and N. Gross, "Acceptance and Diffusion of
Hybrid Corn Seed in Two Iowa Communities," *Iowa Agriculture Experiment Station
Research Bulletin*, no. 372 (January 1950).

4. Kelly Gonsalves, "Google Has More Than 1,000 Artificial Intelligence
Projects in the Works," *The Week*, October 18, 2016, http://theweek.com/
speedreads/654463/google-more-than-1000-artificial-intelligence-projects-works.

5. A rich, entertaining, and ultimately useless debate rages about whether these
sabermetric analysts are better or worse than the scouts. As Nate Silver highlights,
both the *Moneyball* types and the scouts have important roles to play. Nate Silver,
The Signal and the Noise (New York: Penguin Books, 2015), chapter 3.

6. You may counter and say that surely, in order to improve, the prediction
machine needs that past repository of data? This is a subtle issue. Prediction
works best when adding new data does not change algorithms too much—that
stability is an outcome of good statistical practice. That means when you use feedback data to improve the algorithm, it is of most value precisely when what is being
predicted is itself evolving. So if yogurt demand was suddenly shifting with demographics or some other fad, new data will help you improve the algorithm. However,
it does this precisely when those changes mean that "old data" is less useful for
prediction.

7. Daniel Ren, "Tencent Joins the Fray with Baidu in Providing Artificial
Intelligence Applications for Self-Driving Cars," *South China Morning Post*,
August 27, 2017, http://www.scmp.com/business/companies/article/2108489/
tencent-forms-alliance-push-ai-applications-self-driving.

8. Ren, "Tencent Joins the Fray with Baidu in Providing Artificial Intelligence
Applications for Self-Driving Cars."

Chapter 16

1. The theory of adaptation and incentives outlined here comes from Steven Tadelis, "Complexity, Flexibility, and the Make-or-Buy Decision," *American Economic* Review 92, no. 2 (May 2002): 433–437.

2. Silke Januszewski Forbes and Mara Lederman, "Adaptation and Vertical Integration in the Airline Industry," *American Economic Review* 99, no. 5 (December 2009): 1831–1849.

3. Sharon Novak and Scott Stern, "How Does Outsourcing Affect Performance Dynamics? Evidence from the Automobile Industry," *Management Science* 54, no. 12 (December 2008): 1963–1979.

4. Jim Bessen, *Learning by Doing* (New Haven, CT: Yale University Press, 2106).

5. In 2016, Wells Fargo faced massive fraud claims as a result of the actions of account managers who faced incentives to open costly accounts for customers and charge them fees for doing so.

6. This discussion is based on Dirk Bergemann and Alessandro Bonatti, "Selling Cookies," *American Economic Journal: Microeconomics* 7, no. 2 (2015): 259–294.

7. One example is Mastercard Advisors consulting services, which use Mastercard's vast quantity of data to provide a variety of predictions, ranging from consumer fraud to retention rates. See http://www.mastercardadvisors.com/con sulting.html.

Chapter 17

1. As told to Steven Levy. See Will Smith, "Stop Calling Google Cardboard's 360-Degree Videos 'VR,'" *Wired*, November 16, 2015, https://www.wired .com/2015/11/360-video-isnt-virtual-reality/.

2. Jessir Hempel, "Inside Microsoft's AI Comeback," *Wired*, June 21, 2017, https://www.wired.com/story/inside-microsofts-ai-comeback/.

3. "What Does It Mean for Google to Become an 'AI-First' (Quoting Sundar) Company?" *Quora*, April 2016, https://www.quora.com/What-does-it-mean-for-Google-to-become-an-AI-first-company.

4. Clayton M. Christensen, *The Innovator's Dilemma* (Boston: Harvard Business Review Press, 2016).

5. For more on these disruption dilemmas, see Joshua S. Gans, *The Disruption Dilemma* (Cambridge, MA: MIT Press, 2016).

6. Nathan Rosenberg, "Learning by Using: Inside the Black Box: Technology and Economics," paper, University of Illinois at Champaign-Urbana, 1982, 120–140.

7. In the case of video games, because the goal (maximizing score) is closely related to prediction (will this move increase or decrease the score?), the automated process does not separately need judgment. The judgment is the simple recognition that the objective is to score the most points. Teaching a machine to play a sandbox game like Minecraft or a collection game like Pokemon Go would require more judgment, since different people enjoy different aspects of the games. It isn't clear what the goal should be.

8. Chesley "Sully" Sullenberger quoted in Katy Couric, "Capt. Sully Worried about Airline Industry," *CBS News*, February 10, 2009; https://www.cbsnews.com/news/capt-sully-worried-about-airline-industry/.

9. Mark Harris, "Tesla Drivers Are Paying Big Bucks to Test Flawed Self-Driving Software," *Wired*, March 4, 2017, https://backchannel.com/tesla-drivers-are-guinea-pigs-for-flawed-self-driving-software-c2cc80b483a#.s0u7lsv4f.

10. Nikolai Yakovenko, "GANS Will Change the World," *Medium*, January 3, 2017, https://medium.com/@Moscow25/gans-will-change-the-world-7ed6ae8515ca; Sebastian Anthony, "Google Teaches 'AIs' to Invent Their Own Crypto and Avoid Eavesdropping," *Ars Technica*, October 28, 2016, https://arstechnica.com/information-technology/2016/10/google-ai-neural-network-cryptography/.

11. Apple, "Privacy," https://www.apple.com/ca/privacy/.

12. Ibid.

13. The bet is possible because of technological advances in privacy-protecting data analysis, especially Cynthia Dwork's invention of differential privacy: Cynthia Dwork, "Differential Privacy: A Survey of Results," in M. Agrawal, D. Du, Z. Duan, and A. Li (eds), *Theory and Applications of Models of Computation. TAMC 2008. Lecture Notes in Computer Science*, vol 4978 (Berlin: Springer, 2008), https://doi.org/10.1007/978-3-540-79228-4_1.

14. William Langewiesche, "The Human Factor," *Vanity Fair*, October 2014, http://www.vanityfair.com/news/business/2014/10/air-france-flight-447-crash.

15. Tim Harford, "How Computers Are Setting Us Up for Disaster," *The Guardian*, October 11, 2016, https://www.theguardian.com/technology/2016/oct/11/crash-how-computers-are-setting-us-up-disaster.

Chapter 18

1. L. Sweeney, "Discrimination in Online Ad Delivery," *Communications of the ACM* 56, no. 5 (2013): 44–54, https://dataprivacylab.org/projects/onlineads/.

2. Ibid.

3. "Racism Is Poisoning Online Ad Delivery, Says Harvard Professor," *MIT Technology Review*, February 4, 2013, https://www.technologyreview.com/s/510646/racism-is-poisoning-online-ad-delivery-says-harvard-professor/.

4. Anja Lambrecht and Catherine Tucker, "Algorithmic Bias? An Empirical Study into Apparent Gender-Based Discrimination in the Display of STEM Career Ads" (paper presented at the NBER Summer Institute, July 2017).

5. Diane Cardwell and Libby Nelson, "The Fire Dept. Tests That Were Found to Discriminate," *New York Times*, July 23, 2009, https://cityroom.blogs.nytimes.com/2009/07/23/the-fire-dept-tests-that-were-found-to-discriminate/?mcubz=0&_r=0; *US v. City of New York* (FDNY), https://www.justice.gov/archives/crt-fdny/overview.

6. Paul Voosen, "How AI Detectives Are Cracking Open the Black Box of Deep Learning," *Science*, July 6, 2017, http://www.sciencemag.org/news/2017/07/how-ai-detectives-are-cracking-open-black-box-deep-learning.

7. T. Blake, C. Nosko, and S. Tadelis, "Consumer Heterogeneity and Paid Search Effectiveness: A Large-Scale Field Experiment," *Econometrica* 83 (2015): 155–174.

8. Hossein Hosseini, Baicen Xiao, and Radha Poovendran, "Deceiving Google's Cloud Video Intelligence API Built for Summarizing Videos" (paper presented at CVPR Workshops, March 31, 2017), https://arxiv.org/pdf/1703.09793.pdf; see also "Artificial Intelligence Used by Google to Scan Videos Could Easily Be Tricked by a

Picture of Noodles," *Quartz*, April 4, 2017, https://qz.com/948870/the-ai-used-by-google-to-scan-videos-could-easily-be-tricked-by-a-picture-of-noodles/.

9. See, for example, the thousands of citations to C. S. Elton, *The Ecology of Invasions by Animals and Plants* (New York: John Wiley, 1958).

10. Based on discussions with University of Waterloo dean Pearl Sullivan, professor Alexander Wong, and other Waterloo professors on November 20, 2016.

11. There is a fourth benefit to prediction on the ground: sometimes it is necessary for practical purposes. For instance, Google Glass needed to be able to determine whether an eyelid movement was a blink (nonintentional) or a wink (intentional), with the latter being a means by which the device could be controlled. Because of the speed with which that determination needed to be made, sending the data to the cloud and waiting for an answer was impractical. The prediction machine needed to be hosted in the device.

12. Ryan Singel, "Google Catches Bing Copying; Microsoft Says 'So What?'" *Wired*, February 1, 2011, https://www.wired.com/2011/02/bing-copies-google/.

13. See Shane Greenstein for a discussion of why it was unacceptable; "Bing Imitates Google: Their Conduct Crosses a Line," *Virulent Word of Mouse* (blog), February 2, 2011, https://virulentwordofmouse.wordpress.com/2011/02/02/bing-imitates-google-their-conduct-crosses-a-line/; and Ben Edelman for a counterpoint, "In Accusing Microsoft, Google Doth Protest Too Much," *hbr.org*, February 3, 2011, https://hbr.org/2011/02/in-accusing-microsoft-google.html.

14. It is also interesting that Google's attempt to manipulate Microsoft's machine learning did not work very well. Of the one hundred experiments it conducted, only seven to nine actually appeared in Bing search results. See Joshua Gans, "The Consequences of Hiybbprqag'ing," *Digitopoly*, February 8, 2011; https://digitopoly.org/2011/02/08/the-consequences-of-hiybbprqaging/.

15. Florian Tramèr, Fan Zhang, Ari Juels, Michael K. Reiter, and Thomas Ristenpart, "Stealing Machine Learning Models via Prediction APIs" (paper presented at the Proceedings of the 25th USENIX Security Symposium, Austin, TX, August 10–12, 2016), https://regmedia.co.uk/2016/09/30/sec16_paper_tramer.pdf.

16. James Vincent, "Twitter Taught Microsoft's AI Chatbot to Be a Racist Asshole in Less Than a Day," *The Verge*, March 24, 2016, https://www.theverge.com/2016/3/24/11297050/tay-microsoft-chatbot-racist.

17. Rob Price, "Microsoft Is Deleting Its Chatbot's Incredibly Racist Tweets," *Business Insider*, March 24, 2016, http://www.businessinsider.com/microsoft-deletes-racist-genocidal-tweets-from-ai-chatbot-tay-2016-3?r=UK&IR=T.

Chapter 19

1. James Vincent, "Elon Musk Says We Need to Regulate AI Before It Becomes a Danger to Humanity," *The Verge*, July 17, 2017, https://www.theverge.com/2017/7/17/15980954/elon-musk-ai-regulation-existential-threat.

2. Chris Weller, "One of the Biggest VCs in Silicon Valley Is Launching an Experiment That Will Give 3000 People Free Money Until 2022," *Business Insider*, September 21, 2017, http://www.businessinsider.com/y-combinator-basic-income-test-2017-9.

3. Stephen Hawking, "This Is the Most Dangerous Time for Our Planet," *The Guardian*, December 1, 2016, https://www.theguardian.com/commentisfree/2016/dec/01/stephen-hawking-dangerous-time-planet-inequality.

4. "The Onrushing Wave," *The Economist*, January 18, 2014, https://www.economist.com/news/briefing/21594264-previous-technological-innovation-has-always-delivered-more-long-run-employment-not-less.

5. For more, see John Markoff, *Machines of Loving Grace: The Quest for Common Ground Between Humans and Robots* (New York: Harper Collins, 2015); Martin Ford, *Rise of the Robots: Technology and the Threat of a Jobless Future* (New York: Basic Books, 2016); and Ryan Avent, *The Wealth of Humans: Work, Power, and Status in the Twenty-First Century* (London: St. Martin's Press, 2016).

6. Jason Furman, "Is This Time Different? The Opportunities and Challenges of AI," https://obamawhitehouse.archives.gov/sites/default/files/page/files/20160707_cea_ai_furman.pdf.

7. Claudia Dale Goldin and Lawrence F. Katz, *The Race between Education and Technology* (Cambridge, MA: Harvard University Press, 2009), 90.

8. Lesley Chiou and Catherine Tucker, "Search Engines and Data Retention: Implications for Privacy and Antitrust," working paper no. 23815, National Bureau of Economic Research, http://www.nber.org/papers/w23815.

9. Google AdWords, "Reach more customers with broad match," 2008.

10. For a review of antitrust and other implications around algorithms, data, and AI, see Ariel Ezrachi and Maurice Stucke, *Virtual Competition: The Promise and Perils of the Algorithm-Driven Economy* (Cambridge, MA: Harvard University Press, 2016). For a view that perhaps algorithms themselves will be concentrated into a single algorithm, see Pedro Domingos, *The Master Algorithm* (New York: Basic Books, 2015). Finally, Steve Lohr provides an overview of how businesses are preemptively investing in data for strategic advantage; see Steve Lohr, *Dataism* (New York: Harper Business, 2015).

11. James Vincent, "Putin Says the Nation That Leads in AI 'Will Be the Ruler of the World,'" *The Verge*, September 4, 2017, https://www.theverge.com/2017/9/4/16251226/russia-ai-putin-rule-the-world.

12. The reports are: (1) Jason Furman, "Is This Time Different? The Opportunities and Challenges of Artificial Intelligence" (remarks at AI Now, New York University, July 7, 2016), https://obamawhitehouse.archives.gov/sites/default/files/page/files/20160707_cea_ai_furman.pdf; (2) Executive Office of the President, "Artificial Intelligence, Automation, and the Economy," December 2016, https://obamawhitehouse.archives.gov/sites/whitehouse.gov/files/documents/Artificial-Intelligence-Automation-Economy.PDF; (3) Executive Office of the President, National Science and Technology Council, and Committee on Technology, "Preparing for the Future of Artificial Intelligence," October 2016, https://obamawhitehouse.archives.gov/sites/default/files/whitehouse_files/microsites/ostp/NSTC/preparing_for_the_future_of_ai.pdf; (4) National Science and Technology Council and Networking and Information Technology Research and Development Subcommittee, "The National Artificial Intelligence Research and Development Strategic Plan," October 2016, https://obamawhitehouse.archives.gov/sites/default/files/whitehouse_files/microsites/ostp/NSTC/national_ai_rd_strategic_plan.pdf.

13. Dan Trefler and Avi Goldfarb, "AI and Trade," in Ajay Agrawal, Joshua Gans, and Avi Goldfarb, eds., *Economics of AI*, forthcoming.

14. Paul Mozur, "Beijing Wants AI to Be Made in China by 2030," *New York Times*, July 20, 2017, https://www.nytimes.com/2017/07/20/business/china-artificial-intelligence.html?_r=0.

15. "Why China's AI Push Is Worrying," *The Economist*, July 27, 2017, https://www.economist.com/news/leaders/21725561-state-controlled-corporations-are-developing-powerful-artificial-intelligence-why-chinas-ai-push?frsc=dg%7Ce.

16. Paul Mozur, "Beijing Wants AI to Be Made in China by 2030," *New York Times*, July 20, 2017, https://www.nytimes.com/2017/07/20/business/china-artificial-intelligence.html?_r=0.

17. Ibid.

18. Image 37 of Impact of Basic Research on Technological Innovation and National Prosperity: Hearing before the Subcommittee on Basic Research of the Committee on Science, House of Representatives, One Hundred Sixth Congress, first session, September 28, 1999, 27.

19. "Why China's AI Push Is Worrying."

20. Will Knight, "China's AI Awakening," *MIT Technology Review*, November 2017.

21. Jessi Hempel, "How Baidu Will Win China's AI Race—and Maybe the World's," *Wired*, August 9, 2017, https://www.wired.com/story/how-baidu-will-win-chinas-ai-raceand-maybe-the-worlds/.

22. Will Knight, "10 Breakthrough Technologies—2017: Paying with Your Face," *MIT Technology Review*, March–April 2017, https://www.technologyreview.com/s/603494/10-breakthrough-technologies-2017-paying-with-your-face/.

23. Oren Etzioni, "How to Regulate Artificial Intelligence," *New York Times*, September 1, 2017, https://www.nytimes.com/2017/09/01/opinion/artificial-intelligence-regulations-rules.html?_r=0.

24. Aleecia M. McDonald and Lorrie Faith Cranor, "The Cost of Reading Privacy Policies," *I/S* 4, no. 3 (2008): 543–568, http://heinonline.org/HOL/Page?handle=hein.journals/isjlpsoc4&div=27&g_sent=1&casa_token=&collection=journals.

25. Christian Catalini and Joshua S. Gans, "Some Simple Economics of the Blockchain," working paper no. 2874598, Rotman School of Management, September 21, 2017, and MIT Sloan Research Paper No. 5191-16, available at https://ssrn.com/abstract=2874598.

26. Nick Bostrom, *Superintelligence* (Oxford, UK: Oxford University Press, 2016).

27. For an excellent recent discussion of this debate, see Max Tegmark, *Life 3.0: Being Human in the Age of Artificial Intelligence* (New York: Knopf, 2017).

28. "Prepare for the Future of Artificial Intelligence," Executive Office of the President, National Science and Technology Council, Committee on Technology, October 2016.

Index

About the Authors

AJAY AGRAWAL is professor of strategic management and Peter Munk Professor of Entrepreneurship at the University of Toronto's Rotman School of Management and the founder of the Creative Destruction Lab. He is also a research associate at the National Bureau of Economic Research in Cambridge, Massachusetts, and cofounder of The Next 36 and Next AI entrepreneurship programs. Agrawal conducts research on technology strategy, science policy, entrepreneurial finance, and the geography of innovation, and serves on the editorial boards of *Management Science, Strategic Management Journal,* and the *Journal of Urban Economics.* He has presented his research at various institutions including the London School of Economics, London Business School, Harvard University, MIT, Stanford, Carnegie Mellon, Berkeley, Wharton, and the Brookings Institute. Agrawal is cofounder of the AI/robotics company Kindred. The company's mission is to build machines with human-like intelligence.

JOSHUA GANS is professor of strategic management and the holder of the Jeffrey S. Skoll Chair of Technical Innovation and Entrepreneurship at the Rotman School of Management, University of Toronto. Joshua is also chief economist at the University of Toronto's Creative Destruction Lab. Joshua has over 120 peer-reviewed academic publications and is the editor (strategy) of *Management Science.* He also has authored two successful textbooks and written five popular books, including *Parentonomics* (2009), *Information Wants to Be Shared* (2012), *The Disruption Dilemma* (2016), and *Scholarly*

Publishing and Its Discontents (2017). Joshua holds a PhD in economics from Stanford University and, in 2008, was awarded the Economic Society of Australia's Young Economist Award (the Australian equivalent of the John Bates Clark medal).

AVI GOLDFARB is the Ellison Professor of Marketing at the Rotman School of Management, University of Toronto. Avi is also chief data scientist at the Creative Destruction Lab, senior editor at *Marketing Science*, and a research associate at the National Bureau of Economic Research. Avi's research focuses on the opportunities and challenges of the digital economy, with funding from Google, Industry Canada, Bell Canada, AIMIA, SSHRC, the National Science Foundation, the Sloan Foundation, and others. This work has been discussed in White House reports, congressional testimony, European Commission documents, the *Economist*, the *Globe and Mail*, the *National Post*, CBC Radio, National Public Radio, *Forbes*, *Fortune*, the *Atlantic*, the *New York Times*, the *Financial Times*, the *Wall Street Journal*, and many others. He holds a PhD in economics from Northwestern University.